FAMILY LITERACY

FROM Theory TO Practice

ANDREA DEBRUIN-PARECKI

High/Scope Educational Research Foundation
Ypsilanti, Michigan, USA

BARBARA KROL-SINCLAIR

Chelsea, Massachusetts Public Schools
Chelsea, Massachusetts, USA
and
Boston University
Boston, Massachusetts, USA

EDITORS

INTERNATIONAL
Reading Association
800 Barksdale Road, PO Box 8139
Newark, Delaware 19714-8139, USA
www.reading.org

Director of Publications   Joan M. Irwin
Editorial Director, Books and Special Projects   Matthew W. Baker
Production Editor   Shannon Benner
Permissions Editor   Janet S. Parrack
Acquisitions and Communications Coordinator   Corinne M. Mooney
Associate Editor, Books and Special Projects   Sara J. Murphy
Assistant Editor   Charlene M. Nichols
Administrative Assistant   Michele Jester
Senior Editorial Assistant   Tyanna L. Collins
Production Department Manager   Iona Sauscermen
Supervisor, Electronic Publishing   Anette Schütz
Senior Electronic Publishing Specialist   Cheryl J. Strum
Electronic Publishing Specialist   R. Lynn Harrison
Proofreader   Elizabeth C. Hunt

Project Editor   Sara J. Murphy

Cover Design   Linda Steere

Library of Congress Cataloging–in–Publication Data
Family literacy : from theory to practice / Andrea DeBruin-Parecki,
Barbara Krol-Sinclair, editors.
    p. cm.
Includes bibliographical references and indexes.
  ISBN 0-87207-511-7 (pbk.)
  1. Family literacy programs. 2. Reading–Parent participation
  I. DeBruin-Parecki, Andrea. II. Krol-Sinclair, Barbara.
  LC149.F36 2003
  302.2'244--dc21

                                                                    2003004967

Contents

32 21

SECTION III

A Close Look at Diverse Family Literacy Programs

SECTION IV
Evaluating Family Literacy Programs and Their Participants

Foreword

As early as 1908, Edmund Burke Huey wrote of children's learning in school, "It all begins with parents reading to children" (p. 103). Parents are the first teachers their children have, and they are the teachers that children have for the longest time. Parents are potentially the most important people in the education of their children, an idea supported by research that shows a strong link between the home environment and children's acquisition of literacy. Such practices as participating in shared reading, reading aloud, making print materials available, and promoting positive attitudes toward literacy in the home have been found to have a significant effect on children's literacy learning.

However, many different forms of literacy practices that are not school-like exist in families from different cultures. These literacy activities may not influence school success, and conversely, the kinds of literacy practiced in classrooms may have little meaning outside school walls for children from these families. Because of the diversity in the world, we must adopt multiple ways of approaching family literacy and learn these ways from family members and children as well as from agencies, professionals, and scholarly publications. Family literacy must be studied from the widest possible perspective by reporting on cultures in which print is a dominant medium and by respecting cultures in which no books exist but in which storytelling, for example, is a strong part of the cultural environment.

The International Reading Association has devoted a great deal of time to addressing the issue of family literacy. My own interest in the topic was motivated by my appointment as chair of the Family Literacy Commission from 1991 to 1996. I am pleased to see that the Association is continuing its commitment to this important concern with this new volume, which presents a current look at the issues surrounding family literacy. The collection is divided into four sections: Section I deals with theoretical perspectives related to family literacy, section II deals with strategies to promote family literacy, section III looks at the variety of family literacy programs that exist, and section IV investigates ways to evaluate family literacy programs. The book is sensitive to the needs of all families, including those from diverse cultural backgrounds. The volume includes the most current thinking about the topic, and it also presents family literacy theory as it connects to practices. This book provides new and useful information for people training to work with families and young children, people who are already in the family literacy field, and others who wish to assist families in improving their literacy skills and lives.

Family literacy should be viewed by schools and community agencies as one of the most important elements in literacy development, and its concerns need to be treated with the same importance given to issues such as skill development and assessment. Schools need to view family literacy as part of the curricula with coordinators in charge of initiating and supervising programs, and community organizations need to exert energy in this direction as well. It is clear that by attending to the home when we discuss literacy development, whatever strategies we carry out in schools or communities will be more successful.

Lesley Mandel Morrow
Rutgers University
New Brunswick, New Jersey, USA
International Reading Association President 2003–2004

REFERENCE

Huey, E.B. (1908). *The psychology and pedagogy of reading.* New York: Macmillan.

List of Contributors

Mary Bailey
Lecturer in Education
School of Education, University
    of Nottingham
Nottingham, United Kingdom

Dianna Baycich
Literacy Specialist
Ohio Literacy Resource Center
Kent, Ohio, USA

Margaret Cook
Educational Consultant
Wirral, Merseyside, United
    Kingdom

Andrea DeBruin-Parecki
Co-director, Early Childhood
    Reading Institute
High/Scope Educational
    Research Foundation
Ypsilanti, Michigan, USA

Rebecca K. Edmiaston
Assistant Professor, Department
    of Curriculum and Instruction
University of Northern Iowa
Cedar Falls, Iowa, USA

Julia M. Emig
Literacy Specialist
Boston Public Schools
Dorchester, Massachusetts, USA

Billie J. Enz
Associate Division Director
    of Curriculum and Instruction
Arizona State University
Tempe, Arizona, USA

Linda May Fitzgerald
Associate Professor, Early
    Childhood Education
University of Northern Iowa
Cedar Falls, Iowa, USA

Vivian L. Gadsden
Associate Professor of Education
    and Director, National Center
    on Fathers and Families
University of Pennsylvania
Philadelphia, Pennsylvania, USA

Alisa Hindin
Senior Research Associate
Educational Development Center
Maplewood, New Jersey, USA

Christopher Kliewer
Associate Professor of Special
    Education
University of Northern Iowa
Cedar Falls, Iowa, USA

Barbara Krol-Sinclair
Director, Intergenerational
    Literacy Project
Boston University/Chelsea
    Partnership
Boston, Massachusetts, USA

Letta Mashishi
Director, Families Learning
   Together
Soweto, South Africa

Kelly A. McClure
Program Coordinator,
   Intergenerational Literacy
   Project
Boston University/Chelsea
   Partnership
Boston, Massachusetts, USA

Nancy D. Padak
Distinguished Professor,
   Education
Kent State University
Kent, Ohio, USA

Jeanne R. Paratore
Associate Professor of Education
Boston University
Boston, Massachusetts, USA

Maurine V. Richardson
Associate Professor of
   Curriculum and Instruction:
   Reading
University of South Dakota
Vermillion, South Dakota, USA

Donald J. Richgels
Professor, Literacy Education
Northern Illinois University
DeKalb, Illinois, USA

Flora V. Rodríguez-Brown
Professor
University of Illinois at Chicago
Chicago, Illinois, USA

Mary Kathleen Sacks
Associate Professor of Art
Bethel College
McKenzie, Tennessee, USA

Susan Straub
Director, Read to Me Program
Teachers & Writers Collaborative
New York, New York, USA

Introduction

Andrea DeBruin-Parecki and Barbara Krol-Sinclair

Although the term *family literacy* is relatively new, throughout history the practice of family literacy has been consistently present in homes and communities and across generations. Being literate is viewed as "having mastery over the processes by means of which culturally significant information is coded" (DeCastell & Luke, 1983, p. 373). This information can be passed on in a variety of ways such as speaking, drawing, signing, gesturing, singing, and writing. The definition of literacy encompasses much more than conventional types of skills such as reading and writing. A person considered literate in one culture may be considered illiterate when judged by the standards of another culture because adults have always schooled children in some manner to assist them in becoming literate in the ways and traditions of their own cultures.

Although the practice of family literacy may have occurred for generations, the two words were not unified as a concept until 1983, when Denny Taylor published her dissertation, *Family Literacy: Young Children Learning to Read and Write*. The focus of the research she began in 1977 was to "develop systematic ways of looking at reading and writing as activities that have consequences in and are affected by family life" (1983, p. xiii). Her landmark ethnographic study that carefully describes the ways that families support the literacy development of their children is considered to be the starting point for the interest, research, and practice in the area of family literacy today.

Once the term *family literacy* was coined, its meaning became subject to broad interpretation to suit the context in which it was mentioned and implemented, because "no single narrow definition of 'family literacy' can do justice to the richness and complexity of families, and the multiple literacies, including often unrecognized local literacies that are part of their everyday lives" (Taylor, 1997, p. 4). Cultural, linguistic, and familial contexts all influence both the ways in which families share literacy and the content of embedded reading and writing activities.

Because family literacy encompasses a variety of disciplines, including psychology, emergent literacy, beginning reading, anthropology, and sociology (Purcell-Gates, 2000), researchers in these fields began investigating family literacy practices. A wide range of studies concluded that children's success in school can be affected by adult–child interaction around literacy at home (Burgess, 1997; Bus, van IJzendoorn, & Pellegrini, 1995; Heath, 1983; Morrow, 1983; Teale, 1984). The U.S. government embraced this concept, and the Even Start program was founded in 1988 on the premise that the parent is the child's first teacher. Still, there was no universally accepted definition of the concept of family literacy.

The lack of a clear definition has not, however, stopped family literacy programs from emerging all over the world. Some programs must conform to standards placed on them by governments or funders, and others construct unique programs jointly with their participants to focus more specifically on their cultural and individual needs.

Elementary and secondary school teachers and administrators looking for solutions to assist low-achieving students have found family literacy to be a lifeline they can grab (Paratore, 2001). Various stakeholders around the United States and the world have placed high expectations on family literacy to solve a host of social ills through the education of families in a number of areas.

In reality, most educators consider family literacy to be a vague concept that has not linked recent methodologically sound and applicable research with sound practice, effective strategies, and resulting outcomes (Gadsden, 2000; Purcell-Gates, 2000). Programs and strategies first applied in family, school, and community interactions 10 to 15 years ago are not necessarily effective for today's complex families and lifestyles (Springate & Stegelin, 1999). Family literacy must be seen more as a theoretically sound field of research and practice and less as a panacea for curing multiple social and educational dilemmas. This book will attempt to bridge this gap by directly connecting theory to practice in ways that will provide new and useful information for those training to work with families and young children, those already in the family literacy field, and others who wish to assist families in improving their literacy skills and their lives.

Organization of This Book

The first section of the book, titled "Theoretical Perspectives Related to Family Literacy," focuses on the theoretical and historical bases of family literacy. Chapter 1, written by Jeanne R. Paratore, examines the history of research and practice in family literacy. Paratore analyzes the factors that have influenced the growth of family literacy interventions, different types of family literacy programs that frame current practice, and the theoretical and research bases for the various components that make up each program type. She concludes by suggesting future directions for policy, research, and practice to strengthen educators' understanding of this complex field and their ability to support parents' and children's literacy development. Chapter 2 by Donald J. Richgels describes young children's literacy acquisition from a developmental point of view. Richgels examines current understandings of how children from birth to age 8 construct written language knowledge, beginning with very nonconventional behaviors and understandings and moving gradually toward conventional ones. He discusses ways in which parents can build on young children's abilities and knowledge to help them take the next steps in their emergent literacy development.

The second section, "Specific Practices and Strategies Used to Promote Family Literacy in Collaboration With Schools and Communities," presents research findings and specific practices and strategies used to promote family literacy in collaboration with schools and communities. Chapter 3, written by Billie J. Enz, provides a comprehensive research review that establishes a parent's complex and critical role as his or her child's first teacher, describes simple parent–child (from infancy to preschool) language and literacy activities that parents can do within the context of the home, and concludes with practical ways that preschool and primary teachers can support family literacy. In chapter 4, Maurine V. Richardson and Mary Kathleen Sacks focus on children ages 10–18 and how family literacy practices can help to meet the needs of this population. Vivian L. Gadsden, author of chapter 5, examines the conceptual and empirical issues in father involvement and their relevance to family literacy. Fathering and family research, as well as case studies of low-income, minority fathers, are included to address an increasingly prominent shortcoming in family literacy research and practice. In chapter 6, Flora V. Rodríguez-Brown addresses the challenges and questions raised in relation to promoting family literacy with parents who are second language learners. Finally, in chapter 7, Christopher Kliewer examines an often slighted topic— families supporting reading and writing development of children with significant disabilities.

The third section of the book, "A Close Look at Diverse Family Literacy Programs," spotlights a variety of individual family literacy programs both in the United States and around the world. Chapter 8, written by Rebecca K. Edmiaston and Linda May Fitzgerald, describes two major U.S. government-sponsored programs—Even Start and Head Start—and offers specific examples of literacy opportunities provided by the programs. In chapter 9, Susan Straub presents her program, Read to Me, which offers a hands-on series of activities and supervised practice sessions that guide teen parents and other mothers in reading with their babies. Chapter 10, authored by Mary Bailey, offers an account of a program that takes place in the United Kingdom—the Boots Books for Babies Project. This program delivers book packs to the parents or caregivers of babies attending hearing checks at local health centers to increase their awareness of the importance of sharing books with babies and to encourage both the registration of babies with local libraries and the use of library service. Letta Mashishi and Margaret Cook author the section's final chapter in which they examine two very different family literacy programs, one in South Africa and the other in the United Kingdom. They analyze the principles and practices common to both programs, factors in the programs' successes, and the role of cross-cultural experience in reflecting on practice.

The final section of the book, "Evaluating Family Literacy Programs and Their Participants," highlights issues surrounding the evaluation of family literacy programs and their instructional methods. More and more family literacy programs are being held accountable for providing proof of their effectiveness. Even Start legislation, for example, requires each Even Start program to participate in local, state, and national evaluations. It has become imperative for programs to identify and adopt accepted methods of evaluation that match the cultural and individual makeup of participants in their programs. Chapter 12, written by Nancy D. Padak and Dianna Baycich, provides an overview of general guidelines for evaluation, a discussion of the advantages and disadvantages of working with external evaluators, and guidelines for effective evaluation of programs and their children and adult participants. The authors provide references for programs seeking evaluation and assessment tools. In chapter 13, Barbara Krol-Sinclair, Alisa Hindin, Julia M. Emig, and Kelly A. McClure report on a three-year study investigating the use of home-school portfolios in conferences between teachers and immigrant parents participating in a family literacy program. The authors provide a detailed description of how classroom teachers might implement a similar program and include forms, portfolio samples, and transcripts of conversations between parents and teachers about these portfolios. The book's final chapter, written by Andrea DeBruin-Parecki, describes the Adult/Child Interactive Reading Inventory, a research-based observational teaching and learning tool that provides a quantitative and qualitative assessment of interactive storybook reading behaviors between adults and children.

This book is designed to play an important role in building respect for the field of family literacy by providing a research-based discussion of how theory can and should be linked to practice. The field of family literacy has grown by leaps and bounds in recent years due to the attention both popular media and academic research have drawn to the benefits of reading to young children. The International Reading Association and the National Association for the Education of Young Children have validated this in their joint position statement on learning to read and write (1998). The release of the National Research Council Report *Preventing Reading Difficulties in Young Children* (Snow, Burns, & Griffin, 1998) also confirms the widespread support of family literacy. Countries all over the world are becoming aware of the benefits of family literacy programs for families and schools. As you read the following chapters, whether you are a preservice or inservice teacher, administrator, funder, or academic, you will find information sure to be relevant to your needs and the needs of those participating in family literacy programs.

REFERENCES

Burgess, S. (1997). The role of shared reading in the development of phonological awareness: A longitudinal study of middle- to upper class children. *Early Childhood Development and Care, 127/128,* 191–199.

Bus, A.G., van IJzendoorn, M.H., & Pellegrini, A.D. (1995). Joint book reading makes for success in learning to read: A meta-analysis on intergenerational transmission of literacy. *Review of Educational Research, 65*(1), 1–21.

DeCastell, S., & Luke, A. (1983). Defining "literacy" in North American schools: Social and historical conditions and consequences. *Journal of Curriculum Studies, 15,* 373–389.

Gadsden, V.L. (2000). Intergenerational literacy within families. In M.L. Kamil, P.B. Mosenthal, P.D. Pearson, & R. Barr (Eds.), *Handbook of reading research* (Vol. 3, pp. 871–887). Mahwah, NJ: Erlbaum.

Heath, S.B. (1983). *Ways with words: Language, life and work in communities and classrooms.* Cambridge, UK: Cambridge University Press.

International Reading Association and the National Association for the Education of Young Children. (1998). *Learning to read and write: Developmentally appropriate practices for young children.* A joint position statement of the International Reading Association (IRA) and the National Association for the Education of Young Children (NAEYC). Newark, DE: Author; Washington, DC: Author.

Morrow, L.M. (1983). Home and school correlates of early interest in literature. *Journal of Educational Research, 76,* 221–230.

Paratore, J.R. (2001). *Opening doors, opening opportunities: Family literacy in an urban community.* Boston: Allyn & Bacon.

Purcell-Gates, V. (2000). Family literacy. In M.L. Kamil, P.B. Mosenthal, P.D. Pearson, & R. Barr (Eds.), *Handbook of reading research* (Vol. 3, pp. 853–870). Mahwah, NJ: Erlbaum.

Snow, C.E., Burns, M.S., & Griffin, P. (Eds.). (1998). *Preventing reading difficulties in young children.* Washington, DC: National Academy Press.

Springate, K.W., & Stegelin, D.A. (1999). *Building school and community partnerships through parental involvement.* Englewood Cliffs, NJ: Merrill.

Taylor, D. (Ed.). (1983). *Family literacy: Young children learning to read and write.* Portsmouth, NH: Heinemann.

Taylor, D. (1997). *Many families, many literacies: An international declaration of principles.* Portsmouth, NH: Heinemann.

Teale, W.H. (1984). Reading to young children: Its significance for literacy development. In H. Goelman, A. Oberg, & F. Smith (Eds.), *Awakening to literacy* (pp. 110–121). Portsmouth, NH: Heinemann.

SECTION I

Theoretical Perspectives Related to Family Literacy

CHAPTER 1

Building on Family Literacies: Examining the Past and Planning the Future

Jeanne R. Paratore

The role that parents play in their children's education has long been a focus of study by educators and policymakers, particularly regarding efforts to understand high rates of failure among some groups of children. Evidence documenting a relationship between children's early reading success and parents' own reading behaviors has led many educators to seek educational interventions that address the family as a whole rather than the child alone. Sticht and McDonald (1989) were among the earliest educators to refer to such programs as *intergenerational literacy programs*, and subsequently others have referred to them variously as *two-generation programs* (St. Pierre, Layzer, & Barnes, 1998) or as *family literacy programs* (Benjamin & Lord, 1996; Edwards, 1990; Morrow, 1995).

Of particular interest has been the relationship between children's school success and two parent-related factors: parental education and home literacy practices. The importance of the first factor, parental education, is underscored by results from the National Assessment of Educational Progress (NAEP). Over several NAEP administrations, results have consistently shown that children with parents who have higher levels of education have higher rates of performance on achievement tests in all subject areas (Donahue, Voelkl, Campbell, & Mazzeo, 1999). Parents' levels of education also correlate with the degree of parental involvement in their children's schooling. Those without high school diplomas are less likely to attend school events and general or scheduled meetings with teachers and are less likely to serve as volunteers or committee members (National Center for Education Statistics [NCES], 2001). Parents' level of education also has been found to correlate with their personal and parental reading habits. Data indicate that parents who did not complete high school are less likely to read newspapers, magazines, or books (NCES, 2001), and they are less likely to read to their children (NCES, 2000). This finding gains importance when juxtaposed with evidence that children who report having four types of reading materials in the home (books, magazines, newspapers, and encyclopedias) achieve higher reading scores than those who report having fewer reading materials (Donahue, Finnegan, Lutkus, Allen, & Campbell, 2001).

Data that relate parental education to a host of societal issues also have been used to support the need for intergenerational literacy programs. Parents who have not completed high school are more likely to live in poverty. They have substantially higher rates of unemployment and, in cases in which they work, have fewer job opportunities and earn substantially less money than their peers who have completed high school (Children's Defense Fund, 2000). Parents without high school diplomas are also three times more likely than high school graduates to receive public assistance (NCES, 1998). These correlations are important because children who attend schools in lower income communities tend to have lower average reading scores than their peers in higher income school communities (Donahue et al., 2001).

The importance of the second parent-related factor in relation to children's school success, home literacy practices, became a particular focus in 1966 with the publication of Dolores Durkin's oft-cited study on children who read early. In the years since her study, home literacy practices have received substantial support from numerous other investigations. In the published study, Durkin compares the home experiences of early and nonearly readers. She finds that early readers have parents who spend time with them; who read to them; who answer their questions and requests for help; and who demonstrate in their own lives that reading is a rich source of relaxation, information, and commitment.

Durkin's conclusion that home literacy experiences play an important role in children's eventual school success received additional support in many subsequent investigations (e.g., Briggs & Elkind, 1977;

Clark, 1976; Dunn, 1981; Mason, 1980; Morrow, 1983). The accumulated body of evidence led Anderson, Hiebert, Scott, and Wilkinson (1985) to conclude that "the single most important activity for building the knowledge required for eventual success in reading is reading aloud to children" (p. 23). Although this conclusion was challenged in 1994 by Scarborough and Dobrich, a 1995 meta-analysis by Bus, van IJzendoorn, and Pellegrini led to clear and strong support for parent-child storybook reading as an important preschool experience for developing children's reading skills.

As noted previously, important interrelationships exist between home literacy practices and parents' levels of education, with parents who have higher levels of education being substantially more likely to read to their children and to take them to the library than parents with lower levels of education. Taken together, the evidence related to both parental education and home literacy practices argues for parental educational programs designed to accomplish two goals: to help parents advance their own levels of education and to help parents come to understand activities and practices that will help their children attain reasonably high levels of education. Such programs are now commonly referred to as family literacy programs. Although they share a similar descriptor, individual programs differ in the ways they attempt to address their common goals. Some programs offer direct instruction to parents only, with the intention of affecting children's literacy learning through parental actions at home. Other programs provide direct instruction in literacy to parents and children in separate settings and also involve parents and children in joint literacy events and activities that occur at the school. Some programs also require that parents participate in a parenting component, apparently on the basis of an as-yet undocumented assumption that parents who lack literacy proficiency also lack understanding of effective parenting practices. The program model that may be most widely practiced in the United States was first put forth by Sharon Darling and described in an article by Darling and Hayes (1988–1989) at the National Center for Family Literacy. This program model has become the basis for the largest federally funded family literacy initiative—the Even Start Program. This model includes four components: parent literacy education, child lit-

eracy education, parent and child activity time, and parenting education.

In recent years, family literacy programs have proliferated in schools
and communities across the United States and, at the same time, have
become the focus of vigorous debate. Many educators and policymakers view them as the answer to a host of problems associated with
society in general (e.g., unemployment, crime, and poverty) and school
failure in particular. For example, Darling (1997), founder and president of the National Center for Family Literacy, asserts that family literacy is one of the most important initiatives in the effort to reform U.S.
welfare programs and suggests that family literacy programs have the
potential to strengthen family values and functioning and to advance
families toward self-sufficiency. Darling's viewpoint enjoys substantial
U.S. political and legislative support. As a result, family literacy interventions are now singled out as a priority in many federally and state-
funded U.S. reading programs for early childhood, elementary, and
adult education.

Other educators, however, strongly disagree with the claim that education will provide a shield against poverty, low employment, and
other societal problems. Among the most vocal supporters on this side
of the debate, Taylor has relied on a six-year ethnographic study of
families living in poverty (Taylor & Dorsey-Gaines, 1988), as well as
numerous anecdotal accounts collected from parents, teachers, and researchers (Taylor, 1997) to argue that high unemployment and poverty result from inequalities within society that prevent individuals from
achieving economic advancement despite personal motivation or educational attainment. Those sharing this viewpoint (e.g., Auerbach,
1995, 1997) also point to census data indicating that race and gender correlate more highly with unemployment and poverty than education does.

People on each side of the debate differ not only in what they believe
to be the likely outcomes of family literacy intervention programs but
also in their perceptions of the literate lives of families who often are targeted as participants in such programs. For example, Darling and her
colleagues at the National Center for Family Literacy (Darling & Hayes,
1988–1989; Potts & Paull, 1995) describe the daily lives of such families
as essentially devoid of any literate activity and, as a consequence,

unlikely to provide children with sufficient opportunities to acquire basic knowledge about literacy and language. Parents with low literacy, these researchers say, lack the resources to support their children's school success and, as a result, perpetuate an intergenerational cycle of low literacy.

In contrast, researchers such as Heath (1983), Moll and Greenberg (1991), Taylor and Dorsey-Gaines (1988), and Teale (1986) assert that nearly all families embed some forms of literacy and language events within their daily routines. However, these events often are different from those that teachers expect and know, and as a result, the events go unnoticed. Proponents of this viewpoint support their claim with evidence from studies across different cultural, linguistic, and economic groups. They conclude that children fail not because they are language and literacy deprived, but because they are language and literacy different. As such, they enter the schoolhouse doors without knowledge of language patterns and literacy events that are valued and privileged in most classrooms.

Gadsden (1994) summarized the disagreement and dissension that characterizes the work in family literacy. She believes they emerge from two seriously conflicting premises: one that perceives the family's lack of school-like literacy as a barrier to learning, and the other that sees the home literacy practices that are already present—however different they may be from school-based literacy—as a bridge to new learnings. Rather than choosing sides in the debate, however, Gadsden argues that both premises may be useful. She suggests that educators might adopt a reciprocal approach predicated on an understanding that teachers need to instruct parents in school-based literacy *and also* seek to learn about and integrate parents' existing knowledge and resources into school curricula.

Sorting out the differences and disagreements has been difficult because, as noted by both Purcell-Gates (2000) and Gadsden (2000) in their respective research syntheses, the field of family literacy is not one that is rich in rigorously designed, evaluative studies. Instead, it is thick with studies that provide substantial evidence of learning by participants in family literacy programs but that lack a control group that would allow analysis of the extent to which such change can be attributed to the instructional intervention. Despite the methodological weaknesses, the existing studies are useful in examining what benefits might amass for the families who take advantage of family literacy intervention programs. In the remainder of this chapter, my purpose is to try to step back from the political and philosophical debate about family literacy and to look narrowly at practice to examine what seems to work and what does not, as well as to suggest some directions for future research and practice. In doing so, I will examine three types of programs: those that provide comprehensive services to parents and children; those that provide services to parents, and through the parent, with the intent of influencing the literacy achievement of both parents and children; and those that focus on affecting the literacy achievement of the child alone, with the parent as the instrument of change.

Looking at Practice

I begin this exploration with an examination of the results of the U.S. evaluation of the Even Start family literacy program. I choose this as a beginning point for three reasons. First, in comparison to most other family literacy initiatives, Even Start has the most ambitious goal, which is "to help break the cycle of poverty and illiteracy by improving the educational opportunities available to low-income families with limited educational experiences" (St. Pierre, Gamse, Alamprese, Rimdzius, & Tao, 1998). Second, as federally funded initiatives, Even Start programs have grown rapidly since their inception, increasing in service from 76 grantees in 1989 to over 637 grantees in 1996–1997 that serve over 48,000 children and 36,000 adults (1998). The mere scope of the program makes it important. Third, in keeping with U.S. legislative guidelines, Even Start programs uniformly provide families with a range of services, including adult education, parenting education, and early childhood services. As such, it provides a measure of the effectiveness of programs that subscribe to this particular design. The evidence provided here is based on a report of a series of evaluation studies conducted from 1994 to 1997 by St. Pierre and his colleagues (St. Pierre, Gamse, et al., 1998). This report represents the most recent publication of evidence from the research group appointed to conduct a national evaluation of the Even Start program's effects.

Although programs vary widely, St. Pierre, Gamse, et al. (1998) report that more than half of the projects in operation in 1995–1996 offered 32 hours or more of adult education per month, 13 hours or more of parenting education per month, and 34 hours or more of early childhood education per month. However, attendance data provided by individual projects indicate actual participation rates to be substantially lower, with adults participating in an average of 95 hours per year of adult education and 30 hours per year of parenting education. Data related to actual attendance of children in early childhood education were not reported.

Outcome measures suggest that adults participating in Even Start made gains on a measure of reading achievement. However, with the exception of one small-scale study, there is no control group to verify that gains are attributable to Even Start participation. Measures of children's language development and reading readiness show significantly higher performance for Even Start children when compared to children in a randomly assigned control group. However, control group children showed gains in the next year when they entered preschool or kindergarten. On a measure used to assess changes in parenting behaviors, Even Start parents made significant, moderate-sized gains whereas parents in a control group did not achieve similar gains. Finally, both employment status and income increased over time for Even Start parents; however, neither of these indicators was greater than those for control group families.

St. Pierre, Gamse, et al. (1998) also examined the effects of particular programmatic factors and reported that children in programs that occurred in schools or early childhood centers had higher rates of achievement than did children in programs that emphasized home-based services. In addition, families in programs that provided large amounts of time for parents and children together had home environments with more materials, more frequent parent-child learning activities, and better approaches to discipline than families in programs with smaller amounts of parent-child time together. Finally, data related to the importance of parenting education were conflicting. Findings from the first national evaluation show a positive relationship between the amount of parenting education received and children's vocabulary test scores, demonstrating that the more parenting education parents received, the higher their children's vocabulary scores were, data from the second evaluation show no such relationship. St. Pierre, Gamse, et al. (1998) suggest that the different findings may be attributable to a change in the content of the parenting education component:

> If Even Start's approach of training parents to be their children's first and best teachers is to work, then projects need to implement a high-quality, literacy-based parenting education component. In Even Start's early years, projects received strong messages from the federal level to focus on literacy-based parenting education. Once the responsibility for administering Even Start was transferred to the states, technical assistance became less focused and there is anecdotal evidence that parenting education has become more diffuse—a catch-all for a variety of parent-focused services including health education, nutrition education and life skills. If this is so, it helps explain the disappearance in the second national evaluation of the relationship between amount of parenting education and child test gains. (p. 26)

(See chapter 8 for further discussion of Even Start.)

The Basic Skills Agency's Demonstration Programmes developed and implemented in England and Wales (Brooks, Gorman, Harman, Hutchison, & Wilkin, 1996) also are characterized as a comprehensive approach to family literacy. This initiative has two primary goals: "to raise standards of literacy among adults with difficulties and their children, and to extend awareness of the importance of literacy and the role of family literacy" (p. 3). The evaluation report describes the four demonstration programs that are its focus as situated in areas of "multiple deprivation" (1996, p. 4). Parents attended a fixed amount of class time (96 hours). In their separate sessions, they received instruction relevant to their own literacy advancement. Parents also learned about the early stages of literacy and examined ways to help their children achieve academic success. The children-only sessions provided developmentally appropriate instruction in literacy. In the joint sessions, parents worked with their own children and applied what they had learned about helping their children. For children, results indicated greater than expected average improvements on measures of vocabulary, reading, and writing during the course of instruction and 12 weeks after completion of class and indicated normal progress in the next 6 months. For parents, results indicated improved average scores on measures of reading and writing both immediately following the intervention and on the follow-up assessments. In addition, parents reported having greater confidence in their academic and social skills and having increased their levels of involvement in their children's schools. Brooks and colleagues attribute the positive outcomes to a combination of factors, such as the programs' clear aims and objectives, careful selection of program sites, highly qualified and reflective teachers who were responsive to parents' needs and purposes, joint planning between adult basic skills and early years teachers, highly motivated parents, and opportunities for immediate practice of learned strategies during joint parent-child sessions. As in the case of the Even Start investigations, the results are encouraging, but the lack of a control group does not allow a conclusion that gains can be attributed to program effects alone.

Project FLAME (Family Literacy: Aprendiendo, Mejorando, Educando [Learning, Improving, Educating]) represents a second type of family literacy project, one that provides service directly to the parent and intends to reach the child through the parent. This project was developed and implemented by researchers at the University of Illinois. Shanahan, Mulhern, and Rodríguez-Brown (1995) explain that Project FLAME is based on some key assumptions that a supportive home environment is essential to literacy development, that parents can have a positive effect on their children's learning, and that parents who are confident and successful learners will be effective teachers for their children. Shanahan and colleagues note that appropriation of the term *family literacy* "implies specific types of literacy use, motives for learning, and opportunities for shared practice. Simultaneous and connected learning opportunities for children and parents develop social networks of literacy learning and use that will nurture ongoing literacy development" (pp. 40–41). In keeping with the stated assumptions and understanding of family literacy as a construct, teachers provide instruction in English as a second language to Hispanic parents and teach them how to support children's educational success. Teachers emphasize increasing the availability of literacy materials at home, and they teach parents how to both select appropriate books and magazines for children and use the library. The Project FLAME program instructors teach strategies for parent-child storybook reading, for teaching alphabet names and sounds, and for sharing language games and songs. They also teach parents appropriate strategies for contacting and interacting with their children's teachers. Studies of outcomes of Project FLAME (Rodríguez-Brown, Fen Li, & Albom, 1999; Rodríguez-Brown & Meehan, 1998; Shanahan et al., 1995) indicate that it leads to improved English proficiency for parents, statistically significant improvements in children's knowledge of letter names and print and language concepts, more frequent visits by the parents to their children's schools, greater numbers of literacy materials at home, and parents' increased confidence in helping with their children's homework. As is the case with the studies reported previously, the absence of a control group prevents attributing the increases to the effects of Project FLAME alone. Further, in a comparative study of program effects using a class of preschoolers from one of the Project FLAME schools, no significant differences between Project FLAME participants and comparison group children were found. (See chapter 6 for further information on Project FLAME.)

The lack of significant difference in the data could be interpreted in a number of ways. For example, it may be that *both* programs provide children with beneficial services and as such are equally advantageous. Or, it may be that in the short term, programs that offer services only to children are equally successful, but over the long term, differences may be observed. That is, when parents are prepared to support children's literacy learning beyond preschool, benefits may amass for the children in later years. In order to fully interpret the apparent lack of difference in the outcomes, perhaps more detailed and longer-term data are needed.

The Intergenerational Literacy Project (ILP) (Paratore, 1993, 2001) is similar in design to Project FLAME. Its purpose is threefold: to support the literacy development of parents, to help parents support their children's literacy development at home, and to provide parents with information about school culture and ways in which they can help their children succeed in school. Since its inception in 1989, nearly 2,000 parents have participated in ILP, virtually all of whom have been immigrants to the mainland United States, with approximately 75% having been in the United States for fewer than 10 years. Parents attend classes in a building that serves as both an adult and an early childhood education center. Parents participate in six to eight hours of literacy instruction each week. The participants use authentic literacy materials, including readings of adult interest and family literacy support materials. Instructors model parent–child storybook reading, which is discussed in class, and the instructors encourage the participants to borrow books from the program's extensive multilingual and multicultural children's library to share with their children at home. In addition, instructors teach parents how to observe their children's uses of literacy at home and introduce them to the idea of involving their children in the collection of literacy samples in family literacy portfolios. Parents are provided instruction in the purpose of family literacy portfolios and the types of materials to collect, with emphasis placed on the importance of including both samples of children's written work (e.g., drawings, stories, and letters) and parents' own written observations. Each week, parents are asked to share examples from their children's family literacy portfolios with other members of their ILP class and to discuss other uses of literacy that might be documented. Additionally, instructors teach the parents strategies for sharing their children's family literacy portfolios with teachers during informal meetings and in parent–teacher conferences. (See chapter 13 for a more in-depth description of the use of family literacy portfolios.)

Infants and toddlers of parents participating in the ILP attend a separate children's program while their parents attend literacy classes. The children's setting is a literacy-rich environment, directed by an early childhood teacher whose purpose is to optimize children's opportunities to learn about literacy and language through play.

Over the years of the ILP, a diverse collection of evaluation practices have been used to monitor and document its outcomes. These evaluations include evidence of attendance and retention, writing progress for both parents and children, parents' personal uses of reading and writing, parents' engagement of their children in literacy activities, and children's success in school. Documentation has included parents' self-reported data; reading and writing samples from parents and children; interviews with parents, teachers, and children; questionnaires completed by parents and teachers; and school records. The findings from a series of studies (Melzi, Paratore, & Krol-Sinclair, 2000; Paratore, 1993, 1994, 2001; Paratore, Melzi, & Krol-Sinclair, 1999) indicate that parents achieve rates of attendance and retention that exceed those of traditional adult basic education, they increase their use of reading and writing outside of class to achieve personal goals (thereby making print literacy a more frequent routine in their daily lives), and they increase the frequency with which they engage their children in literacy events (e.g., storytelling, writing, and talking about experiences) in general and storybook reading in particular. Once again, the results are encouraging and suggest the potential for family literacy interventions to have beneficial outcomes; however, the absence of a control group prevents attributing gains to the effects of project participation alone.

A third type of family literacy program focuses primarily on teaching parents to implement activities at home that will improve their children's early literacy knowledge. Such projects do not have as a goal the advancement of parents' own literacy abilities. A project recently reported by Jordan, Snow, and Porche (2000), Project EASE, represents this type of program. This project was implemented within a community of primarily European American families with a median income well above the poverty level. The project was conducted within four of nine elementary schools that were chosen because they were designated as Title I schools and, therefore, had a higher incidence of poverty than other schools in the district. A large percentage of children in the focal schools performed within the bottom quartile on standardized tests. Children in the families that participated were all attending half-day kindergarten in one of the four schools. A total of 248 children served as project participants—177 students in a group that received the intervention and 71 students in the control group. The intervention comprised 5 one-month units that included a parent education session during which literacy activities were modeled, opportunities to practice those activities with the child were given, and scripted activities for use at home were distributed weekly by the teachers. Using an experimental design that included pre- and posttesting of children's language and literacy knowledge, Jordan and colleagues reported "striking" (2000, p. 537) impact of participation in the intervention. Children in the treatment group demonstrated statistically significant gains greater than their control group peers on measures of language and literacy. In addition, Jordan and colleagues found that the amount of participation mattered. Those families who participated in more of the intervention activities had greater gains than those who participated in fewer. Further, positive effects were greatest for those children who began the project with the lowest levels of achievement on pretest measures. Jordan and colleagues suggest that their results are especially important because of the nature of the sample participants. The participants were not the neediest families; rather, they were considered to be moderate to low-risk for learning failure and from families with median family incomes above the poverty level and access to good schools. Jordan and colleagues note that even in families with these advantages, their evidence suggests "room for parental involvement to improve children's school performance" (p. 538).

In another example of this program type, Morrow and Young (1997) examined the effects on children's literacy of their parents' involvement in developmentally appropriate literacy activities, including parent–child storybook reading, recording environmental print, journal writing, storytelling, and the use of children's magazines as a home-school connection. Monthly meetings with teachers, parents, and children together provided opportunities for parents and children to share ideas, for teachers to find out what parents and children wanted to learn, and for parents and children to work together. The family program was developed as a complement to a literature-based classroom program, which included literacy centers, teacher-modeled literature activities, and child-centered writing and reading appreciation periods. The program was implemented in a high-poverty urban school district with mostly African American and Latino families. Children in 6 first-grade classes were randomly assigned to treatment and control groups. Twelve children from each classroom were randomly selected for the data pool. Children in the treatment group participated in both the school and home programs, whereas children in the control group participated in the school program only. Outcome measures indicated that children in the experimental group outscored their control group peers on all achievement measures and on teacher ratings of interest and motivation.

Keeping Up With the Children (KUC) (Brooks et al., 2002) is a third example of a family literacy program that has been developed to help parents help their children. It introduces parents to what Corno (1989) describes as "classroom literacy" (p. 29) by providing them with information about the structure and teaching methods of the classroom literacy and numeracy programs. Brooks et al. note that the program's

> most innovative feature was to take the literacy hour or the daily maths session and adapt them, using adult content, but keeping the same pedagogy, so that parents experienced, directly the ways in which their children were now being taught. (2002, p. 12)

Questionnaire data from a total of 246 parents, interview data from 10 local coordinators and 30 program staff, and observations by researchers of 31 instructional sessions examined effects of the program on parents' interactions with their children and their children's teachers. Results indicate that parents acquired increased confidence in helping their children, as well as increased knowledge and understanding of how children learn and ways to help their children learn.

Learning From Practice

What does this brief summary of the effects of different program models teach us about practice, and what questions does it leave unanswered? First, when outcomes are considered in relation to literacy-related goals and objectives for children, it is fair to say that all program models are successful in achieving some level of success. In each case, evidence exists that efforts to involve parents in their children's literacy learning result at least in the short-term in higher levels of performance for children on literacy-related measures. In the few cases where comparison data are available, these levels of achievement surpass that of comparison group peers (Jordan et al., 2000; Morrow & Young, 1997; St. Pierre, Gamse, et al., 1998). The evidence presented by St. Pierre and colleagues that the early gains of children diminish over a relatively short period of time is troubling but not surprising. It speaks to the importance and persistence of the factors that put children at risk for school failure in the first place—in particular, the effects of poverty and language and cultural differences on school-based learning. The evidence underscores the need for serious and determined examination of ways to extend home-school intervention efforts beyond the preschool and primary grade years. (See chapter 4 for suggested strategies for home–school collaborations with families of adolescents.)

Second, although evidence related to gains in parents' literacy abilities is less both in size and methodological rigor by comparison to data on children, the results from the various program types remain consistent—adults make measurable gains in literacy abilities in relatively short periods of time. One might speculate that time spent by parents on their own literacy and time spent supporting their children's literacy combine to increase parents' opportunities to practice reading and writing, and as a result, lead to more rapid learning gains (Paratore, 1993).

Third, when effects of family literacy interventions on non-literacy-related outcomes are examined, the results are far less positive. Despite allocation of a sizeable amount of programmatic time to parenting education, no convincing evidence exists that Even Start programs have an impact on parenting abilities or that any changes in parents' employment or income status can be attributed to participation in any of the family literacy programs.

So, what do the data mean for future policy, research, and practice? Although there is a clear need for more and better data, the current evidence suggests some future steps. First, there is good reason to continue to support family literacy interventions aimed at increasing the literacy knowledge of both children and adults. The decision to design and implement such programs as short-term interventions, however, may underestimate the persistence of the recognized risk factors in children's school success and parents' economic stability. Reconceptualizing the interventions as multiyear efforts will require not only a greater economic commitment by schools and funding agencies but also adjustments to popular program models. For example, it may not be reasonable to expect parents to maintain a multiyear commitment to literacy classes that require attendance four or five days a week when they also need to attend to a full range of economic, personal, and family responsibilities. Rather, it may be necessary to consider a multiphase model that decreases in instructional intensity over a period of years, while still offering consistent and routine instruction.

Second, for children enrolled in school beyond the preschool and kindergarten levels, models that require on-site parent-child activity time during the school day may diminish the amount of instructional time available for high-quality, teacher-led instruction and cause fragmentation in children's school-based academic programs. Multiyear engagement will require a plan for modifying or meeting the requirement for joint parent-child activities outside the child's regular school day without imposing a further burden on parents who already have many family and employment responsibilities.

Third, achieving more lasting gains may require greater reciprocity in learning between parents and teachers. That is, as family literacy programs are currently implemented, they largely conform to what Swap (1993) refers to as programs for transmitting rather than transforming knowledge. The burden for change rests primarily, often even exclusively, on the shoulders of parents. They are expected to incorporate school-like literacy and learning routines within the fabric of their everyday lives. Data document that parents who participate in family literacy programs are relatively successful at doing this. They increase the amount of time they spend in parent-child storybook reading, storytelling, language games, and library visits—all practices that have been proven to support children's school success. Despite these additions to their home literacy lives, it is likely that they and their children continue to use language and literacy in ways that are quite different from what teachers expect and encourage in classrooms, and despite the newly developed areas of congruence, it is likely that there remains much that is disparate between home and school. Increased efforts by teachers to learn about and build on the multiple ways in which parents and children use literacy outside school may help children to maintain, even increase, the gains they make during initial family literacy interventions. The model in Figure 1.1 for extending the literacy context to include both home and school literacies proposed by Shockley, Michalove, and Allen (1995) provides an excellent starting place.

Fourth, the lack of evidence of measurable outcomes related to parenting education may suggest the need to reexamine and rethink this program requirement. Is it accurate to assume that parents who lack English literacy and language knowledge also lack adequate parenting

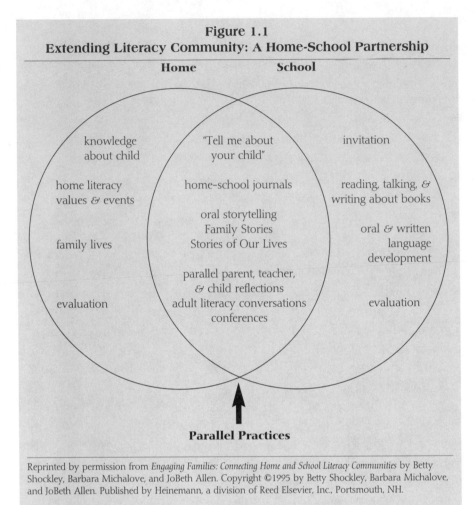

Figure 1.1
Extending Literacy Community: A Home-School Partnership

Home   School

knowledge   "Tell me about   invitation
about child   your child"

home literacy   home-school journals   reading, talking, &
values & events   writing about books

                       oral storytelling
                       Family Stories   oral & written
family lives   Stories of Our Lives   language
                                                  development

                       parallel parent, teacher,
                       & child reflections
evaluation   adult literacy conversations   evaluation
                       conferences

Parallel Practices

Reprinted by permission from *Engaging Families: Connecting Home and School Literacy Communities* by Betty Shockley, Barbara Michalove, and JoBeth Allen. Copyright ©1995 by Betty Shockley, Barbara Michalove, and JoBeth Allen. Published by Heinemann, a division of Reed Elsevier, Inc., Portsmouth, NH.

abilities? Can the time allocated to parenting education be more effectively spent in activities more directly and centrally related to improving adults' and children's literacy and language abilities? Given the limited amount of time available for any educational intervention, and the evidence that suggests that more instructional time leads to greater learning gains (e.g., Jordan et al., 2000; Melzi et al., 2000), further investigation of the benefits of this particular program component is an important consideration.

Conclusion

Most children in today's classrooms are achieving success in learning to read and write. However, most is not all, and as teachers, we have the responsibility to serve *every* child who enters our classrooms. There is good evidence that some children fail not because they lack intellectual ability or motivation to learn, but rather, at least in part, because their home and school learning lives lack congruence. It is true that such failure often occurs from generation to generation in families that are economically poor or linguistically and culturally different. What is not true is that parents are to blame for such cycles of failure or that the cycle of failure can be stopped by "fixing" the parent. Rather, the evidence suggests a problem far more complex than that—one that requires much more than short-term change to children's home literacy experiences. The evidence related to family literacy interventions tells us that such programs may provide children with a better starting point for learning. However, to the extent that such interventions stand alone and outside the context of the child's full and long-term educational program, the gains are likely to be erased long before the completion of the early school years. If we expect our educational and economic investment to pay off, it is likely that we will need to conceptualize parents and children as learning partners well into the elementary school years.

REFERENCES

Anderson, R.C., Hiebert, E.H., Scott, J., & Wilkinson, I.A.G. (1985). *Becoming a nation of readers. The report of the Commission on Reading.* Washington, DC: National Institute of Education.

Auerbach, E. (1995). Deconstructing the discussion of strengths in family literacy. *Journal of Reading Behavior, 27*(4), 643–661.

Auerbach, E. (1997). Reading between the lines. In D. Taylor (Ed.), *Many families, many literacies: An international declaration of principles* (pp. 71–81). Portsmouth, NH: Heinemann.

Benjamin, L.A., & Lord, J. (Eds.). (1996). *Family literacy: Directions in research and implications for practice.* Washington, DC: U.S. Department of Education, OERI.

Briggs, C., & Elkind, D. (1977). Characteristics of early readers. *Perceptual and Motor Skills, 44,* 1231–1237.

Brooks, G., Cole, P., Davies, P., Davis, B., Frater, G., Harman, J., et al. (2002). *Keeping up with the children.* London: Basic Skills Agency.

Brooks, G., Gorman, T., Harman, J., Hutchison, D., & Wilkin, A. (1996). *Family literacy works: The NFER evaluation of the Basic Skills Agency's Demonstration Programmes.* London: Basic Skills Agency.

Bus, A.G., van IJzendoorn, M.H., & Pellegrini, A.D. (1995). Joint book reading makes for success in learning to read: A meta-analysis on intergenerational transmission of literacy. *Review of Educational Research, 65*(1), 1–21.

Children's Defense Fund. (2000). *State of America's children.* Washington, DC: Author.

Clark, M.M. (1976). *Young fluent readers: What they can teach us.* London: Heinemann.

Corno, L. (1989). What it means to be literate about classrooms. In D. Bloom (Ed.), *Classrooms and literacy* (pp. 29–52). Westport, CT: Ablex.

Darling, S. (1997, April). *Opening session speech.* Paper presented at the 6th Annual Conference on Family Literacy, Louisville, KY.

Darling, S., & Hayes, A. (1988–1989). *Family Literacy Project final project report.* Louisville, KY: National Center for Family Literacy.

Donahue, P.L., Finnegan, R.J., Lutkus, A.D., Allen, N.L., & Campbell, J.R. (2001). *The nation's report card: Fourth-grade. Reading 2000.* Washington, DC: National Center for Education Statistics.

Donahue, P.L., Voelkl, K.E., Campbell, J.R., & Mazzeo, J. (1999). *NAEP 1998: Reading report card for the nation.* Washington, DC: National Center for Education Statistics.

Dunn, N.E. (1981). Children's achievement at school-entry age as a function of mothers' and fathers' teaching sets. *The Elementary School Journal, 81,* 245–253.

Durkin, D. (1966). *Children who read early: Two longitudinal studies.* New York: Teachers College Press.

Edwards, P.A. (1990). *Parents as partners in reading: A family literacy training program.* Chicago: Children's Press.

Gadsden, V.L. (1994). *Understanding family literacy: Conceptual issues facing the field.* Philadelphia: University of Pennsylvania National Center for Adult Literacy.

Gadsden, V.L. (2000). Intergenerational literacy within families. In M.L. Kamil, P.B. Mosenthal, P.D. Pearson, & R. Barr (Eds.), *Handbook of reading research* (Vol. 3, pp. 871–888). Mahwah, NJ: Erlbaum.

Heath, S.B. (1983). *Ways with words: Language, life and work in communities and classrooms.* Cambridge, UK: Cambridge University Press.

Jordan, G.E., Snow, C.E., & Porche, M.V. (2000). Project EASE: The effect of a family literacy project on kindergarten students' early literacy skills. *Reading Research Quarterly, 35,* 524–546.

Mason, J.M. (1980). When do children begin to read: An exploration of four-year-old children's letter and word reading competencies. *Reading Research Quarterly, 15,* 203–227.

Melzi, G., Paratore, J.R., & Krol-Sinclair, B. (2000). Reading and writing in the daily lives of Latino mothers who participate in a family literacy program. In T. Shanahan & F.V. Rodríguez-Brown (Eds.), *49th yearbook of the National Reading Conference* (pp. 178–193). Chicago: National Reading Conference.

Moll, L.C., & Greenberg, J.B. (1991). Creating zones of possibilities: Combining social contexts for instruction. In L.C. Moll (Ed.), *Vygotsky and education: Instructional implications and applications of sociohistorical psychology* (pp. 319–348). New York: Cambridge University Press.

Morrow, L.M. (1983). Home and school correlates of early interest in literature. *Journal of Educational Research, 76,* 221–230.

Morrow, L.M. (Ed.). (1995). *Family literacy connections in schools and communities.* Newark, DE: International Reading Association.

Morrow, L.M., & Young, J. (1997). A collaborative family literacy program: The effects on children's motivation and literacy achievement. *Early Child Development and Care, 127/128,* 13–25.

National Center for Education Statistics (NCES). (1998). *The condition of education.* Washington, DC: Author.

National Center for Education Statistics. (2000). *The condition of education.* Washington, DC: Author.

National Center for Education Statistics. (2001). *The condition of education.* Washington, DC: Author.

Paratore, J.R. (1993). Influence of an intergenerational approach to literacy on the practice of literacy of parents and their children. In C. Kinzer & D. Leu (Eds.), *Examining central issues in literacy, research, theory, and practice* (pp. 83–91). Chicago: National Reading Conference.

Paratore, J.R. (1994). Parents and children sharing literacy. In D. Lancy (Ed.), *Children's emergent literacy: From research to practice* (pp. 193–216). Westport, CT: Praeger.

Paratore, J.R. (2001). *Opening doors, opening opportunities: Family literacy in an urban community.* Boston: Allyn & Bacon.

Paratore, J.R., Melzi, G., & Krol-Sinclair, B. (1999). *What should we expect of family literacy? Experiences of Latino children whose parents participate in an intergenerational literacy project.* Newark, DE: International Reading Association; Chicago: National Reading Conference.

Potts, M.W., & Paull, S. (1995). A comprehensive approach to family-focused services. In L.M. Morrow (Ed.), *Family literacy connections in schools and communities* (pp. 167–183). Newark, DE: International Reading Association.

Purcell-Gates, V. (2000). Family literacy. In M.L. Kamil, P.B. Mosenthal, P.D. Pearson, & R. Barr (Eds.), *Handbook of reading research* (Vol. 3, pp. 853–870). Mahwah, NJ: Erlbaum.

Rodríguez-Brown, F., Fen Li, R., & Albom, J.A. (1999). Hispanic parents' awareness and use of literacy-rich environments at home and in the community. *Education and Urban Society, 32,* 41–57.

Rodríguez-Brown, F., & Meehan, M.A. (1998). Family literacy and adult education: Project FLAME. In M.C. Smith (Ed.), *Literacy for the 21st century: Research, policy, practices and the National Adult Literacy Survey* (pp. 175–193). Westport, CT: Greenwood.

Scarborough, H.S., & Dobrich, W. (1994). On the efficacy of reading to preschoolers. *Developmental Review, 14,* 245–302.

Shanahan, T., Mulhern, M., & Rodríguez-Brown, F. (1995). Project FLAME: Lessons learned from a family literacy program for minority families. *The Reading Teacher, 48,* 40–47.

Shockley, B., Michalove, B., & Allen, J. (1995). *Engaging families: Connecting home and school literacy communities.* Portsmouth, NH: Heinemann.

Sticht, T.G., & McDonald, B. (1989). *Making the nation smarter: The intergenerational transfer of literacy.* San Diego: Institute for Adult Literacy.

St. Pierre, R.G., Gamse, B., Alamprese, J., Rimdzius, T., & Tao, F. (1998). *National evaluation of the Even Start family literacy program: Evidence from the past and a look to the future.* Washington, DC: U.S. Department of Education Planning and Evaluation Service.

St. Pierre, R.G., Layzer, J.I., & Barnes, H.V. (1998). Regenerating two-generation programs. In W.S. Barnett & S.S. Boocock (Eds.), *Early care and education for children in poverty: Promises, programs, and long-term results* (pp. 99–122). Albany, NY: State University of New York Press.

Swap, S.M. (1993). *Developing home-school partnerships: From concepts to practice.* New York: Teachers College Press.

Taylor, D. (Ed.). (1997). *Many families, many literacies: An international declaration of principles.* Portsmouth, NH: Heinemann.

Taylor, D., & Dorsey Gaines, C. (1988). *Growing up literate: Learning from inner-city families.* Portsmouth, NH: Heinemann.

Teale, W.H. (1986). Home background and young children's literacy development. In W.H. Teale & E. Sulzby (Eds.), *Emergent literacy: Writing and reading* (pp. 173–206). Westport, CT: Ablex.

CHAPTER 2

Emergent Literacy

Donald J. Richgels

L iteracy is not an either–or phenomenon; young children are not either readers and writers or nonreaders and nonwriters. Rather, literacy is better characterized as a gradually emerging compe-tence. It develops along a broad continuum on which fall such varied processes as pretend reading of favorite storybooks, scribble writing, sounding out unfamiliar words, and invented spelling (Teale, 1987). In order for parents and teachers to know where children fall on this con-tinuum and to appreciate what children can do on their own and what they can do with just the right kinds of adult support, early literacy researchers have described phases of typical literacy development. McGee and Richgels (2000), for example, describe the literacy knowledge and behaviors of beginners, novices, experimenters, and conventional readers and writers. Dorn and Soffos (2001) present a very helpful con-tinuum, concentrating just on writing development, with phases for emergent writers, beginning early writers, late early writers, and transi-tional writers. A continuum of children's development in early reading and writing is found in a 1998 joint position statement of the International Reading Association (IRA) and the National Association for the Education of Young Children (NAEYC) titled *Learning to Read and Write: Developmentally Appropriate Practices for Young Children.* The position statement describes five phases of development: awareness and explo-ration, experimental reading and writing, early reading and writing, tran-sitional reading and writing, and independent and productive reading and writing.

A careful comparison of these descriptions of early literacy reveals basic agreement about benchmarks on the continuum of emergent literacy development. The authors of all three descriptions agree, as well, that they describe not a lock–step sequence of achievements but a complex unfolding of many kinds of knowing and many abilities such that no single snapshot of that process adequately captures the complexity. For example, children may appear to be at one place on an emergent literacy continuum when they read or write with specific kinds of help, with particular materials, and for certain purposes, and they may appear to be at another place when they read or write with other help, materials, or purposes. The descriptions, with their phases and benchmarks, are meant as guides for observers and helpers of young children, not as prescriptions of what children must do and when they must do it. They give parents and teachers rough indicators of children's current notions about literacy and skills with reading and writing; they also suggest potential next steps for children under appropriate supportive conditions that observant parents and teachers can then provide.

Overview of Literacy Development

This overview will use IRA and NAEYC's phases of development, but it also will include some descriptors or benchmarks from McGee and Richgels (2000). Greater consideration will be given to the first three phases (awareness and exploration, experimental reading and writing, and early reading and writing) because they—more than the last two phases—are represented mostly by emerging, not-yet-conventional literacy understandings and products and because fostering parents' and teachers' recognition of the authenticity and worthiness of such understandings and products is one of the purposes of this chapter.

Because the knowledge and abilities that comprise literacy benchmarks are so many and so varied, it is helpful to organize them within broad areas. This chapter will use McGee and Richgels's (2000) organization of literacy knowledge and abilities in terms of forms of written language (how it looks, from the shapes of alphabetic letters to the distinguishing looks of lists and stories and poems and reports), the meanings of written language (how it communicates, from the meanings of individual words to the themes of a story or the findings and conclusions of a report), meaning-form links in written language (how a text's meanings are determined by its forms, from the combination of letters that spell a word to the arrangement of ideas that signal a type of argument), and the functions of written language (what it accomplishes, from purposes that also are served by spoken language to those that are unique to written language).

PHASE 1: AWARENESS AND EXPLORATION

Awareness and exploration involve special attention to the wide variety of print and its many uses that children in most modern cultures see all around them, from product names on toys to directives on highway signs and from team insignia on athletic uniforms to print in children's books. Awareness implies a conscious knowing that something special is going on with these pervasive examples of written language, that grown-ups in children's lives are responding differently to writing than to other phenomena in the environment, that grown-ups want children to be involved in some of those responses, and even that grown-ups are expecting special, exploratory responses by children to some of those examples of written language.

Learning to read and write frequently requires conscious attention to language features that are used automatically and unconsciously in spoken language (phonemes—the sound units of which words are built—are just one such feature, and phonemic awareness is just one kind of consciousness raising required to read and write). So children's beginning to be aware of and to explore any aspect of written language is a very significant development, one often underappreciated because of beginners' unconventional and primitive-looking writing and reading products. Some onlookers would even deny (wrongly) that children are reading or writing in this phase.

Observant parents and teachers realize, however, that real writing and reading is happening whenever children consciously intend to convey meaning by their marks or to retrieve meanings by their interactions with print. A 4-year-old preschooler, for example, when asked to write a story, responded, "I know what story I should write...*Robin Hood*...and I should write the end part," and she did (McGee & Richgels, 1996, p. 217). The child wrote mostly with pictures and mock letters, but it is clear that she consciously conveyed meaning. Writing in the form of drawing is typical at this phase and does not detract from the importance of this child's communicative intention. Scribble writing, writing with mock letters, and pretend storybook reading also demonstrate intentional communication using written signs and so are legitimate writing and reading in this phase.

This sort of awareness does not necessarily originate in the actions of the child. It may begin with others' actions. A child, for example, may see a mother pause to read the print on a movie theater marquee or on a movie poster before deciding what movie to see and wonder, "What is she doing? Why is she doing that? What is she paying attention to?" The mother is demonstrating a function of written language—that it provides information. The child may come to recognize forms of written language, the block letters in rows on a marquee and the eye-catching print always combined with pictures on a movie poster. The meaning-form links on the poster enable easier reading than the block letters on the marquee; even a very young child can read the poster if the pictures are familiar from other contexts, such as movie advertising on television or a familiar cartoon, book, or television program from which the movie was adapted. Similarly, a parent may invite a child to pay attention to a logo by saying, for example, "Look at that *m* and here's another one! What kind of candy is this?" (M & Ms). This parent talk emphasizes meaning-form links—that the presence of those *m*s signifies a specific brand of candy—and it helps children achieve a benchmark of the awareness and exploration phase, reading uniquely configured print by attending to such visual features as size, font, and color (McGee & Richgels, 2000).

The IRA and NAEYC joint position statement (1998) lists other benchmarks of this phase, including children's ability to

- enjoy listening to and discussing storybooks
- understand that print carries a message
- engage in reading and writing attempts
- identify labels and signs in their environment
- participate in rhyming games
- identify some letters and make some letter–sound matches
- use known letters or approximations of letters to represent written language (especially meaningful words like their name and phrases such as "I love you"). (p. 8)

These abilities themselves represent development; that is, they are not equally sophisticated just because they all appear on the awareness and exploration list. Understanding that print carries a message, for example, is more sophisticated than just enjoying listening to and discussing storybooks. This is the difference between, on the one hand, a child's listening to a story being read no differently than the child would listen to a story being told and, on the other hand, a child's sitting up to see the pictures in a book and even pointing to some print in an illustration or at the bottom of the page while asking the reader, "What's this say?"

Participating in rhyming games means being able to recognize or even to make rhymes. This recognition involves a conscious awareness of the phonemic structure of words that spoken language does not require, but that learning to read often does require. Consider, for example, a child who hears the rhymes at the ends of the lines of a poem and explores how that works by sometimes supplying the rhyming word before his or her parent reads it. This child is on the way to being able to participate in talk about the first sound in a word or the sound that a letter makes. Such talk is often an important part of formal reading instruction in school. Other benchmarks of awareness and exploration are given in Table 2.1. (See chapter 3 for further discussion and activities related to the benchmarks.)

Strategies for Supporting Awareness and Exploration. Providing the best support for children's literacy development in the awareness and exploration phase is largely a matter of creating opportunities for children to engage in explorations of the kinds described above, observing how they respond to those opportunities, and building on the abilities they display with encouragement, modeling, and scaffolding for next-step literacy activities (McGee & Richgels, in press). A crucial factor is how parents and teachers talk to children. (See chapters 3 and 9 for discussion of parent–child communication.)

Whitehurst and Lonigan (1998) list several contributors to early reading and writing success. Three of the strongest contributors are phonological and phonemic awareness, alphabet knowledge, and spoken language ability. Compared to the first two factors, the spoken language factor is too often neglected or taken for granted by educators.

The relationship between spoken language development and written language development works in many ways. Two ways that

TABLE 2.1
Benchmarks and Strategies to Support Children in the Awareness and Exploration Phase of Literacy Development

Phase	Benchmarks	Strategies for Support
Awareness and Exploration	**Meanings** Conscious knowledge of the uniqueness of written language Intention to convey meanings with written marks and to retrieve meanings from print Pretend storybook reading Environmental print reading Writing labels for pictures **Forms** Writing by drawing, scribbling, and making mock letters Knowing some letter names Signature writing Knowing rudiments of story structure, such as *beginning, middle,* and *end* **Meaning–Form Links** Playing rhyming games Segmenting words by phonemes Knowing some sound-letter correspondences **Functions** Enjoying listening to and discussing storybooks Writing and reading as part of imaginative play Controlling others and self—using signs (for example, to prohibit or warn) and lists Reading and writing in family routines, such as grocery shopping or holiday observance	Creating opportunities for children's reading and writing Observing what children do with reading and writing during those opportunities Responding to what children do with encouragement, modeling, and scaffolding Enriching spoken vocabulary Providing decontextualized language experiences Waiting for and listening to children's contributions to conversation Extending children's comments Frequently reading and discussing storybooks Rereading favorite storybooks with follow-up of children's interests and abilities shown in earlier readings

Adapted from IRA & NAEYC (1998) and McGee & Richgels (2000).

depend on conscious efforts by parents and teachers are vocabulary enrichment and use of decontextualized language. Parents and teachers can monitor and fashion their talk with children to enrich the children's vocabularies and to provide practice in communicating about content beyond the here and now. Reading and writing require both richer vocabulary and more decontextualized language than spoken language does because written language must stand on its own. Whatever input readers receive from writers is unalterable, limited to the words on the page. Those words have to be more numerous and more powerful because they do all the work. Unlike with spoken language, in which speakers help one another and refer to shared context during a conversation, readers cannot ask for clarification from writers, who usually are in a different place and time.

Snow, Dickinson, and their colleagues, using data from their longitudinal Home–School Study of Language and Literacy Development, emphasize the importance to children's literacy development of particular kinds of spoken language that require planning and effort by adults. Snow, Tabors, Nicholson, and Kurland (1994) identify spoken language skills, especially vocabulary skills and the production and understanding of extended discourse, as being strongly related to literacy achievement in the school years. Dickinson and Sprague (2001) identify the use of rare words and a willingness to wait for and listen to children's responses as important factors in children's ongoing literacy development. This is true of both preschool teachers' conversations with students during free play and parents' conversations with children during meals. About free–play conversations, Dickinson and Sprague write,

> our analyses...revealed the importance of the frequency with which [teachers] extended children's comments and engaged children in cognitively challenging conversations (conversations about nonpresent topics that encouraged reflection on language or discussed things thought to be generally true about the social or physical world). (pp. 270–271)

Such talk can often begin in books, with talk about the form and content of what parents and teachers read to children. It can build on children's existing focus on meanings and functions. Children already know how to convey ideas and get things done with speech. A majority of even 2-year-olds' utterances begin with an idea in their heads that they want to put in someone else's head. And when children hear another person make some string of sounds, they know to try to retrieve an idea that began in the speaker's head. This is meaning making, the heart and soul of spoken language. They know how to get things done with speech, whether with a direct "Gimme juice!" or an indirect "How about we play tag?" This is functionality, the driving force of most language.

A child usually doesn't say "Car!" without wanting someone to look at his or her toy car, to hand over a toy car, to look at a passing automobile, or to understand that Grandpa just departed in such a vehicle. Similarly, when an adult says "Car!" even a very young child looks around to see what he or she might be labeling with that string of three sounds, and a slightly older child will expect to see a picture of, a toy version of, or a two-ton instance of that 4-wheeled, internal-combustion-engine-driven vehicle that has come to have that name in English. How fitting it is, then, to combine this behavior with print, to say "Car!" while directing a child's attention to a picture and accompanying word label in a picture dictionary or to write car on a card and attach the card to a picture of a car or to a toy car.

Similarly, children know early on that spoken words matter. For example, they know that "Cindy stepped into the car" has a different meaning from "Cindy stepped on the car." How fitting it is, then, while reading to point to the printed words More than anything else, Becky wanted the toy car for her birthday below a picture-book illustration of a girl looking at a whole department store window full of toys, only one of which is a toy car. Repeated exposure to such pointing and to such imprecise relationships between illustrations and text help children learn that printed words matter—that the meanings in books are determined by the words written there, not just by the illustrations. They learn that, in fact, the words may tell what really matters in the illustrations.

Conversation embedded in book reading is consistent with one characteristic of the awareness and exploration phase listed earlier, that "children can enjoy listening to and discussing storybooks" (IRA & NAEYC, 1998, p. 8). At its most basic level, this means that parents and teachers of young children must frequently read storybooks to the children and discuss the storybooks in comfortable settings and with enjoyable books. At school, this may involve small groups rather than large groups; at home, it usually involves one-on-one lap reading. Once a parent, teacher, or child has chosen a quality storybook, the adult should read the book in an interactive way and for the purpose of enjoyment. Interactive storybook reading means not reading straight through a book. It involves asking children questions about the illustrations, word meanings, their plot expectations, and the feelings that the story and its characters and events evoke. It means pausing to let children appreciate an illustration, absorb a plot development, or react to a character. Interactive storybook reading means making time for children's comments and questions and responding to children's observations, reactions, and questions. (See chapter 14 for discussion of effective storybook reading strategies.)

Such reading is only a beginning point. Many books warrant rereadings, depending on children's responses to initial readings, their interests, and the nature of their engagements in the initial reading. Many children have favorite storybooks to which they ask parents and teachers to return over and over again. Some become favorites for children's reading on their own, using a variety of pretend storybook reading strategies (Sulzby, 1985). For example, if a child's engagement with a book during a first interactive reading includes pointing to and asking about or commenting about a character in many of the illustrations in which that character is represented, then the teacher or parent in a rereading of that book can point to depictions of that character and others and ask the child to identify them and share his or her feelings about them and knowledge about their roles in the story's unfolding. If some illustrations include objects that the child might not know, an adult reader can use the child's interest in illustrations to develop vocabulary. The adult can point out the items, ask what they are, answer his or her own questions, and if there are subsequent readings of the book or if the same objects recur in later pictures, prod the child's later naming of the objects.

Similarly, if interaction with a child over a first reading of a book reveals the child's interest in printed words, whether in illustrations or in the text, then the parent or teacher can return in later readings to word reading. Again, the adult reader will ask first about the word or words that originally interested the child and then will expand to other words of similar interest, length, spelling, or structure, initially asking and answering his or her own questions about those words and later prodding the child to answer them.

This attention to print can lead to another characteristic of the awareness and exploration phase, "understand[ing] that print carries a message" (IRA & NAEYC, 1998, p. 8). When, after talking about a word, an adult reader resumes reading the text in which the word is located, the adult can pause, point to the word, and comment, "Oh, there's that word we talked about!" Then, the adult will read the word with emphasis and finally, retrace and read in a normal manner the sentence that contains the word. The adult's moving a hand below a line of text while reading further emphasizes the connection between the text and the message in a storybook. As the book becomes more familiar because of repeated readings, or as words recur that are familiar from the sorts of interactions just described, the adult can pause and expect the child to supply the words. These strategies for supporting awareness and exploration are summarized in Table 2.1 (see page 33).

Phase 2: Experimental Reading and Writing

With experimental reading and writing, children interact more proactively with written language. They know more of the basics of how reading and writing work, such as letter-sound correspondences and left-to-right progression, and they begin to apply that knowledge in ways that show they are testing what they know and using it to suit their communicative purposes. Children at the earlier awareness and exploration phase are aware of literacy around them; in contrast, experimenters know more about the process of becoming readers and writers. This process includes enjoyment of new abilities and powers (reading and writing abilities confer greater involvement in one's social milieu and even more control over it). It also includes experimenters' appreciation that they do not yet read and write like grown-ups do. The experimenter "approaches reading and writing more tentatively, more thoughtfully, in a more testing way than before" (McGee & Richgels, in press).

Jason and Freddy were students in a kindergarten where I was an observer and helper for one year. Their drawing and writing of a plan for building an incubator are examples of experimenters at work. (See Richgels [2002] for more about this episode and Richgels [2003] for an in-depth description of my year in their kindergarten class.) Jason intended to show the plan to his grandfather and get his help building an incubator. He asked about his writing L+ for *light*, "Could Grandpa read that?" Jason's invented spelling demonstrated his knowledge about meaning–form links. He knew that his choice of letters was important in getting his grandfather to read his writing and to arrive at the important understanding that a light bulb is an essential part of an incubator. Jason also showed that he knows the recording and reporting functions of written language, that he could collect and preserve information (how to build an incubator) for later use by putting it in writing. Other benchmarks of the experimental reading and writing phase are listed in Table 2.2.

How Experimenters Spell. Let us look at spelling as an area where experimentation easily shows itself. (Space limits allow only this one extended example. That it is a writing example should not suggest that experimenters do not also read. Again, see Table 2.2 for examples of both reading and writing by experimenters.) Whereas in the awareness and exploration phase, young writers use some of the few letters they know in order to write a small set of words, often including their names and other meaningful names—such as *Mom*, *Dad*, and brothers' or sisters' names—as experimenters, they will use a growing set of known letters to write an almost unlimited number of words, whatever words they need in order to express themselves. They do this by using their increasing knowledge of letter-sound correspondences in a process known as invented spelling.

Frequently, inventive spellers know that they do not know how to spell like grown-ups do. They will ask for help spelling words, but if given encouragement and example, they also will begin to experiment, using what they do know in ways that communicate to their satisfaction. Let's return to Jason and Freddy's story. After Jason wrote L+ for *light*, he wanted to write *bulb*.

He asked me, "Now how do you write *bulb*?" But he had a theory for how to begin: "Oh, a *B*? *B*? What's after the *B*?"

"Buhlllll, lllll," I said.

"*L*?" asked Jason.

"Mmm hmm," I answered. "And what do you hear at the end of *bulb*?"

"*B*."

TABLE 2.2
Benchmarks and Strategies to Support Children in the Experimental Reading and Writing Phase of Literacy Development

Phase	Benchmarks	Strategies for Support
Experimental Reading and Writing	**Meanings** Retelling of simple storybooks and informational books Finding ways to create texts that they know others will be able to read **Forms** Using knowledge of left-to-right and top-to-bottom progression and other concepts of print Writing most letters of the alphabet Using a variety of text formats, such as lists, letters, stories, poems, charts **Meaning–Form Links** Well-developed phonemic awareness, as shown, for example, by phoneme substituting Knowing beginning sounds and making rhymes Speech-to-print matching, including concept of word as shown in finger-point reading and writing that shows word boundaries Nearly complete knowledge of sound-letter correspondences Automatic reading and writing of high-frequency words, such as *the, and, said* Using invented spelling Using specialized literary language, such as *He said, And then,* and *Dear Grandma* **Functions** Conscious use of written language for its unique functions, such as recording and reporting Enjoying listening to book reading Testing knowledge about writing and reading (experimenting)	Continuing the support given in the awareness and exploration phase Seeing reading and writing as experimenters do and satisfying their needs, not the adult helper's.

Adapted from IRA & NAEYC (1998) and McGee & Richgels (2000).

"Another *B*!" I confirmed.

"A pattern!" said Jason's friend Freddy, who was also writing *bulb* as BLB.

"That's it?" asked Jason.

"It looks like a pattern! You're right, Freddy," I said.

"B-L-B-L-B-L—" said Jason.

But earlier, before he had written Lt, Jason had written a backwards *3*, so I knew he intended *light bulb* to be plural. Now I said, "Okay, now you wanted it to be *light bulb***s**—"

"'Three light bulbs,'" Jason read.

"—right? Because there's three of them. So what do you need at the end of—"

"*S*," said Jason before I finished.

"—*light bulb*?" I finished. And I confirmed: "An *S*."

"*S*," echoed Freddy.

Both boys ended up with BLBS.

In his writing of BLBS for *bulbs*, Jason displayed several more characteristics of an experimenting writer. He knew the alphabet well enough to be able to name letters easily and write them fluently (knowledge of forms). Jason was able to discover what letter's name contains a sound that he was attempting to spell, as he did with the letter *B* for the beginning sound. His increasing phonemic awareness allowed him to concentrate on one sound at a time in the word *bulb* and in the names for the letters he scanned as he searched for a letter-sound correspondence (knowledge of meaning–form links). Jason wanted to write a meaningful list of materials as part of his incubator plan (knowledge of meanings and functions of written language), and he had two ways of satisfying that desire: asking a more knowledgeable writer for help and using his own developing handwriting ability and knowledge of letters and sounds. He knew he did not know how to spell *bulb*, but he was willing to experiment with what he did know. Even when he had a good invented spelling, BLB, he was willing to do more with adult assistance, adding one more letter to make the word plural.

Strategies for Supporting Experimenters. Adults who wish to support experimenters' literacy growth will do as they do for children in the previous phase; they will provide opportunities to read and write, observe what children do, and build on observed abilities by encouraging, modeling, and scaffolding for next-step literacy activities. However, an experimenter is more needy. Compared to a child at the awareness and exploration phase, an experimenter is more aware of the processes that he or she does and does not control. This leads to asking the kinds of questions that Jason did in the exchange previously described ("Now how do you write *bulb?*" "What's after the *B?*"). So parents and teachers must be ready to enter the process where the experimenter is and provide just the right questions and support to satisfy the experimenter's needs, not the adult's. For example, I was able to scaffold Jason's spelling of four sounds in *bulbs* (**BLBS**), but I was prepared to stop there, not venturing into vowel spelling.

Although unconventional, most experimenters' reading and writing attempts are more accessible to adults than reading and writing attempts in the previous awareness and exploration phase. That is, adults are more likely to be able to read what experimenters have written and to see what parts of text they are using in their reading. Most adults would be able to read *Lt BLBS*. Similarly, most adults would recognize that although experimenters usually cannot read the word *what* out of context, they can use the repeated phrase in a pattern book such as *Brown Bear, Brown Bear, What Do You See?* (Martin, 1967) to read "Yellow Duck, Yellow Duck, What do you see?" (n.p.).

Experimenters' processes and the tremendous strides they make along the literacy continuum are very visible. This makes the experimental reading and writing phase very exciting to adult observers and helpers, whether they are teachers or parents. Strategies for supporting experimental reading and writing are summarized in Table 2.2 (see page 39).

PHASE 3: EARLY READING AND WRITING

With early reading and writing, children have sufficient reading and writing skills and strategies to be able frequently to read and write with confidence and fluency, even if not always in fully conventional ways. They become more able to orchestrate the many and varied processes involved in reading and writing. More frequently, their knowledge of forms, meaning making, meaning-form links, and language functions come together in satisfying, successful reading and writing performances.

For example, a child may read simple texts written for beginning readers by relying on some high-frequency words known by sight and on sounding out some phonetically regular words. Or, a child may write multisentence entries in a daily school journal in a way that is readable by others (many correctly spelled words, some invented spellings, and such basics of punctuation and capitalization as capital letters at sentence beginnings and periods, question marks, or exclamation points at sentence endings) and may be able to read his or her own entries and talk about them with another person. Other benchmarks of the early reading and writing phase are given in Table 2.3.

Text Reading by Early Readers. Let us consider text reading (as opposed to word reading) as an area in which the characteristics of the early reading and writing phase are readily discernable. (The choice of this extended reading example should not suggest that children in this phase do not also write. Again, see Table 2.3.) McGee and Richgels (in press) state,

> Early readers are more prolific and fluent than are experimental readers. Several key abilities and understandings about the workings of written language begin to fall into place and work together, so that the child is able to read more kinds of text and do so smoothly and with increasing confidence.

For example, the early reader can read a sufficient number of words on sight (automatically, without sounding out or otherwise analyzing them) so that many "easy reading" texts are accessible. Because most such sight words are high-frequency words, a relatively high percentage of words in a given text is likely to require no conscious work; for example, early readers probably will not stumble over *the, and,* or *is.* In addition, early readers know a sufficient number of letter–sound correspondences and know enough about word structure (how to recognize root words and common prefixes and suffixes) so they quickly decode words that they cannot read on sight by using such knowledge.

"Easy reading" is a category of texts (some even bear the label "Easy-to-Read" or "I Can Read") that have supportive illustrations, simple sen-

TABLE 2.3

Benchmarks and Strategies to Support Children in the Early Reading and Writing Phase of Literacy Development

Phase	Benchmarks	Strategies for Support
Early Reading and Writing	Successful merging of **meaning making** strategies, **form** knowledge, **meaning-form links,** and **functionality**	Continuing the support given in earlier phases
	Frequent, confident, fluent reading and writing for a variety of purposes	Conversing about meanings, forms, meaning-form links, and functions of written language, for example, in the context of shared writing and interactive writing.
	Orchestrating multiple processes	
	Reading simple texts written for beginning readers	
	Writing multisentence texts on personally meaningful topics	Long-term scaffolding in the context of written-language learning routines, such as parent-child storybook reading or classroom center activities
	Knowing many sight words for reading and writing	
	Using sophisticated invented spelling	
	Using basic punctuation and capitalization	
	Rereading, predicting, questioning, and using context to comprehend	
	Using sound-letter correspondences, word parts, and context to identify unknown words	

Adapted from IRA & NAEYC (1998) and McGee & Richgels (2000).

tences, few unfamiliar or difficult words, and clear messages. Both word identification and comprehension are facilitated, not hindered, by the book's structure and language.

Early readers' greater ease with reading connected text as opposed to isolated words moves comprehension of the text's message to the foreground. The message becomes more apparent, and its primary place in what reading is all about is reinforced. As these elements begin to fall into place, early readers read more and more texts and thus gain wider experience with genres and with purposes for reading. Early readers will not depend only on familiar, favorite books that they can read by pretend reading. They will not be limited to reading only isolated, familiar words from texts. Early readers may choose an easy-to-read text, such as *Three by the Sea* (Marshall, 1981). Page 20 of this book has an illustration of a rat walking and carrying a polka-dot bag and an umbrella. The text description is as follows:

> A rat went for a walk.
> "What a fine day," he said.
> "The sun is shining
> and all is well."

As an experimenter, a child may have been able to approximate the message of this text, doing a pretend reading, especially if the child had heard it read many times. Or, an experimenter may have pointed to and read words he or she knew by sight, possibly *A, he, said*, and *and*. But, as an early reader, the child will attempt a whole-text reading, even if the book is not familiar. Most words (*for, a, what, he, said, the, is, and*, and *all*) will be sight words, over which he or she will not hesitate at all. *Went, fine, day, sun*, and *well* may be readable using letter–sound correspondences and familiarity with some written English word patterns (silent *e, -ay*, and double final consonants). The picture context gives a clue for *walk*. *Shining* is the most difficult word. Even though the picture context of an umbrella suggests rain, not sunshine, the surrounding words suggest shining: *The sun is* almost requires *shining*, and reading on (to *all is well*) confirms that the sun is not setting or hiding and that, therefore, the umbrella is to keep sun, not rain, off the rat. Knowledge of word structure may provide additional help with *shining*, enabling the reader to see *-ing* as a common, readable word ending.

Strategies for Supporting Early Reading and Writing. As in the earlier two phases of literacy development, parents' and teachers' support in this phase depends on informed observation, providing of functional uses of written language, and social interaction, such as occurs during interactive storybook reading and shared writing. Such interaction can include conversation about meanings, forms, meaning-form links, and functions. With shared writing, an adult and children write together; the children provide many if not all of the ideas, and the adult does the actual writing (Van Allen & Van Allen, 1982). The adult models and talks explicitly about spelling and composing processes. This evolves into interactive writing as children show that they can do some of the writing themselves (Button, Johnson, & Furgerson, 1996).

Such an evolution is typical of long-term routines that can support all aspects of children's early reading and writing and all phases of emergent literacy (Richgels, 1995). Over several months, an adult provides for predictable, repeated actions, props, people, and language around a routine home or classroom event. In homes, these might be mealtime, bedtime, and storybook reading routines; in classrooms, they might be opening-of-the day activities, storybook reading, and some kinds of center activities. (See Ninio and Bruner [1978] for a description of an at-home book reading routine and Richgels [2003] for descriptions of several kindergarten classroom routines.) All these routines can involve both spoken and written language. At first, the adult and children learn together the ways of the routine, how to use the objects, and what to say, write, or read. Early on, the adult does most of the doing, saying, reading, and writing. Over time, as the children show greater competence, the adult gradually withdraws, and the children do more. In the end, after several months of the routine, the children can use both spoken and written language independently, even outside the routine. Children have mastered the actions and language that at first the adult had to provide. Strategies for supporting early reading and writing are summarized in Table 2.3 (see page 43).

PHASES 4 AND 5: TRANSITIONAL READING AND WRITING AND INDEPENDENT AND PRODUCTIVE READING AND WRITING

Two additional phases of literacy development take children beyond the topic of this chapter—emergent literacy. With the transitional reading and writing phase and the independent and productive reading and writing phase, children become conventional—even very versatile and sophisticated—readers and writers. Most adults, for example, would describe what children do in the transitional phase as "really reading and really writing." Children in these phases may read unfamiliar books with more demanding vocabulary and text structures than in the

TABLE 2.4
Benchmarks and Strategies to Support Children in the Transitional Phase and the Independent and Productive Reading and Writing Phase of Literacy Development

Phases	Benchmarks	Strategies for Support
Transitional Reading and Writing	Conventional reading and writing Reading of unfamiliar books Spelling based on knowledge of high-frequency letter patterns and word structure Reading with even greater word identification, fluency, and comprehension than in the early reading and writing phase Writing with awareness of audience Proofreading final drafts of writing Spending increased time on reading Reading as research	Continuing the support given in earlier phases Facilitating reading and writing workshops Making available a wide variety of reading materials Providing for reading and writing across the school curriculum
Independent and Productive Reading and Writing	Greater independence in writing and reading than in earlier phases Spending less energy on *how-tos*, more on personal purposes for reading and writing, including enjoyment Using appropriate word identification and comprehension strategies automatically Using narrative and expository text structures as aids to comprehension during reading and coherence in writing Making meaning across texts	Continuing the support given in earlier phases Providing for reading and writing as part of thematic units of study Providing for reading and writing in multiple genres

Adapted from IRA & NAEYC (1998) and McGee & Richgels (2000).

early reading phase because of their ability to choose appropriate word identification strategies for unknown words and fix-up strategies for self-diagnosed misreadings. Transitional writers may spell most words conventionally using familiarity with high-frequency letter patterns and knowledge of how to break multisyllabic words into spellable parts.

Independent and productive reading and writing is just that. Children in this phase read and write strategically; they plan and execute their reading and writing based on conscious goals and deliberate selections from a repertoire of strategies. They read and write more and more on their own; they need to spend less energy on the *how-tos* of reading and writing and can devote more energy to gaining information, finding enjoyment, and establishing and maintaining ties with others through their reading and writing. A child in this phase may read series books with devotion and total involvement or write poems or persuasive essays that have a powerful impact on others. Other benchmarks of the transitional phase and the independent and productive phase of reading and writing and a very few selected strategies for supporting literacy development in those phases are provided in Table 2.4.

Conclusion

This chapter ends as it began, with a reminder that its descriptions, with their phases and benchmarks, are meant as guidelines, not prescriptions. *Developmental* does not mean *sequential*. A continuum, such as the five phases described in this chapter, is arranged sequentially for easy presentation and comprehension, but children will move back and forth between phases. Each reading and writing episode is influenced by the amount of support children receive and by other considerations, such as purposes for reading or writing. Most important are where children's reading and writing *usually* fall on an emergent literacy continuum and their long-term progress, over months or even years.

REFERENCES

Button, K., Johnson, M.J., & Furgerson, P. (1996). Interactive writing in a primary classroom. *The Reading Teacher, 49*, 446–454.

Dickinson, D.K., & Sprague, K.E. (2001). The nature and impact of early childhood care environments on the language and early literacy development of children from low-income families. In S.B. Neuman & D.K. Dickinson (Eds.), *Handbook of early literacy research* (pp. 263–280). New York: Guilford.

Dorn, L.J., & Soffos, C. (2001). *Scaffolding young writers: A writers' workshop approach.* York, ME: Stenhouse.

International Reading Association and the National Association for the Education of Young Children. (1998). *Learning to read and write: Developmentally appropriate practices for young children.* A joint position statement of the International Reading Association (IRA) and the National Association for the Education of Young Children (NAEYC). Newark, DE: Author; Washington, DC: Author.

McGee, L.M., & Richgels, D.J. (1996). *Literacy's beginnings: Supporting young readers and writers* (2nd ed.). Boston: Allyn & Bacon.

McGee, L.M., & Richgels, D.J. (2000). *Literacy's beginnings: Supporting young readers and writers* (3rd ed.). Boston: Allyn & Bacon.

McGee, L.M., & Richgels, D.J. (in press). *Designing early literacy programs: Strategies for at-risk preschool and kindergarten children.* New York: Guilford.

Ninio, A., & Bruner, J. (1978). Antecedents of the achievement of labeling. *Journal of Child Language, 5,* 1–15.

Richgels, D.J. (1995). A kindergarten sign-in procedure: A routine in support of written language learning. In K.A. Hinchman, D.J. Leu, & C.K. Kinzer (Eds.), *Perspectives on literacy research and practice* (44th yearbook of the National Reading Conference, pp. 243–254). Chicago: National Reading Conference.

Richgels, D.J. (2002). Informational texts in kindergarten. *The Reading Teacher, 55,* 586–595.

Richgels, D.J. (2003). *Going to kindergarten: A year with an outstanding teacher.* Lanham, MD: Scarecrow Press.

Snow, C.E., Tabors, P.O., Nicholson, P., & Kurland, B. (1994). SHELL: Oral language and early literacy skills in kindergarten and first-grade children. *Journal of Research in Childhood Education, 10,* 37–48.

Sulzby, E. (1985). Children's emergent reading of favorite storybooks: A developmental study. *Reading Research Quarterly, 20,* 458–481.

Teale, W.H. (1987). Emergent literacy: Reading and writing development in early childhood. In J.E. Readence & R.S. Baldwin (Eds.), *Research in literacy: Merging perspectives* (36th yearbook of the National Reading Conference, pp. 45–74). Chicago: National Reading Conference.

Van Allen, R., & Van Allen, C. (1982). *Language experience activities* (2nd ed.). Boston: Houghton Mifflin.

Whitehurst, G.J., & Lonigan, C.J. (1998). Child development and emergent literacy. *Child Development, 69,* 848–872.

LITERATURE CITED

Marshall, E. (1981). *Three by the sea.* New York: Dial.

Martin, B., Jr. (1967). *Brown bear, brown bear, what do you see?* Austin, TX: Holt, Rinehart and Winston.

Specific Practices and Strategies Used to Promote Family Literacy in Collaboration With Schools and Communities

CHAPTER 3

The ABCs of Family Literacy

Billie J. Enz

> One-year-old Annie is sitting on the bedroom floor reading *The Itsy-Bitsy Spider*. The book has a detachable spider, which can travel up and down the waterspout. As she "reads" she bounces the spider from page to page, and talks to herself, "ider up—ider out!"

Though quite young, Annie has learned a lot about literacy. She knows how to turn the pages, and she knows that when she turns pages, they tell a story. Annie knows that the pictures in this book tell a story about a spider. Yes, Annie has learned a lot about literacy. How did Annie learn all this?

In the last two decades, educators have learned a great deal about how children learn language and become literate. We have learned that becoming literate is an ongoing process that actually begins at birth. (See chapter 2 for discussion of early literacy and chapter 9 for discussion of strategies for parents to support their young children's language and literacy development.) Most important, we have come to realize that parents are their children's first teachers (Christian, Morrison, & Bryant, 1998; Epstein, 1995; Hart & Risley, 1995; Sulzby, Teale, & Kamberelis, 1989).

Language Is the Foundation

The thousands of hours of parent–child interactions, from a child's birth through the preschool years, provide the foundation for language and literacy. From birth, children's brains begin to set the stage for talking and reading. Research shows that infants' brains seek patterns in the sounds of language, and by six months of age, their brains have already created permanent neural networks that recognize the subtle sounds and rhythmic patterns of their native language(s). By nine months of age, babies begin to distinguish syllables, which soon enables them to detect word boundaries. Prior to this, "hereisyourrattle" was a pleasant tune to babies, but it was not explicit communication. After auditory boundaries become apparent, babies will hear distinct words: "Here / is / your / rattle." As sounds become words that are frequently used in context to label specific objects, the acquisition of word meaning begins. At about one year, babies usually recognize and have cognitive meaning for words that are frequently used in their homes. Their receptive, or listening, vocabulary grows rapidly (Cowley, 1997; Shore, 1997; Sylvester, 1995).

As children acquire language, they are able to share with others what they feel, think, believe, and want. Although most children begin to use their expressive, oral vocabulary in the second year of life, research has long documented that children differ in their ability to learn and use new words (Smith & Dickinson, 1994). In an effort to understand what accounts for these differences, researchers Hart and Risley (1995) documented parent–child interactions during the first three years of children's lives. The research team observed 42 families from different socioeconomic and ethnic backgrounds for one hour each month for two-and-a-half years. Their data revealed vast differences in the amount of language spoken to children. What they found was interesting: regardless of all the other differences found between families (education level, parents' intelligence quotients [IQs], socioeconomic level, and/or race), the best predictor of academic performance was the sheer amount of talk that was directed at the babies. A lot of baby-directed talk resulted in better academic performance and higher IQ scores for the children. The highest IQ among the children who were talked to the most during the first three years of life was 150, but the lowest IQ among the children of nontalkative parents was 75. Compare the following mothers' baby-directed talk. What child will most likely have the largest vocabulary?

Mom 1: OK, Crystal. Let's eat.

Mom 2: OK, Paulie. It's time to eat our lunch. Let's see what we are having. Yes, let's have carrots.

Mom 3: OK, Teryl. It's lunchtime. Are you hungry? Mommy is so hungry! Let's see what we have in the refrigerator today. What is this? It's orange. Could it be peaches? Could it be apricots? Let's see! See the picture on the jar? That's right, it's carrots.

Appendix A, The Talking Home (see page 63), shows how parents can view each room in their home as special places to nurture talk.

Reading Begins With Representational Thinking

The ability to read relies on a reader's brain's ability to substitute symbols for real objects. From 12 to 36 months of age, normal brain maturation allows young children to develop the ability to substitute real objects for pictures of objects. Shortly thereafter, the brain is further able to substitute pictures of objects for symbols—letters and words. This ability is called representational thinking. Learning to read depends on the brain's ability to mentally substitute a symbol for the real thing. Between ages 2 and 3, children who live in a print-rich environment have learned the following (Kotulak, 1997; Sylvester, 1995):

- A photograph of a cat is not the same thing as a real cat, but it is a representation of a real cat.
- The sound of /c/a/t/ stands for the picture of the cat or the real cat.
- A string of symbols is not just a bunch of squiggly lines but stands for a word—*cat*—that, in turn, stands for a picture of a cat or the real cat.

Often children begin to make this connection through becoming aware of environmental print. Environmental print (EP) refers to print that occurs in real-life contexts (e.g., the word *Pepsi* on a soda can or *McDonald's* on a sign in front of a restaurant). Children begin to recognize EP at a very early age. Research has shown that many 3- and 4-year-olds can recognize and know the meanings of common product labels, restaurant signs, and street signs (Goodman, 1986; Mason, 1980; McGee, Lomax, & Head, 1988). Even if children do not say the correct word when attempting to read such print, they usually will come up with a related term. For example, when presented with a Pepsi can, the child might say "soda" or "Coke." The following vignette from Vukelich, Christie, and Enz (2001) illustrates a shopping trip that included EP recognition:

> Tiffany (2 and a half years old) is sitting in the grocery cart as her sister, Dawn (5 years old), picks up a box of Cheerios.
>
> "No, Dawn," says Tiffany as she vigorously shakes her head.
>
> Dawn replies, "Well, then, what?"
>
> Tiffany points to a brightly colored box with a rabbit gracing the front, "Dat Tics." [It's Trix, Tiffany's favorite cereal.] Dawn places the box in the cart as Tiffany nods in approval. (p. 1)

Tiffany's ability to read the print/picture of the cereal box enables her to select her favorite cereal. Initially, young children attend to the entire context of EP—logos, colors, shape, and size—rather than just the print (Masonheimer, Drum, & Ehri, 1984). As they grow older, children begin to recognize increasingly decontextualized forms of print. Research has revealed a general developmental progression of EP recognition: actual three-dimensional object, two-dimensional color picture of complete logo, stylized "word art" text from logo, text in generic font (Cloer, Aldridge, & Dean, 1981; Kuby, Aldridge, & Snyder, 1994). Figure 3.1, EP Recognition Development, provides an example of this process.

Often, parents are surprised when their children begin to recognize EP. Children usually read EP before they are able to read print in books. Parents can help children learn to read by using simple and fun EP activities which are identified in the "As Children Grow" charts at the end of this chapter (see Appendix B, pp. 64–67).

It's As Simple As A, B, C

Clearly, parents play a critical role as their children's language teachers (Cowley, 1997). We also now know that parents are their children's first literacy teachers. (See chapter 9 for discussion of strategies to support parents in working with their children.) This poses a challenge: Although virtually all parents want their children to become successful readers, not all parents feel confident or know how to be literacy

Figure 3.1
EP Recognition Development

Level 1: Real object—a three-dimensional model of a stop sign

Level 2: Actual stop sign in color

Level 3: Black-and-white stylized print

Level 4: Black-and-white "generic" print

STOP

teachers. As educators, we must help parents understand the crucial role they play in helping their children become successful readers, *and* we must build parents' knowledge of how to support their children's literacy development (Epstein, 1995). In addition, we must help parents realize how their simple, everyday interactions with their children actually establish the foundation for literacy. We need to encourage parents to view their home interactions with children as natural opportunities to enhance language and explore literacy (Enz & Stamm, 2003). Parents need to know that, for most children, learning to read is a combination of A, B, and C. (See Appendix B for "As Children Grow" charts that describe age-appropriate language and literacy activities for children and family members.)

A Stands for Attention: Research demonstrates that children's attention spans correlate to their ability to learn (Kotulak, 1997). The good news is that helping children increase their ability to pay attention can be accomplished through two-way conversations and by reading appropriate storybooks with them, talking about the story with them, and listening to their responses.

B Stands for Bonding: Research reveals that children who bond with their parents and family are able to learn new information more quickly than children who feel insecure. The good news is that reading and talking to your child helps them feel more secure (Dickinson & Tabors, 2000; Enz & Stamm, 2003; Shore, 1997).

C Stands for Communication: Research also tells us that communicating and IQ are highly correlated. Parents who talk to their children (a lot) and also listen *carefully* when their children talk generally have children who achieve well in language- and literacy-related tasks in school (Hart & Risley, 1995). Storybook reading is an ideal vehicle for improving communication.

Fortunately, storybook interactions provide the greatest opportunities for blending the ABCs.

STORYBOOK INTERACTIONS

In recent years, virtually hundreds of studies have revealed that home literacy experiences, or the lack of them, profoundly influence children's later literacy development (Bus, van IJzendoorn, & Pellegrini, 1995; Christian et al., 1998; Griffin & Morrison, 1997). What these studies have found is that the most effective way parents can help children learn to make the connections between the spoken and written word is through storybook reading. Unfortunately, Enz and Stamm (2003) have found that many parents become frustrated with storybook time when their children do not respond enthusiastically. Fortunately, storybook reading is a skill that parents can learn (DeBruin-Parecki, 1999). In most cases, parents need to learn the following:

- How to read in a way that encourages their children to stay engaged
- How and when to ask questions that encourage comprehension
- How to select age-appropriate storybooks

In 1994, researchers conducted a study with 167 2- and 3-year-old children enrolled in Head Start programs that documented how specific storybook strategies affected young children's literacy skills (Whitehurst et al., 1994). For over a year, 94 of these children received special dialogic reading experiences both at home and in school; the remaining 73 children received their standard reading experiences—listening to the story without a specific focus on content or illustrations. Dialogic reading involves parents engaging children throughout the storytime. For instance, parents ask their child to

- describe the illustrations,
- describe what they think is happening on the page, and
- predict what might happen next.

In addition, parents also are encouraged to add information or to share their feelings about the story. The following vignette from Vukelich and colleagues (2001) presents an example of dialogic reading. Observe the young mother using the dialogic reading strategies to keep Tate (2 years old) and Darrin (4 years old) engaged in the story by asking them to find labeled objects, interpret the illustrations, and predict what will happen next.

> "How many frogs are trying to help this duck? Let's count them." [Tate and Darrin use their fingers to count the fearless frogs].
>
> "What animal do you think will try to help next? [The children guess a pig.]
>
> "You're right. It was the pink pig. It's a silly looking pig, too."
>
> "How many animals do you think will be on the next page? Let's count together. Yes, that's right—five."
>
> "Darrin, how would you have helped the duck? That's a great idea."
> (p. 222)

After they had read the story, the two very happy children asked to have it read *again*.

In the study conducted by Whitehurst and colleagues (1994), children in the dialogic reading group scored higher in many areas of literacy development. For instance, they experienced a 93% increase in their ability to link sounds and letters—a critical preliteracy skill. Whitehurst and colleagues concluded that the simple dialogic reading technique was effective because it simultaneously combined interaction of visual stimulation of the illustrations, the words from the text, and the emotional security of being embraced by a family member. These interactions increased attention span, helped to bond parent and child, and increased communication.

In addition to dialogic reading strategies, there are other techniques parents may use to create a wonderful storybook reading time (Vukelich, Christie, & Enz, 2001). The following techniques will be helpful to parents:

Frequency over duration: Young children have short attention spans, so it is better to read for short periods of time (5 minutes) two or three times a day instead of 30 minutes at once.

Read familiar books: Read the same books again and again because children learn new things each time they hear a story and look at the pictures. Repeated reading often encourages children to retell the story in their own ways.

Books, books, and more books: Children need a number of storybooks with which to interact. Public libraries offer wonderful opportunities to check out several new books each week.

Book handling: Let children handle the books. This encourages children to stay involved and helps teach them the concepts of book handling.

Read with enthusiasm: Taking on the voices of the three little pigs and the wolf is fun and exciting and brings the story to life.

Play with literature: Children can retell stories using dramatic play, puppets, and/or drawings about their favorite parts of the story.

Sharing Instructional Materials and Offering Guidance

"In some schools there are still educators who say, '*If* the family would just do its job, we could do our job.' And there are still families who say, 'I raised this child; now it is your turn to educate her'" (Epstein, 1995, p. 702). (See chapter 8 for a description of family literacy programming.) Most often, children who need the most help come from families that need the most support. Schools and centers that wish to make a significant difference in the lives of these children must find ways to offer support and forge successful school-family partnerships. Fortunately, most early childhood educators find that educating a child requires at least two teachers—the one at school and the one at home. The following ideas offer concrete suggestions that teachers may use to help parents fulfill their role as their children's first teachers.

Preschool teachers frequently recommend that parents read to their young children (Enz & Searfoss, 1996). Unfortunately, many parents face great financial hardships and cannot provide a large number of quality reading materials in their homes. (See chapters 10 and 11 for descriptions of family literacy programs that support parents.) Further, parents may not know how to encourage and engage their children's interest in reading (Richgels & Wold, 1998). (See chapter 14 for description of, assessment of, and support for effective read-aloud strategies.) To help parents fulfill their role as partners in literacy programs, it is vital for teachers to work with these families to offer easy access to books and guidance in how to use them (McGee & Richgels, 1996).

CLASSROOM LENDING LIBRARY

Susan Neuman's 1999 study examined the effect of flooding over 330 child-care centers with storybooks. The results of her study confirm that children who have access to high-quality storybooks and teachers who are trained to support their storybook interactions score significantly higher on several early reading achievement measures than children who have not experienced high-quality storybooks and trained teachers. In other words, it is critically important for young children to have easy access to high-quality storybooks. (See chapter 10 for a description of a program that provides books to families with young children.) Further, it is essential that parents and child-care providers know how to support children's early interactions with print. Though most public schools possess libraries, children generally are restricted to borrowing only one or two books a week. Some childcare centers use public libraries with similar restrictions. Although this procedure may be appropriate for older children who can read chapter books, this quantity is insufficient for young children who are learning how to read. Each young child should have the opportunity to have at least one new book an evening. One way to ensure early literacy development at home and foster the home–school connection is through a classroom lending library. A classroom lending library allows each child to check out a new book each day, thus ensuring that all parents have an opportunity to read to their children frequently.

Managing the classroom lending library requires that all books contain a library pocket and identification card. The teacher also needs to create a classroom library checkout chart. When a child borrows a book, he or she simply removes the book's identification card and replaces it in his or her name pocket, which is on the classroom checkout chart. At a glance, the teacher can easily see what book each child has checked out.

The rules that accompany the classroom lending library are simple. A child may borrow one book each day. When the book is returned, the child may check out another. Teaching the children to manage the checkout routine is easy. When the children enter the classroom in the morning, they return their books to the library by removing the book's identification card from their name pocket. They then place the identification card back in the book's library pocket, and finally, they place the book back on the shelf. The children may select new books anytime throughout the day.

BOOK BAGS

Yet another way to encourage family participation and successfully engage and guide parents' literacy interactions with their children is through book bags (Vukelich, Christie, & Enz, 2001). Book bags, like writing briefcases, may be checked out of the classroom lending library for a week at a time. Book bags contain a collection of high-quality books and offer informal, interactive activities for extending children's language and literacy acquisition. When designing the bags, teachers need to consider their children's developmental stages, interests, experiences, and literacy levels. The book bags (nylon gym bags) typically contain three or four books and activities inspired by a specific theme. Some bags contain tape recorders and the tapes that accompany the books. The tapes and tape recorders are particularly important for parents who may not be able to read English. Each bag also contains an inventory that helps parents and children keep track of and return materials assigned to each bag.

The book bag project has been highly successful in many teachers' classrooms (Richgels & Wold, 1998). The book bags supply parents with the appropriate materials and explicit guidance which, in turn,

- empowers and motivates them to become teachers of their own children,
- encourages them to provide supportive home learning environments, and
- expands their knowledge of how to interact with their children.

VIDEOTAPE

As more schools have access to video cameras, another option an early childhood teacher may consider is creating a video-lending section for the classroom library. Videotape has the potential to become an exceptional tool for teaching parents about storybook reading skills. Teachers may wish to videotape themselves reading an exciting storybook. While reading books to the children, the teachers have the opportunity to demonstrate oral fluency, enthusiasm, and the use of different voices to make the story characters come alive. In addition, the teacher can illustrate how open-ended, predictive questioning strategies can facilitate children's active involvement during storytime (Christie, Enz, & Vukelich, 2002). Likewise, using retelling prompts, teachers can demonstrate how children discuss story events with one another and share their unique and meaningful perspectives. These informal, instructive videos may have a significant impact for helping parents improve and expand their own storybook reading skills. Children may check out both the videotape and the storybook. The video and accompanying storybook may be stored in a large plastic self-sealing bag.

Conclusion

Cullinan refers to the parents' nurturing role in their child's literacy development as "planting the seeds of literacy" (1992, p. 2). Almost all parents want to plant these seeds, but many are unsure of the best way to begin. Similarly, most parents and other primary caregivers vastly underestimate the importance of their role in helping children to become competent language users. Families play a critical role in nurturing young children's literacy learning. Early childhood teachers must be prepared to reach out to parents to form two-way partnerships aimed at building parents' awareness of the important role they play in their children's literacy learning and providing them with strategies for nurturing their children's early reading, writing, and speaking development.

REFERENCES

Bus, A.G., van IJzendoorn, M.H., & Pellegrini, A.D. (1995). Joint book reading makes for success in learning to read: A meta-analysis on intergenerational transmission of literacy. *Review of Educational Research, 65*(1), 1–21.

Christian, K., Morrison, F., & Bryant, F. (1998). Predicting kindergarten academic skills: Interaction among child-care, maternal education, and family literacy environments. *Early Childhood Research Quarterly, 13*, 501–521.

Christie, J., Enz, B., & Vukelich, C. (2002). *Teaching language and literacy: From pre-school through elementary school.* Boston: Allyn & Bacon.

Cloer, T., Aldridge, J., & Dean, R. (1981). Examining different levels of print awareness. *Journal of Language Experience, 4*(1&2), 25–34.

Cowley, F. (1997, Spring/Summer). The language explosion [Special issue]. *Newsweek: Your Child, 16*, 18–22.

Cullinan, B. (1992). *Read to me: Raising kids who love to read.* New York: Scholastic.

DeBruin-Parecki, A. (1999, August). *The Adult/Child Interactive Reading Inventory: An assessment of joint storybook reading skills* (Tech Rep. No. 2-004). Ann Arbor, MI: Center for Improvement of Early Reading Achievement.

Dickinson, D., & Tabors, P. (2000). *Beginning literacy with language: Young children learning at home and school.* Baltimore: Brookes.

Enz, B.J., & Searfoss, L. (1996). Expanding our views of family literacy. *The Reading Teacher, 49*, 576–579.

Enz, B.J., & Stamm, J. (2003, April). *The first teacher project.* Paper presented at the Association of Early Childhood International Conference, Phoenix, AZ.

Epstein, J. (1995). School/family/community partnerships: Caring for the children we share. *Phi Delta Kappan, 76*, 701–712.

Goodman, Y. (1986). Children coming to know literacy. In W.H. Teale & E. Sulzby (Eds.), *Emergent literacy: Writing and reading* (pp. 1–14). Westport, CT: Ablex.

Griffin, E., & Morrison, F. (1997). The unique contribution of home literacy environment to differences in early literacy skills. *Early Child Development and Care, 127/128*, 233–243.

Hart, B., & Risley, T. (1995). *Meaningful differences in the everyday experience of young American children.* Baltimore: Brookes.

Kotulak, R. (1997). *Inside the brain: Revolutionary discoveries of how the mind works.* Kansas City, MO: Andrews McMeel.

Kuby, P., Aldridge, J., & Snyder, S. (1994). Developmental progression of EP recognition in kindergarten children. *Reading Psychology International Quarterly, 15,* 1–9.

Mason, J. (1980). When do children begin to read: An exploration of four-year-old children's letter and word reading competencies. *Reading Research Quarterly, 15,* 203–227.

Masonheimer, P., Drum, P., & Ehri, L. (1984). Does environmental print identification lead children into word reading? *Journal of Reading Behavior, 16,* 257–271.

McGee, L.M., Lomax, R., & Head, M. (1988). Young children's written language knowledge: What environmental and functional print reading reveals. *Journal of Reading Behavior, 20,* 99–118.

McGee, L.M., & Richgels, D.J. (1996). *Literacy's beginnings: Supporting young readers and writers* (2nd ed.). Boston: Allyn & Bacon.

Neuman, S. (1999). Books make a difference: A study of access to literacy. *Reading Research Quarterly, 34,* 286–311.

Richgels, D.J., & Wold, L. (1998). Literacy on the road: Backpacking partnerships between school and home. *The Reading Teacher, 52,* 18–29.

Shore, R. (1997). *Rethinking the brain: New insights into early development.* New York: Families and Work Institute.

Smith, M., & Dickinson, D. (1994). Describing oral language opportunities and environments in Head Start and other preschool classrooms. *Early Childhood Research Quarterly, 9,* 345–366.

Sulzby, E., Teale, W., & Kamberelis, G. (1989). Emergent writing in the classroom: Home and school connection. In D.S. Strickland & L.M. Morrow (Eds.), *Emerging literacy: Young children learn to read and write* (pp. 63–79). Newark, DE: International Reading Association.

Sylvester, R. (1995). *A celebration of neurons: An educator's guide to the human brain.* Alexandria, VA: Association for Supervision and Curriculum Development.

Vukelich, C., Christie, J., & Enz, B. (2001). *Helping young children learn language and literacy.* Boston: Allyn & Bacon.

Whitehurst, G.J., Epstein, J.N., Angel, A., Payne, A.C., Crone, D., & Fischel, J.E. (1994). Outcomes of an emergent literacy intervention in Head Start. *Journal of Educational Psychology, 84,* 541–556.

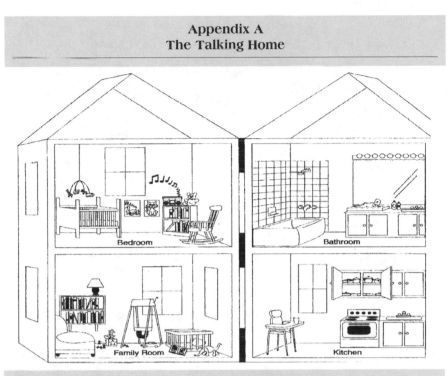

Bedroom Talk

Label and describe toys and talk about their colors, textures, and special features. For example, say, "Look how the jack-in-the-box jumps!"

Label and describe clothes and talk about the color, style, and textures. For instance, say "Today, we are wearing a warm, wooly sweater because it is cool outside."

Bathroom Talk

Label and describe the activities of bath time. For instance, note the slippery soap, warm water, bubbles in the water, and ticklish feeling from washing your toes.

With water toys, talk about the pouring water, the swimming diver, and the floating duck.

Family Room Talk

Talk about the toys, read storybooks, watch children's videos and discuss the characters, and watch children's television and discuss the actions of characters.

Ask your child to pick up toys by describing them. For instance, ask "José, please pick up the toy that has four blue wheels."

Kitchen Talk

Talk about the food you are preparing for meals and the color, texture, smell, and taste.

Talk about how small you are cutting the pieces and how you are cooking the food.

Describe how to set the table, and demonstrate how to say "please" and "thank you" while sharing food at the table.

Appendix B
As Children Grow: Age-Appropriate Language and Literacy Activities

Birth to One Year

Babies	Books for babies should
Gain visual perception much more quickly than was once believed	Feature single objects of familiar household items on each page. Stark contrasting colors are best.
Are learning the labels for objects in their environment	Include familiar objects. Often, only one object is pictured on a page–objects such as a sock, a shoe, a cup.
Explore their world physically and with their senses and see books as objects to be manipulated, tasted, and torn	Be sturdy, made of thick cardboard, cloth, or washable plastic.
Discriminate textures	Build on babies' sensory exploratory approach (e.g., *Pat the Bunny*).
Have very short attention spans	Have very few pages or are designed to be shared only a few pages at a time. Plot and sequence are not important.

Language and literacy activities for babies and their families include

- **Recognition and labeling games:** Using age-appropriate storybooks, ask the child, "Where is the kitty?" "What does the kitty look like?" Board books that show familiar animals are ways to reinforce object recognition and labeling.

- **Photobook stories:** Show the photobook of family members. Seeing family members in a book fascinates babies. Ask, "Where is Daddy? Can you find Daddy in the picture?"

- **Talking:** Babies love to hear the sound of their native language. Babies also need to see how the sounds of their language are produced, and the sounds and words of their native language are best learned in pleasant face-to-face interactions.

Suggested books for babies:
Aber, L. (2000). *The color of my wings*. New York: Reader's Digest Children's Books.
Davenport, A. (1999). *Teletubbies love to roll!* New York: Scholastic.
Hood, S. (1998). *Match shapes with me*. New York: Reader's Digest Children's Books.
Hood, S. (1999). *1, 2, 3, Count With Me*. New York: Reader's Digest Children's Books.
Miller, M. (1998). *Baby faces*. New York: Little Simon.
Weeks, S. (2001). *Happy colors*. New York: Reader's Digest Children's Books.

(continued)

One to Two Years

Toddlers	Books for toddlers should
Begin to enjoy the sounds of their language	Feature rhyming or alliterating words (e.g., "Annie's alligator ate ants.").
Begin to handle books and learn conventions of print	Be made of plastic, cloth, cardboard, or sturdy paper. These types of books will not tear as toddlers touch, point, and turn the pages.
Delight in participation	Be interactive. For example, *Where's My Fuzzy Blanket?* gives toddlers great enjoyment as they open the book's cupboard doors and toy boxes in their search for the soft blue blanket.
Are moving from the babbling period to real words, and they label familiar people (e.g., "Mama" and "Dada").	Encourage adult and child labeling.

Language and literacy activities for toddlers and their families include

- **Read– and sing–aloud books:** Since toddlers' brains are working to distinguish differences between sounds, it is important to read books and poems with a lot of rhymes. It is also good to read the book format of songs that they already know.

- **Puppets:** Many young children can speak through the mouth of a puppet in ways they cannot speak on their own. Puppets provide children with another means of dramatizing a good story. Manufactured puppets are available from many sources; for example, most early childhood equipment catalogs and teacher stores include puppets for retelling children's old favorites. Hand or finger puppets can be constructed easily from such household items as small paper bags, socks, gloves, or boxes.

Suggested books for toddlers:
Aruego, J., & Dewey, A. (1989). *Five little ducks.* New York: Crown.
Christelow, E. (1989). *Five little monkeys sitting in a tree.* New York: Houghton Mifflin.
Daniel, A., & Daniel, L. (1993). *This old man.* Bothell, WA: Wright Group.
Raffi & Westcott, N.B. (1987). *Down by the bay.* New York: Crown.

(continued)

Appendix B (continued)
As Children Grow: Age-Appropriate Language and Literacy Activities

Two to Three Years

Young preschoolers	Books for young preschoolers should
Begin to express their early awareness of writing	Allow for scribbling. Many parents give children several blank pages (folded and stapled) to write on. This way, children can express themselves while their books stay free of marks.
Recognize familiar logos and graphic symbols	Feature environmental print (E.P.). Parents may also wish to create their own EP picture books.
Enjoy listening to storybooks and can retell familiar stories.	Have a clear plot and sequence and distinct characters.

Language and literacy activities for young preschoolers and their families include

- **Creative dramatics:** Because young preschoolers can now use symbolic substitution in dramatic play (e.g., a block becomes a phone), families can encourage dramatic play. Creative dramatics is the informal dramatizing with no printed script or memorized lines. Stories that are good for dramatizing need dialogue and action characters who say and do something. Sometimes props are used; sometimes the children use their imaginations. For example, they can imagine the bears' bowls, chairs, and beds when acting out *The Three Bears* or the Troll's bridge when dramatizing *The Three Billy Goats Gruff.*

- **Sorting game:** Because young preschoolers can categorize and classify, you can sort cards or coupons with logos into specified categories, such as "Food or Toys," "Eat or Don't Eat," and so on. You may change the sorting categories and cards periodically.

- **Shopping trip:** Because young preschoolers can recognize familiar products, when shopping with your child ask him or her to help you find favorite foods. You will be surprised at how many items he or she recognizes.

Suggested books for young preschoolers:
McGrath, B.B. (1999). *Pepperidge Farm Goldfish fun book.* New York: Harper Festival.
McGrath, B.B. (2000). *Kellogg's Fruit Loops! counting fun book.* New York: Harper Festival.
Muldrow, D. (1998). *The Pokèmon book of colors.* New York: Golden Books.
Muldrow, D. (1998). *The Pokèmon counting book.* New York: Golden Books.
Wade, L. (1998). *The Cheerios play book.* New York: Simon & Schuster.

(continued)

Three to Five Years

Preschoolers	Books for preschoolers should
Start to write notes and begin to recognize letters	Feature the alphabet.
Begin to "read" familiar storybooks	Have repeated lines and predictable text.
Enjoy private time to read and look at a wide variety of books	Be plentiful! It is time for parents to get a library card.
Realize that print is very functional and is used to accomplish important tasks	Include functional print (e.g., children's cookbooks)

Language and literacy activities for preschoolers and their families include

- **Making a home library:** Set aside a special place for your child's books. Create a nook for books in his or her play space. The area you choose should be easily accessible; the more often he or she passes the personal library as he or she plays with toys, the more likely he or she will be to stop and select a book to read with you or to look through on his or her own.

- **Making book collections:** Help your child organize his or her books so he or she can quickly find favorite titles. Go through his or her collection frequently and try to focus attention on books he or she might have overlooked or forgotten.

- **Create a reading corner:** Find a place—a favorite easy chair or a corner of a couch—where the two of you can routinely read books together. It should be cozy, comfortable, and well lit.

- **The exotic library corner:** For variety, you might create an exotic locale that makes reading an irresistible adventure. Build a story tent by throwing a sheet over your kitchen table (keep a flashlight in the tent). Or, make a reading nest of an old comforter and throw pillows.

- **Cooking:** Read recipes together. Cooking allows children to experience functional print. It also includes math (measurement, counting, determining how much is needed so that everyone gets a piece), social skills (following the recipe together, eating), health and safety habits (nutrition and preparing food), and eating the food they enjoyed making.

Suggested books for preschoolers:
Aylesworkth, J. (1995). *Old black fly.* New York: Henry Holt.
Bonne, R. (1961). *I know an old lady who swallowed a fly.* New York: Scholastic.
Daniel, A., & Daniel, L. (1993). *This old man.* Bothell, WA: Wright Group.

CHAPTER 4

Making a Future for the Adolescent Through Literacy: Family, School, and Community

Maurine V. Richardson and Mary Kathleen Sacks

There is widespread agreement among educators that the practice of family literacy must focus on the needs, interests, and literacy routines of all family members, regardless of their ages (Cairney, 1995; Epstein, 2001). The majority of family literacy research and resulting instructional programs, however, have concentrated primarily on families with children from birth to age 9 (Hendrix, 2000; Purcell-Gates, 2000). Those efforts directed at adolescents most often focus on the goal of supporting teen parents in sharing literacy with their own children (e.g., Johnson, Pflaum, Sherman, Taylor, & Poole, 1996; Neuman, Celano, & Fischer, 1996). (See chapter 9 for a description of this type of program.) As a result, little data exist concerning the impact of the involvement of nonparenting adolescents in family literacy interventions. At the same time, there is substantial evidence indicating that many parents are faced with the barriers of limited literacy and/or English that challenge their efforts in supporting their middle- and high-school-aged children's home literacy and school success (Finn, 2001; Greenberg, Macías, Rhodes, & Chan, 2001; Melby & Conger, 1996; Newburger & Curry, 2000).

This chapter attempts to bridge the gap between what we know about the role of families in adolescents' literacy development and current knowledge about effective family literacy interventions in order to support both the academic achievement and home literacy practices of middle school and high school students.

Effects of Family on Adolescents' School Performance

Evidence suggests that effects resulting from the practice of family-based literacy with young children can have consequences extending into adolescence. Enz and Searfoss (1995) reported that an informal 1990 survey with 400 tenth graders revealed that 70% of students who were struggling readers in high school revealed that they had not been read to by their parents when they were in the elementary grades. Ninety-six percent of accelerated readers reported having been read to by their parents on a regular basis during their elementary years.

Ample evidence exists to indicate that families continue to play an important role in supporting students' academic success during their middle and high school years (Epstein, 2001; Henderson & Berla, 1994; Hickman, Greenwood, & Miller, 1995; Keith, Reimers, Fehrmenn, Pottebaum, & Aubey, 1986; Stevenson & Baker, 1987). Data from the 1998 National Assessment of Educational Progress (NAEP) writing and reading assessments indicate that a range of home literacy practices emphasized with younger children are equally important for adolescents (National Center for Education Statistics [NCES], 1999a, 1999b). For example, in homes in which students reported having 25 or more books, students at all three levels assessed (fourth, eighth, and twelfth grades) had higher scores in reading and writing than did those students who reported having fewer than 25 books or no books. Students from homes containing a wide range of literacy materials, students who reported reading for fun on their own, and students who said they had read five or more books outside of school in the previous month also outperformed their peers at all three grade levels in reading and writing. Further, the extent to which students engaged in discussion about school at home correlated with stronger performance in both reading and writing:

> Students in all three grades who discussed studies at home at least weekly had higher reading scores than did students who did so less frequently.

At grades 8 and 12, students who did this almost every day had the high-est reading scores. (NCES, 1999a, p. 11)

Although typically the types of parent support described here are carried over from the elementary years and are built on practices already in place, evidence suggests that high school is not too late for families to implement such measures. Epstein (2001) cites Lee's 1994 research demonstrating that

> family involvement in monitoring and interacting with students about homework and, particularly, family discussions about schoolwork, cours-es, grades, and the future have positive effects on high school students' report card grades and attitudes about school and teachers, even after sta-tistically accounting for family involvement and student outcomes in the middle grades. (p. 55)

Data indicate that families' emphasis on learning and home envi-ronments are more significant factors in student achievement or par-ent involvement than is a parent's education level (Becker & Epstein, 2001; Henderson & Berla, 1994). For parents whose experiences with formal education may have been negative or for parents who speak lit-tle English or have little understanding of their role in U.S. schools, however, the extent to which schools reach out to them is critical. Becker and Epstein found that teachers who actively used parent in-volvement strategies employed those strategies effectively regardless of the education level of their students' parents. Teachers who did not actively reach out to parents, however, judged families with higher levels of education as more likely to participate in school, given the opportunity, than parents with less education. Schools and the strate-gies teachers use to involve parents, then, are key determinants of the extent to which families take an active role in supporting their adoles-cent children's academic performances. As Dauber and Epstein (2001) note,

> The data are clear that the schools' practices to inform and involve par-ents are more important than parent education, family size, marital status, and even grade level in determining whether inner-city parents stay involved with their children's education through the middle grades. (p. 218)

Despite the clearly critical role that parents play in adolescents' school success, data suggest that middle and secondary school teachers and administrators are far less likely than their elementary school counterparts to reach out to involve parents in children's education in meaningful ways (Catsambis & Garland, 1997; Rioux & Berla, 1993; Swap, 1993). In their examination of teachers' efforts to involve parents in inner-city elementary and middle schools, Epstein and Dauber (2001) note that

> elementary and middle school teachers do not report much difference in their schools' programs to communicate with parents (r 5 2.121, not significant). Specific communication practices, however (including informal notes, telephone calls, the actual number of children's families involved in parent-teacher conferences), are used significantly more often by elementary grade teachers than by their middle-grade counterparts (r 5 2.232). (p. 141)

One successful initiative to build connections between schools and the families of middle school students is Teachers Involve Parents in Schoolwork (TIPS), developed by Epstein (Epstein, 2001; Rioux & Berla, 1993). Epstein created TIPS in response to research findings showing that, when early elementary teachers gave parents directions and specific suggestions for supporting their children's reading at home, parents were more likely to be involved in their children's reading at home than they were without teachers' suggestions. Because of this parental involvement, children's reading achievement increased. The TIPS process expanded the existing home-school linkages by offering strategies for parents in other content areas and in higher grades. Teachers Involve Parents in Schoolwork consists primarily of homework assignments that incorporate extensive information for parents, including a message to parents identifying the topic of the assignment, clearly stated objectives, unambiguous instructions for parents and students, and an opportunity for parents to comment on the assignment. Most important, with TIPS, the responsibility for completing homework remains with the students, while parents serve as sounding boards for their children. Teachers Involve Parents in Schoolwork is a process, rather than a fixed program, and individual schools adapt it to include homework assignments consistent with the schools' curricula and to meet the needs of their own teachers and families (Rioux & Berla, 1993). For parents who may have limited English literacy, assignments can be sent home in families' native languages or with instructions for students to read and explain the directions to their parents.

Another initiative to build home-school collaborations with families of middle school students was a book talk program developed by a classroom teacher and a librarian (Morris & Kaplan, 1994). Teachers introduced students in class to 15 books selected by the program developers. Students were then asked to take an annotated booklist home to discuss with a parent with whom they would be reading. Parents and children prioritized five choices from the list. Teachers then assigned each student to a book from among their choices, and each child was grouped with nine students who would read the same book. Parents and students were given three weeks to read their books, and then informal book talk sessions for all participants were held at the school. Each group of 10 students and their parents who had read a specific book met in its own classroom with a facilitator who began the discussion with general questions about the book. Parents and students soon took over the conversation. Morris and Kaplan (1994) note that both parents and students enjoyed the book talks and that parents reported being surprised at their children's understanding of what they had read. The book talk sessions were followed up by class assignments in which students wrote letters to their parents with comments about the books. The success of the initial project led to the program's expansion, and increasing numbers of school personnel, including administrators and math teachers, volunteered to serve as facilitators in subsequent sessions.

Rioux and Berla (1993) write that

> conventional wisdom has it that parent-family involvement in schools declines as the student moves from elementary to middle school and that by the time of high school it has all but disappeared. Conventional wisdom in this case is nearly right. Involvement has not disappeared but it is hard to find. It is hard to find commitment and high quality operating programs. (p. 205)

Although the importance of school-based parent involvement initiatives for families of middle and high school students has been well documented, there is ample room for both innovation and research into effective school practices to build partnerships with families.

Effects of Family on Adolescents' Home Literacy Practices

The prominence of the role parents play in adolescents' literacy development extends beyond school. Although little research has focused directly on parent-child literacy interactions with adolescents (Chandler, 1999), anecdotal evidence shows that parents strongly influence both the amount and types of out-of-school reading in which their older children engage. Adolescents' reading, especially reading for pleasure, is a primary concern of parents (Katz & Johnson-Kuby, 1995). In her study of first-year college students enrolled in a reading workshop, Henry (1995) discovered that mothers who were avid readers themselves were the students' greatest source of out-of-school reading referrals. Cherland (1994), in examining the relationship between adolescent girls' reading habits and their sense of identity, found that mothers encouraged and influenced daughters' reading of fiction. Fathers were unlikely to read fiction, and neither parent encouraged sons to read, even though fiction reading was valued for daughters by both parents. Finders (1995) studied middle school girls' uses of literacy in their daily lives and found that many of her informants had strong reading relationships with their mothers well into adolescence. Carlsen and Sherrill (1988) elicited literacy autobiographies from undergraduate and graduate students over several years to determine how they became avid readers. Family played a prominent role in encouraging the students' love of reading, as shown in the following anecdotes:

> Our home was always full of books, most of which my parents had acquired at household goods sales. At the time when my friends were reading love romances, I was pouring through *Robinson Crusoe* and *Crime and Punishment.* (p. 59)

> I advanced from a single book to a whole box of books that belonged to my brother. The summer after tenth grade I started reading books which were around the house—Fitzgerald, Salinger, Wolfe, Ibsen. (p. 60)

In one of the few studies focused on connections between parents' and adolescents' reading, Chandler (1999) examined the extent to which parents influenced high school students' out-of-school reading for pleasure. Chandler's initial intent was to study the responses of students who chose to read Stephen King novels outside school to determine how their engagement in this fiction could inform teachers' understanding of how to motivate students to respond as avidly to in-school texts. On learning that two thirds of the students she was studying had become fans of King's through their parents' recommendations, Chandler reflected:

> Conversations with my own former students echoed in my head–times when I teased them about the "trash" they were reading or refused to approve a choice they wanted to make. At the time, it didn't occur to me that I might be judging parents' or other family members' tastes as well as my students'. I'm sure my careless comments did nothing to bridge the gap between home and school for teenagers, a subject that surfaced frequently in my conversations with student informants, particularly when they talked about the difference between acceptable school reading and the reading that other people did. (p. 235)

Chandler points out that school reading materials are not typically the books that students or their families would choose to read for pleasure and that the school practice of analyzing what is read is not reflected in students' pure pleasure reading out of school. She notes, "These teenagers' reading relationships with their parents serve as a reminder that outside school, people's transactions with texts are often different than the ones we favor in English classrooms" (p. 236). Parents and other family members, then, are often the primary sources of adolescents' out-of-school reading material and the inspiration for middle and high school students to become lifelong readers.

Many parents are not able to actively support their adolescents' literacy through shared reading and book referrals because they do not read well themselves, they are not avid readers, or they are not able to read in the same language in which their children read (Gonzalez et al., 1995; Heath, 1983; Taylor & Dorsey-Gaines, 1988). A substantial body of evidence, however, indicates that families can and do support adolescents' literacy in a variety of other ways (Gonzalez et al., 1995; Heath, 1983; Taylor & Dorsey-Gaines, 1988). Ways in which families support literacy include storytelling, discussion, and sharing of cultural information and practices, all of which foster adolescents' narrative abilities, senses of identity, and abilities to negotiate within their communities (Gee, 1989).

Literacy Efforts With Families of Adolescents

As previously noted, the great majority of family literacy programs have focused on families with preschool- or elementary aged children. Handel (1995, 1999) developed one of the few initiatives directed at supporting parent–child literacy with adolescents by adapting the existing Family Reading Program for use with middle school families.

The original Family Reading Program began in 1986 and has been implemented across the United States. The program includes interactive workshops for parents, centered on building their understanding of children's literature and strengthening their own reading comprehension through a cognitive strategies approach. Workshops are followed by opportunities for parents to engage in read-alouds with their children, and parents are provided with support and scaffolding throughout the read-aloud process.

In adapting the Family Reading Program for use in an inner-city middle school, Handel built on both the existing structure of the program and the work of the National Center for Service Learning in Early Adolescence (NCSLEA). The center's "concept of service as fulfilling both emotional and academic needs of young adolescents was adopted as a guiding framework" (Handel, 1995, p. 530). Handel determined that the students themselves would serve the participant roles that parents did in the original model, and a key addition included offering the students opportunities to engage in service by acting as reading partners with younger children.

The final program consisted of three major elements: ongoing professional development for middle school teachers, middle school students serving as reading helpers to younger children, and family involvement. Teachers were introduced to the Family Reading program processes and were provided collaboration time to determine how they would apply these processes in working with their students. The teachers then led within the language arts block Family Reading program workshops for middle school students that introduced the concepts of the program, encouraged students to reflect on their own experiences with picture books as young children, provided opportunities for students to read and discuss picture books, and helped students plan for their read-aloud sessions with kindergarten and first-grade students. Students participated in five classroom reading sessions each year of the ongoing program. To bring families into the process, teachers sent middle school parents information about the program on an ongoing basis, encouraged them to participate in the workshops with their adolescent children, and invited them to a Family Reading program demonstration. Although only three parents actively participated in the first year, attending workshops and engaging in elementary read-alouds, Handel noted that their involvement was important:

> By entering directly into the literacy area, these adults served students in several ways: as colearners and role models in their classroom participation; as instructors when they shared effective ways to work with children in the debriefing sessions; and as community validators of the students' efforts when they praised the seventh graders' purposefulness and behavior. (1995, p. 538)

Results after the first two years of the project suggest that teaching Family Reading program strategies to adolescents and having them apply what they have learned in reading with younger children is an effective means of building students' awareness of reading strategies. Handel found that the majority of students were using the strategies to which they had been introduced in the workshops in their read-aloud sessions. Students themselves also included family in their learning. Half the participating middle school students chose to take Family Reading program books home to share with their siblings. Handel also reported that efforts were underway to involve more parents directly as learners with their middle school children (1995).

In another initiative, Cairney (1995) responded to high school parents' requests to adapt an existing family literacy program for parents of elementary school students to families with secondary school students. The resulting project, Effective Partners in Secondary Literacy Learning (EPISLL), was implemented in a high school in the suburbs of Sydney, Australia, with an initial learner population of 17 parents (nearly all of whom had left high school before graduation) and their 57 adolescent children. The goals of EPISLL included increasing parents' and community members' awareness of the importance of reading and writing in their daily lives and strengthening parents' participation in their children's schooling. Parents and their adolescent children attended short presentations on such topics as goal setting and making use of community resources, participated in discussions with one another of how these strategies might be implemented in families' daily lives, and practiced newly acquired strategies. Parent–child homework assignments were integral to the project and included such tasks as discussing the issues presented in that day's session, practicing strategies discussed in small groups, and talking about school with one another. In each subsequent session, parents began by meeting for a half hour to discuss the home assignment they had shared with their children.

Results from the initial project indicate that EPISLL positively influenced parents, teachers, and students. Here are some of the key findings:

> Parents gained new strategies to use to assist their children.
>
> Parents experienced improved communication with their children and better personal relationships with them.
>
> Parents gained new knowledge about literacy and learning.
>
> [Teachers demonstrated] an increased understanding of parent perceptions and expectations of schooling.
>
> [Teachers] changed attitudes and expectations concerning the significant roles that parents play in student learning.
>
> Students acquired new skills as results of their parents' involvement (e.g., study skills).
>
> Students showed evidence of raised expectations. (Cairney, 1995, p. 524)

The program has since been expanded for use in approximately 50 communities. Despite a limited number of efforts, then, there is evidence that family literacy initiatives can be used with parents and adolescent students in order to strengthen both parents' and children's literacy, to build home–school collaborations, and to reinforce understanding between parents and children.

Suggestions for Working With Families

A key strength of families in supporting the literacy development of their middle school and high school children is that routine uses of reading and writing are already in place (Taylor & Dorsey-Gaines, 1988). As is consistent with evidence from family literacy programs aimed at families with younger children, efforts directed at families are most effective when they build on existing literacy practices (Auerbach, 1989; Paratore, 2001). (See chapters 5, 6, and 11 for further support of this point.) Programs that work with families can, and should, encourage parents to include adolescents deliberately in daily literacy routines, such as writing shopping lists; reading newspapers and mail; writing letters, notes, and messages; and reading for pleasure.

Expanding on families' shared experiences provides another entry into supporting literacy among parents and adolescents. Families can be encouraged to use a range of materials and strategies to investigate family history, including digging through artifacts, such as old letters and photo albums, reading and discussing books about their families' cultures and customs, exploring the Internet for genealogical data, and interviewing older family members to strengthen understanding of the experiences that have shaped their families. Photo albums and treasured gifts can provide the basis for families to revisit and perhaps write about special occasions they have shared. Adolescents can join with their parents in planning future family gatherings or trips through books, magazines, and maps. Parents with limited literacy and/or little English proficiency can benefit from instruction that helps parents strengthen their own reading and writing, informs them about school culture, teaches strategies for monitoring their children's homework, and emphasizes the ways in which literacy can be infused throughout daily routines (Delgado-Gaitan, 1990; Paratore, 2001; Purcell-Gates, 1995; Rodríguez-Brown & Mulhern, 1993; see also chapter 6).

Data suggest that parents continue to have a strong impact on their children's reading at home well into adolescence. In recent years, mother-daughter book clubs, first popularized in *The Mother-Daughter Book Club: How Ten Busy Mothers and Daughters Came Together to Talk, Laugh and Learn Through Their Love of Reading* (Dodson & Barker, 1997), have sprung up across the United States, most begun by groups of mothers who followed the procedures mapped out by Dodson and Barker. Such reading partnerships can provide families with opportunities to become part of a larger reading community, to encounter new books, and to engage in meaningful discussions around literacy. A wealth of bibliographies directed at both girls' and boys' reading can provide the means for parents and children in both gender-specific and gender-mixed groups to build a love of reading, a wider range of literature, and an appreciation for one another. (See Figure 4.1 for suggested booklists.)

At the same time, adolescents hold a special place in society, sandwiched between the dependence of childhood and the responsibility of adulthood. Moje (2002) notes that

> because youth typically have more independent free time with peers than do children (whose activities are usually mediated and regulated by adults), youth have more opportunities to construct new and different literacy practices and to read and write a wider range of texts than do children. (p. 218)

Adolescents are establishing their independence and determining their own interests separate from their families. Rather than existing as sources of separation, older children's involvements can serve as the bases for designing family literacy efforts that will build on adolescents' interests within the framework of existing family literacy routines. For example, parents and adolescents can be encouraged to write letters

---

Figure 4.1
Booklists for Parents and Adolescents

Beers, K., & Lesesne, T. (2001). *Books for you: An annotated book list for senior high* (14th ed.). Urbana, IL: National Council of Teachers of English.

Dodson, S. (1998). *100 books for girls to grow on*. New York: HarperCollins.

International Reading Association. (2002). *Young adults' choices for 2002*. Newark, DE: Author.

Lipson, E.R. (2000). *The New York Times parent's guide to the best books for children*. New York: Three Rivers Press.

Odean, K. (1998). *Great books for boys: More than 600 books for boys 2–14*. New York: Ballantine.

Odean, K. (2002). *Great books for girls: More than 600 recommended books for girls ages 3–14*. New York: Ballantine.

Roslow, L.A. (2003). *Good reads for lifelong readers: An annotated thematic bibliography for ABE, ESL, GED, and teens*. Englewood, CO: Libraries Unlimited.

to each other or to adopt dialogue journals as a means of addressing issues that may be difficult to discuss face to face. Parents can seek information and elicit opinions from middle and high school students, encouraging them to share what they read, what they listen to, what they choose to do in their free time, and what they value in family discussions and activities.

Families have unique perspectives on adolescents. Efforts that build on existing home literacy routines, that strengthen parents' knowledge about their children's literacy, that help develop their own reading and writing, and that bolster parents' influence as reading guides for their children can strengthen the literacy of all family members and add to the base of families' shared experiences.

Suggestions for Schools

Substantial evidence indicates that adolescents often find school literacy practices at odds with their interests and needs (e.g., Moje, 2002; Sullivan, 1991), as reflected in a position statement on family–school partnerships issued in 2002 by the International Reading Association:

> Activities to develop family–school partnerships also need to look different at the elementary, middle, and high school levels. Not only do adolescents' needs and abilities differ from those of young students, their relationships with family members and educators change as they mature. The failure to include older students in family–school activities may partially account for the dramatic decline in working partnerships as students move through the grades. (n.p.)

Families can provide a wealth of information on effective ways to support adolescents' literacy that both build on home cultural and literacy practices and reflect students' interests.

School efforts that seek out parents, that attempt to build on reading and writing at home, and that incorporate parents and students into school decision making, in addition to well-established practices of informing parents of school curricula and student achievement, are steps to developing true home–school partnerships (Ashton & Cairney, 1999; Rutherford, Anderson, & Billig, 1997; Swap, 1993). The home-school partnership model, developed by Swap (1993) for use in schools at all grade levels, consists of four major components that are especially applicable to middle schools and high schools seeking to bridge the gap between home and school. The model consists of creating two-way communication, enhancing learning at home and at school, providing mutual support, and making joint decisions. The first element, creating two-way communication, requires that schools move beyond the "school-to-home transmission model" (p. 29) of information sharing and begin to elicit information from parents about students' strengths, needs, and home literacy practices. Enhancing learning at home and at school brings parents beyond the realm of mere monitors of homework so they become informed partners who extend the school curricula into routine family activities, as well as active participants in school life through volunteer opportunities, attendees at school events, and advisors to curricula development. With the component of mutual support, schools reach out to help parents meet their own needs, by providing educational programs for parents, including instruction in language and literacy, networking opportunities, or other necessary services. Parents, in turn, actively support school goals through such activities as fundraising, participation in committees, volunteering, and participation in conferences and school events. The fourth crucial element, making joint decisions, brings parents and school personnel together as collaborators in problem solving and planning at the levels of individual students, classrooms, and schools (Swap, 1993). This approach to home-school collaboration helps parents develop the tools they may need to support their children, while building on the experiences and knowledge that families bring to their children's education.

Chandler (1999) writes,

> As a teacher I probably gave more credit to parents who resembled my mother in terms of education and social class. One of the most significant themes of this study for me is that parents who don't fit that profile still have a great deal to offer their children in terms of literacy support—and their children's teachers in terms of feedback. Although most of these family conversations took place over texts that schools would not sanction, they built skills that teachers could easily tap in the classroom. (p. 238)

True home–school partnerships allow schools and teachers the freedom to build instruction that has as its core the values, home literacy practices, needs, and interests of adolescents and their families.

Suggestions for Communities

In many ways, adolescents' forays into the community at large are manifestations of their burgeoning independence from their families. Strategies, however, can be introduced at the community level to support the practice of parent–child literacy with families of middle and high school students. Alvermann, Young, and Green (1997) developed and studied book clubs, called R&T (Read and Talk) Clubs, for adolescents. The clubs were held in public libraries. Twenty-two middle and high school students met weekly with a facilitator in one of four different groups to discuss books they had read. Each member of the group determined individually what he or she would read, with the exception of one common text that three of the four groups decided to read at one point. Discourse styles varied among the groups, with two groups choosing to follow the established school practice of taking turns to talk and the other two groups embracing the opportunity to speak out as they chose.

Parents were at the periphery of Alvermann, Young, and Green's investigation; the parents' role was merely to comment on the impact of their children's participation in the project. As a result, the findings do not include any reports of increased discussion about reading between parents and students. The body of evidence supporting parents' role as discussants with adolescents (e.g., Chandler, 1999; Finders, 1995; Henry, 1995), however, suggests that providing occasions for middle and high school students to engage in out-of-school reading and discussion about books would increase opportunities for parents and adolescents to engage in discussion or shared reading.

Conclusion

The evidence is clear that parents play crucial roles in their adolescents' school achievements. At the same time, literacy activities unrelated to school may make up the major component of adolescents' reading and writing and are certainly reflective of self-initiated literacy (Alvermann, 2001). Moje (2002) notes,

> I watch youth who seem unmotivated to read books in school devouring books outside of school.... I listen to them comparing types of texts, at times dismissing texts that progressive educators exhort educators to offer.... Why is there such a disparity in what we observe youth doing in ethnographic studies with literacy outside of school, as they engage with particular kinds of texts, and what we observe them doing in formal, standardized, constrained literacy activities? (p. 220)

As middle and high school students gain independence and increasingly rely on out-of-school literacy experiences as means of defining themselves and of determining the ways they will use reading and writing in their lives, the role of families as providers of the great portion of adolescents' nonacademic literacy experiences becomes increasingly critical. Despite the prevailing emphasis on supporting families' literacy interactions with their young children, evidence of both home-school collaborations and home uses of reading and writing clearly points to the efficacy of working with families to foster shared literacy with adolescents. Family literacy efforts that build on families' routine uses of reading and writing, that support both parents' and students' literacy development, and that address the interests of middle and high school students in addition to bringing parents into closer contact with their children's schools, can only serve to enhance adolescents' desire and ability to be effective readers and writers as they move from childhood to adulthood, to autonomy, and, in many cases, to their own roles as parents.

REFERENCES

Alvermann, D.E. (2001). Reading adolescents' reading identities: Looking back to see ahead. *Journal of Adolescent & Adult Literacy, 44*, 676–690.

Alvermann, D.E., Young, J.P., & Green, C. (1997). *Adolescent's negotiations of out-of-school reading discussions* (Reading Research Report No. 77). Athens, GA: National Reading Research Center.

Ashton, J., & Cairney, T.H. (1999, July). *Making judgements: An analysis of school and teacher discourses of home-school partnerships.* Paper presented at the 7th Conference of the International Federation for the Teaching of English, Warwick, England.

Auerbach, E.R. (1989). Towards a socio-contextual approach to family literacy. *Harvard Educational Review, 59*, 165–181.

Becker, H.J., & Epstein, J.L. (2001). Parent involvement: A survey of teacher practices. In J.L. Epstein (Ed.), *School, family, and community partnerships: Preparing educators and improving schools* (pp. 101–119). Boulder, CO: Westview Press.

Cairney, T.H. (1995). Developing parent partnerships in secondary literacy learning. *Journal of Reading, 38,* 520–526.

Carlsen, G.R., & Sherrill, A. (1988). *Voices of readers: How we come to love books.* Urbana, IL: National Council of Teachers of English.

Catsambis, S., & Garland, J.E. (1997). *Parental involvement in students' education during middle school and high school* (Report No. 18). Washington, DC: Center for Research on the Education of Students Placed at Risk.

Chandler, K. (1999). Reading relationships: Parents, adolescents, and popular fiction by Stephen King. *Journal of Adolescent & Adult Literacy, 43,* 228–239.

Cherland, M.R. (1994). *Private practices: Girls reading fiction and constructing identity.* London: Taylor & Francis.

Dauber, S.L, & Epstein, J.L. (2001). Parents' attitudes and practices of involvement in inner-city elementary and middle schools. In J.L. Epstein (Ed.), *School, family, and community partnerships: Preparing educators and improving schools* (pp. 205–220). Boulder, CO: Westview.

Delgado-Gaitan, C. (1990). *Literacy for empowerment: The role of parents in children's education.* London: Falmer.

Dodson, S., & Barker, T. (1997). *The mother-daughter book club: How ten busy mothers and daughters came together to talk, laugh and learn through their love of reading.* New York: HarperCollins.

Enz, B.J., & Searfoss, L.W. (1995). Let the circle be unbroken: Teens as literacy learners and teachers. In L.M. Morrow (Ed.), *Family literacy connections in schools and communities.* Newark, DE: International Reading Association.

Epstein, J.L. (2001). Perspectives and previews on research and policy for school, family, and community partnerships. In J.L. Epstein (Ed.), *School, family, and community partnerships: Preparing educators and improving schools* (pp. 38–74). Boulder, CO: Westview Press.

Epstein, J.L., & Dauber, S.L. (2001). School programs and teacher practices of parent involvement in inner-city elementary and middle schools. In J.L. Epstein (Ed.), *School, family, and community partnerships: Preparing educators and improving schools* (pp. 134–154). Boulder, CO: Westview Press.

Finders, M.J. (1995). *Just girls: Hidden literacies and life in junior high.* New York: Teachers College Press.

Finn, J.D. (2001). School noncompletion and literacy. In C.F. Kaestle, A. Campbell, J.D. Finn, S.T. Johnson, & L. Mikulecky (Eds.), *Adult literacy and education in America* (pp. 41–71). Washington, DC: National Center for Education Statistics.

Gee, J.P. (1989). Two styles of narrative construction and their linguistic and education implications. *Journal of Education, 171,* 97–115.

Gonzalez, N., Moll, L., Tenery, M.F., Rivera, A., Mendon, P., Gonzales, R., et al. (1995). Funds of knowledge for teaching in Latino households. *Urban Education, 29,* 443–470.

Greenberg, E., Macías, R.F., Rhodes, D., & Chan, T. (2001). *English literacy and language minorities in the United States.* Washington, DC: National Center for Education Statistics.

Handel, R.D. (1995). Family reading at the middle school. *Journal of Reading, 38,* 528–540.

Handel, R.D. (1999). *Building family literacy in an urban community.* New York: Teachers College Press.

Heath, S.B. (1983). *Ways with words: Language, life, and work in communities and classrooms.* Cambridge, UK: Cambridge University Press.

Henderson, A.T., & Berla. N. (1994). *A new generation of evidence: The family is critical to student achievement.* St. Louis, MO: Danforth Foundation; Flint, MI: Mott (C.S.) Foundation.

Hendrix, S. (2000). Family literacy education–Panacea or false promise? *Journal of Adolescent & Adult Literacy, 43,* 338–346.

Henry, J. (1995). *If not now: Developmental readers in the college classroom.* Portsmouth, NH: Heinemann.

Hickman, C.W., Greenwood, G.E., & Miller, M.D. (1995). High school parent involvement: Relationships with achievement, grade level, SES, and gender. *Journal of Research and Development in Education, 28,* 125–134.

International Reading Association. (2002). *Family-school partnerships: Essential elements of literacy instruction in the United States.* A position statement of the International Reading Association. Newark, DE: Author.

Johnson, H.L., Pflaum, S., Sherman, E., Taylor, P., & Poole, P. (1996). Focus on teenage parents: Using children's literature to strengthen teenage literacy. *Journal of Adolescent & Adult Literacy, 39,* 290–296.

Katz, A., & Johnson-Kuby, S.A. (1995). Visit from the vampire. *Journal of Adolescent & Adult Literacy, 39,* 156–159.

Keith, T.A, Reimers, T.M, Fehrmenn, P., Pottebaum, S., & Aubey, L. (1986). Parental involvement, homework, and TV time: Direct and indirect effects on high school achievement. *Journal of Educational Psychology, 78,* 373–380.

Melby, J.N, & Conger, R. (1996). Parental behaviors and adolescent academic performance. A longitudinal analysis. *Journal of Research on Adolescence, 6,* 113–37.

Moje, E.B. (2002). Re-framing adolescent literacy research for new times: Studying youth as a resource. *Reading Research and Instruction, 41,* 211–228.

Morris, N.C., & Kaplan, I. (1994). Middle school parents are good partners for reading. *Journal of Reading, 38,* 130–131.

National Center for Education Statistics. (1999a). *The NAEP 1998 reading report card: National and state highlights.* Washington, DC: Author.

National Center for Education Statistics. (1999b). *NAEP 1998 writing: Report card for the nation and the states.* Washington, DC: Author.

Neuman, S.B., Celano, D., & Fischer, R. (1996). The children's literature hour: A social-constructivist approach to family literacy. *Journal of Literacy Research, 28,* 499–523.

Newburger, E.C., & Curry, A.E. (2000, March). Educational attainment in the United States (update). *Current Population Reports* (Report No. P20–536). Washington, DC: U.S. Census Bureau.

Paratore, J.R. (2001). *Opening doors, opening opportunities: Family literacy in an urban community.* Boston: Allyn & Bacon.

Purcell-Gates, V. (1995). *Other people's words. The cycle of low literacy.* Cambridge, MA: Harvard University Press.

Purcell-Gates, V. (2000). Family literacy. In M.L. Kamil, P.B. Mosenthal, P.D. Pearson, & R. Barr (Eds.), *Handbook of reading research* (Vol. 3, pp. 853–870). Mahwah, NJ: Erlbaum.

Rioux, J.W., & Berla, N. (1993). *Innovations in parent & family involvement.* Princeton Junction, NJ: Eye on Education.

Rodríguez-Brown, F.V., & Mulhern, M.M. (1993). Fostering critical literacy through family literacy: A study of families in a Mexican-immigrant community. *Bilingual Research Journal, 17*(3–4), 1–16.

Rutherford, B., Anderson, B., & Billig, S. (1997). *Parent and community involvement in education.* Washington, DC: Office of Educational Research and Improvement.

Stevenson, D.L., & Baker, D.P. (1987). The family-school relation and the child's school performance. *Child Development, 58,* 1348–1357.

Sullivan, A.M. (1991). The natural reading life: A high-school anomaly. *English Journal, 80*(6), 40–46.

Swap, S.M. (1993). *Developing home-school partnerships: From concepts to practice.* New York: Teachers College Press.

Taylor, D., & Dorsey-Gaines, C. (1988). *Growing up literate: Learning from inner-city families.* Portsmouth, NH: Heinemann.

CHAPTER 5

Expanding the Concept of "Family" in Family Literacy: Integrating a Focus on Fathers

Vivian L. Gadsden

Within the past 10 years, there has been increased attention from researchers, practitioners, and policymakers to fathers' involvement in children's learning and their contributions to child and family well-being. Fathers' contributions, fathering and family researchers and practitioners agree, extend beyond expectations of fathers as financial contributors and include their role in children's cognitive, social, physical, and emotional development and in family learning and functioning (Amato & Gilbreth, 1999; Gadsden & Ray, 2002; Garfinkel & McLanahan, 2000). More recent studies, such as Nord, Brimall, and West's 1997 research on father involvement in children's schools, denote the positive effects of father participation in children's schooling. Despite growing interest in these issues and the implications of father involvement for the larger discussion of family involvement and family literacy, relatively little research has examined issues of fathers and literacy—fathers as learners, as family members, and as parents of children learning literacy. Similar to other areas of research that address the needs of children and families, research on literacy has typically focused on the literacy levels and educational attainment of mothers—historically the primary caregivers to children—to predict children's literacy development and school achievement. Beyond a few studies (e.g., Hiebert & Adams, 1987; Ortiz, Stile, & Brown, 1999) that compare mothers' and fathers' perceptions of children's literacy abilities and performance, only a handful of reports provide any conceptual or empirical analysis on the different kinds of interactions between fathers and their children learning literacy; the effects of father involvement or approaches to involving fathers in family literacy; and the ways in which interactions between fathers and their families might facilitate fathers' individual learning, support children's literacy, and enhance family learning more broadly.

This chapter examines father involvement as an increasingly critical area of research, practice, and policy by exploring the ways in which discussions on fathering may be understood and integrated with conceptual and practical frameworks of family literacy. Specifically, the chapter focuses on fathers with respect to their own literacy; their roles or potential roles in the transmission of literacy practices, behaviors, and beliefs to children and other family members; and their roles in the construction and maintenance of family cultures (Gadsden, 1998) in which literacy, schooling, identity, and academic achievement are prominent. In addressing the growing body of research on fathers, this chapter attempts to move the discourse about family literacy beyond the important focus on mothers and children alone. Instead, it broadens the scope to address "parent" and "family" as a more expansive and encompassing context to practice, use, and interpret literacy and to explore the range of interactive and supportive relationships that contribute to the learning and teaching of literacy for different family members across genders, ages, and generations.

The premise of this chapter is that families constitute a fundamental social system that promotes, disrupts, or mediates the learning and literacy experiences of its members and in which there are exchanges of knowledge, resources, and services. Fathers are situated at different locations within this system, depending on accepted traditions, societal expectations, relationships with family members, and cultural and social practices within the family. Fathers—through their presence or absence, their involvement or distance—are a critical subset of adults whose uses of and interactions around literacy help to frame literacy expectations and goals of both individual family members and the entire family unit.

The chapter is divided into four parts. I begin by providing a background of and context for research, practice, and policy analyses on father involvement. The second part summarizes past and current research studies that focus on father–child interactions around literacy as well as conceptual issues in crafting a family literacy framework that addresses fathers as learners and supporters of literacy development. The third part draws from research, practice, and policy discussions among a specific subset of fathers—low-income, African American fathers—who have been a major focus in discussions on fathering and family structure and who, given family literacy's targeting of low-income families, are likely to be among those whose children and families may be engaged in family literacy programs. I use accounts from interviews with these fathers, all of whom were participants in a fathering program (The Father and Literacy Study), to explore the question: What are the issues faced by young, poor fathers that interfere with their engagement with their children? In the fourth section, I conclude by offering closing reflections about fathering and family literacy and considerations for research, practice, and policy discussions.

In addition to the four areas, the chapter will address some complexities and challenges that are inherent in studying father–child literacy. The discussion will be grounded in analyses that point to a range of potential, though modestly explored, directions for parent–child literacy, for example, the different ways in which parents and other family members transfer literacy knowledge to children, children's motivations to read and the relationship of these motivations to parents' beliefs about the value and usefulness of literacy, the nature and content of literacy in homes that are diverse in cultural history and language, and parents' reasons for engaging in their children's literacy development. Drawing from research in fathering, family studies, and intergenerationality within families, the chapter is intended to provide a context for investigating and addressing potentially prominent shortcomings in family literacy research and practice: the relative absence of a discussion on father–child learning or the role of fathers in children's academic achievement.

Research on Father Involvement: Background and Contextual Issues

The years since the early 1990s have been marked by the most sustained effort to date to study fatherhood and to change policies that affect fathers. Indeed, U.S. policy initiatives of the 1990s began to engage several central debates regarding fathering: What constitutes being a responsible parent? What is responsible fathering? What are the individual and collective roles that men and women assume around the health and well-being of children? How do families and society work together—or at cross-purposes—to protect children and promote their development? Until the beginning of the 1990s, the cultural debate was organized around a gender-oriented view of parenting roles inside and outside the family: What (if anything) should mothers do *outside* the family? What (if anything) should fathers do *inside* the family (Doherty, Kouneski, & Erickson, 1998)? What role should fathers play in the everyday lives of their children, beyond the traditional breadwinner role? How much should fathers emulate the traditional nurturing activities of mothers, and how much should they represent a traditional masculine role model image to their children?

There is no single impetus for the current shift in interest in fathers and families. R. Smith (personal communication, April 18, 1998) suggests that the apparent increase in attention toward father involvement can be traced to an intersection of concerns about father absence, family formation, the decline of marriage and increase in divorce, and the vulnerability of communities, particularly low-income, minority communities. One such concern centered solely on divorce and the consequences for children when fathers leave the household. A second concern addressed father absence as an indicator of larger cultural problems and the decline of the so-called Western tradition; erosion in the quality of life for children and families was attributed primarily, if not solely, to the increased absence of fathers. A third concern was child well-being in the face of growing child poverty, as reflected in three primary areas: (1) the specific relationships between father absence and child and family poverty (e.g., the problems faced by poor mothers and children resulting from the loss of income); (2) poor fathers, often never married, for whom the problems and barriers presented by race, unemployment, and intergenerational hardship served as obstacles to their supporting their children; and (3) child support enforcement.

A growing area of inquiry in human development and family studies, father involvement represents a challenging and multifaceted issue. Although public discussions focus on the concept of responsible fathering, research studies are still unclear about what the characteristics of a responsible or competent father actually are (Gadsden, Fagan, Ray, & Davis, in press; Lamb, 2000; Levine & Pitt, 1996; Pollack, 1995). The use of the term *responsible fathering* reflects a recent shift among academics and professionals away from value-free language toward a more explicit value-advocacy approach. In addition, the burgeoning interest in fathering has generated concern from different segments of the academic world and within society. Some alliances, for example, women's and mothers' rights groups, argue that the emphasis on the role of fathers in families may feed longstanding biases against female-headed, single-parent families; that services for fathers might be increased at the expense of services for single mothers; and that the profatherhood discourse might be used by fathers' rights groups who are challenging custody, child support, and visitation arrangements after divorce.

On the other hand, some feminist psychologists have argued for greater emphasis on fathering, suggesting that involved, nurturing fathers will benefit women as well as children (Phares, 1997; Silverstein, 1996). Others argue that only an ecologically sensitive approach to parenting, which views the welfare of fathers, mothers, and children as intertwined and interdependent, can avoid a zero-sum approach to parenting in which fathers' gains become mothers' losses (e.g., Doherty, Kouneski, & Erickson, 1998). These issues are often addressed along two lines of inquiry—father presence and father caregiving—which are discussed below. (For more information on these issues, visit the website of the National Center on Fathers and Families [NCOFF] at the University of Pennsylvania at http://www.ncoff.gse.upenn.edu.)

PATERNAL PRESENCE

From the 1960s to the 1990s, research on structural patterns within families, particularly mother-headed, poor families, focused on father absence. Since that time, interpretations of fathering have focused on fathering as existing along a continuum, with high-level presence and activity at one end and little to no contact at the other (see background information for the establishment of NCOFF, 1994). The shift to an emphasis on father presence rather than absence allows the observer to denote the variability and elasticity of fathers' engagement in the lives of their children and families and to examine whether, when, and how different points along the continuum are affected by or affect the well-being of children, families, and fathers themselves.

Over the past two decades, researchers have refined their efforts to distinguish among various types of father involvement. The resulting literature allows researchers to define and describe father–child presence with greater precision (Parke, 1996, 2000). Lamb and his colleagues (Lamb, Pleck, Charnov, & Levine, 1985) in the mid-1980s offered the most influential schema to date. Their framework includes three elements: (1) responsibility, (2) availability, and (3) engagement. Responsibility refers to the role that a father plays in ensuring that the child is cared for and arranging for the availability of resources. Availability, a related concept, concerns the father's potential for interaction, by virtue of being present or being accessible to the child (irrespective of whether direct interaction is occurring). Engagement refers to the father's direct interaction or contact with his child through caregiving and shared activities. In the past, family and child development studies rarely collected information on all these aspects of father–child involvement. However, social and behavioral scientists have come to a general consensus that measuring these three aspects of father–child relations provides the best opportunity for an assessment of the potential impact of fathers' behaviors on child development.

Responsibility is one of the least studied and understood aspects of fathering. As noted above, this form of involvement refers to the managerial functions of parenting, including the ways in which fathers organize opportunities for their children to participate in a wide range of activities and experiences. Two types of management are important to consider: intrafamily management and extrafamily management. In intrafamily management, parents organize the child's home environment by making certain parts of the home (such as the playroom) and/or certain objects (such as toys and games) available, while limiting access to other parts (such as the dining room) and/or objects (such as guns and fragile objects). Intrafamily management also includes regulation of access to schools, churches, and organized recreational opportunities (e.g., sports), as well as informal walks, trips, and outings. In extrafamily management, fathers play the role of provider and/or restrictor of opportunities for interaction with other social agents and institutions outside the family. This management includes providing access to other play and recreational partners by regulating children's contact with different individuals.

Measures of father availability focus on the potential for interaction when the father is available or accessible to the child. Availability typically quantifies the number of hours or days that fathers are physically present and potentially available for activity or interaction with their children, regardless of whether interaction actually takes place (Lamb, 1987). Examples of this type of availability are reading the paper while the child plays nearby or cooking a meal while the child does homework. Pleck (1997) suggests that fathers' availability has increased from one half that of mothers prior to the 1980s to nearly two thirds as much as mothers in the 1990s. It is difficult to determine why these changes in fathers' availability have occurred, but it appears that they may reflect an increase in maternal work outside the home, as well as a change in societal expectations of fathers' involvement with their children and their role in helping their partners.

Often, father availability is measured only in families in which the father coresides with the child (e.g., in two-parent, married-couple families). The assumption is that coresidence equals involvement. Some studies (e.g., Cochran, 1997; Johnson, 1998) suggest that actual availability may be as great when the father is not a coresident (e.g., the father is absent by divorce or by virtue of not marrying the mother of his child). However, in most instances, paternal availability may be affected negatively when fathers do not live with their children because nonresident fathers are reportedly less involved with their children and at greater risk of losing regular contact with them over time (Furstenberg & Weiss, 2000; McLanahan & Sandefur, 1994).

Research on father engagement makes a specific distinction between *fatherhood* and *fatherwork*. Hawkins and Dollahite (1997, pp. 20–21) suggest that positive (generative) fathering is best conceived as *fatherwork* (i.e., sustained efforts men actually undertake with and for children) rather than as *fatherhood* (i.e., structural arrangements and cultural or normative expectations). Although Hawkins and Dollahite acknowledge that the structural aspects of fatherhood (e.g., marriage, paternity, and coresidence) can be important, direct and indirect fatherwork (those father–child interactions and child-maintenance activities that long have been recognized as having substantial influence on child development) should form the core of any father presence construct.

PATERNAL CAREGIVING

Fathering researchers (Palkovitz, 1997; Parke, 2000) typically refer to fathers' caregiving in ways that are similar to maternal caregiving: father caregiving provides for children's basic needs, including feeding them, ensuring they get sufficient rest, and protecting them from danger. Caregiving also involves nurturing expressions and behaviors that convey to children a sense of emotional engagement, love, attachment, and security. Such behaviors involve culturally appropriate physical acts of affection and comfort (such as touching, hugging, kissing, and cuddling), verbal expressions (such as comforting with reassuring words and sounds), and behaviors that help to maintain communication between children and caregivers (including listening and giving timely responses to children's concerns). In addition, caregiving involves generativity, that is, psychological and emotional investment in the caregiving role and in the children for whom one provides such care (Erikson, 1969; Erikson & Erikson, 1981). Finally, paternal caregiving includes the managerial tasks that permit caregivers to cooperatively and consistently meet children's basic needs (such as shopping for food and clothing).

The quality of caregiving and parenting can have a profound effect on children. Children who receive inconsistent, neglectful, or inadequate physical and emotional caregiving are at greater risk for negative developmental outcomes (McLoyd, 1990; Ray & McLoyd, 1986). In high-risk communities characterized by chronic long-term poverty, a nurturing and supportive parent is the single most important source of resiliency in children (Luthar & Zigler, 1991; Wakschlag & Hans, 1999).

Research on fathers' caregiving tends to describe the frequency of care and the task performed but does not focus on the quality of father care or its relationship to child outcomes (Davis & Perkins, 1996). The bulk of this research focuses on fathers and children who reside together. Although some studies conducted in the early 1990s (e.g., Seltzer, 1991) suggest that divorced fathers who do not live with their children are at risk of becoming less involved as their children grow older, findings from longitudinal studies (e.g., McLanahan & Teitler, 1998) suggest that many unmarried fathers are likely to be as involved with their children at the end of the child's first year as they are two years later. However, in general, researchers have not investigated the degree to which unmarried fathers are able to sustain a consistent caregiving role over the first 18 years of a child's life.

An important exception comes from data in the longitudinal, intergenerational study of children born to low-income, African American adolescent mothers that was undertaken by Furstenberg in the 1980s and has continued to the present (Furstenberg & Harris, 1993; Furstenberg & Weiss, 2000). Although the studies are not specifically an investigation of caregiving, they suggest that unmarried fathers' involvement with children decreases during the critical years of childhood and adolescence. The authors reported that, by the time the children reached adolescence, only 46% of fathers in the study were in contact with them, and only 14% lived with them.

In another recent study, Coley and Chase-Lansdale (2000) found that the nature or type of father involvement is as important as the level of involvement. In this multigenerational study of 135 low-income, minority fathers in Baltimore, Maryland, the authors found that father characteristics, household composition, and family relationships were important predictors of father involvement. Employed fathers were seven times as likely as unemployed fathers to have moved from low involvement to high involvement or to have always been involved. Fathers with at least a high school education were less likely to reduce involvement over time. Paternal age, child's age, and maternal personal and familial resources were not significant predictors of involvement. Married or coresident fathers were more likely to be highly involved than nonresident fathers were, regardless of their involvement at the time of birth. The presence of a new maternal partner or of the child's maternal grandmother did not decrease father involvement. Mothers' reports of emotionally close relationships with fathers suggested that such relationships increased the likelihood that fathers would be highly involved, regardless of involvement at birth or whether they lived with the child's mother. Coley and Chase-Lansdale suggest that the first few years after the child's birth provide a window for intervention to increase father involvement.

In less economically advantaged families, many fathers reportedly play a critical role in caring for young children. In one study (Hans, Ray, Bernstein, & Halpern, 1995), low-income, unmarried African American mothers stated that, after themselves, fathers were the most frequent providers of care to very young children. A majority of mothers (53%) indicated that fathers provided solo care to toddlers at least one or two days per week. Cohen (1998) found that 43% of low-income fathers, compared to 24% of more economically advantaged fathers, cared for their young children while their wives worked. In addition, 42% of fathers in blue-collar and service occupations, compared to 18% of fathers in managerial and professional jobs, reported looking after their children while their wives worked (U.S. Census, 1997).

FATHER INVOLVEMENT IN CHILDREN'S ACADEMIC ACHIEVEMENT

The most comprehensive study to date on the relation between father involvement and children's academic achievement was conducted by Nord, Brimhall, and West (1997). They found that fathers from two-parent families who are moderately or highly involved in school are significantly more likely to have children who receive mostly high marks, enjoy school, and never repeat a grade. Nonresident fathers' involvement in school also predicts the same outcome measures for children. In their study of 11- to 14-year-old children, Grolnick and Slowiaczek (1994) found that fathers who participated in school activities had children with a higher degree of self-perceived academic competence and greater self-regulation. Father involvement in intellectual and cultural activities at home also was related to children's perceived academic competence. In a recent study of prekindergarten Head Start children, a positive association was found between high-level participation in a father involvement project and children's mathematics readiness change scores (Fagan & Iglesias, 1999).

In early work on this topic, Cohen (1987) investigated the degree of parents' influence on their children's educational aspirations. Using data collected from questionnaires assessing intelligence quotient (IQ), grades, and general demographic information on almost 7,000 white, male and female, preadolescent and adolescent students, Cohen found that daughters modeled their parents more than sons, and sons were more influenced by their parents' definitions of educational success. Mothers and fathers did not differ in the strength of their influence on children. The intergenerational effects of either parent's encouragement were found to be equally strong.

Both the U.S. representative study undertaken by Nord and her colleagues (1997) and an earlier Head Start study by Gary, Beatty, and Weaver (1987) examined the extent to which fathers were involved in their children's schools. The studies showed that fathers were less involved than mothers in all types of school activities, including acting as volunteers and attending class events, parent-teacher conferences, and general school meetings. Fathers without high school educations were also much less likely to be involved in their children's schools than fathers with higher levels of education (Nord et al., 1997). Although nonresident fathers were found to be substantially less involved in the child's schools than coresident fathers, their involvement was by no means trivial to children's achievement or behavior in school.

ISSUES OF RACE AND POVERTY

Not unlike the challenges facing families in general, issues of race, poverty, culture, language, and access determine a range of life experiences, opportunities, and problems for children. Such issues concern whether and to what degree boys and girls—particularly those in low-income neighborhoods—are victimized by the residual effects of racial discrimination, poverty, and father absence over time and through generations. Even when researchers control for poverty, the findings are mixed; however, researchers (e.g., Hans, Ray, Bernstein, & Halpern, 1995) are close to unanimous in citing the potentially harmful effects of father absence on children's development when coupled with poverty and recognize that minority children and their families have higher rates of poverty and father absence. Because of welfare reform and other U.S. federal legislation, the issues facing these families and the significance of father absence has received increased attention by both researchers and the popular press. (See the discussion later in this chapter.)

A criticism of much of the research on fathering is that the larger problems of father involvement have been positioned exclusively within the context of low-income fathers who live apart from their children, that is, nonresident, noncustodial fathers. A related criticism is that the attention to these fathers has been shaped primarily by policy demands in relationship to U.S. federal legislation such as welfare reform. There are multiple reasons for the enormous interest in poor fathers. First, the children of poor mothers are poor, and the fathers of these children are equally poor. Second, fatherhood issues are tied to welfare reform, with expectations being high that the two, when combined, will result in reductions of pregnancies outside marriage. Because fathers have been considered the culprits in the rise of welfare-dependent families (Mincy & Dupree, 2000), observers expect that if these fathers become financially responsible for their children, the need for government support to these families will decrease. In addition, poor fathers—particularly poor, unwed fathers—constitute the group about whom U.S. federal and state policymakers or researchers are least aware or knowledgeable. The Family Support Act of 1988, which made public the problems of child support but which was focused mostly on divorced men (many of whom were financially capable of supporting their children), makes no distinctions between poor men and middle-income men who could contribute financially to their children. At the time, child support efforts did not consider in-kind contributions of fathers in determining child support awards.

The assumptions that contribute to these criticisms are well worth noting. However, it is also important to note that a range of debilitating social and structural barriers—resulting from poor quality schools, inaccessibility to other public institutions, and problems of employment and employability—contribute to the precarious situations of these fathers. Of equal significance is the fact that the fathers who are the center of attention are disproportionately of racial or ethnic minorities, residents of urban settings, and intergenerationally poor.

Beginning in the early 1990s, several researchers (e.g., Furstenberg & Harris, 1993; Lerman & Ooms, 1993) began to stress the importance of studying the long-term consequences of father absence on children's development into adulthood, perceptions of family, relationships within the family unit, and families' abilities to achieve family equilibrium or organization over the long term. The child's ability to chart his or her future as learner, provider, and parent and to develop expectations of father behavior may be limited by the absence of a father or male fig-

ure who can and does model economically and emotionally supportive behavior. In father-absent, poor families, the normal patterns of
family reorganization after any kind of adversity may disappear. The
result may be sustained disorganization that makes the family vulner-
able to stress and poverty imprinted in the lives and minds of children. For lack of resources and knowledge about how to identify and
best use these resources, the family's life course may exist in a state of
relative disorganization intergenerationally (Anderson, 1999; Hill, 1986;
Hogan, Hao, & Parish, 1990).

Fathers and Literacy Within the Family

Parents—mothers in particular—are considered to be children's first
teachers, the transmitters of beliefs, practices, and knowledge, such as
literacy knowledge. Most family literacy programs serve mothers, primarily because mothers have traditionally been children's primary or
sole caregivers. Some problems associated with engaging fathers stem
from the unavailability of fathers who serve as the family's primary
breadwinners; in other cases, fathers live outside the home and are either not considered important by program staff, difficult to reach, or
not accessible. Moreover, when fathers do not coreside with children or
when they have antagonistic relationships with their children's mothers, practitioners are often hesitant to involve fathers or are uncertain
about what the boundaries of their relationship with families in conflict
should be. In addition, involving fathers in programs raises questions
about how gender is discussed and approached within the interventions themselves. These questions concern the content of program instruction and how boys and girls (or men and women) learn literacy,
the instructional materials that are most useful for boys versus girls
(or men versus women), and the nature of interactions between parent and child. Among the other questions raised is how prepared programs are to involve fathers, an increasing number of whom are
children's primary caregivers or want to be involved more actively in
their children's development (Gadsden & Ray, 2002).

Although the focus on fathers is not entirely new to literacy research
and practice, an identifiable emphasis on fathers in the literature has
not been present. Durkin (1966) examined the nature of both fathers'
and mothers' interactions in the early literacy development of inner-city

and middle-income children. However, the individual, gendered activities of fathers were not isolated. In other words, Durkin was primarily concerned with the result of the interactions of fathers as one of the two parents engaged with children and was less interested in whether there were specific practices, interactions, and experiences that were unique to fathers versus mothers in shaping children's literacy.

In 1987, Hiebert and Adams moved Durkin's research a small step further by paying attention to whether there was a difference in mothers' and fathers' perceptions of children's literacy abilities and performance. They found that both parents tended to overestimate children's literate abilities. In the late 1980s and early 1990s, Taylor (1983, 1990) and Taylor and Dorsey-Gaines (1988) examined the complexity of the relationships between African American parents and children and among family members. Like Durkin (1966), they rarely referred to gender differences in their references; however, they addressed a range of cultural issues that form the basis for interactions and that, by extension, are significant to understanding how fathers are integrated in family life. Bowman's review (1995) of the literature on African American families, as well as Gadsden and Bowman's review (1999), suggest that examining the role of fathers in children's education, schooling, and literacy development is critical for deconstructing fathers' participation in literate activities, the barriers they face as a result of low literacy, and their perceptions of the role they play in their children's literacy development. These factors may affect whether and how well children are prepared for school, as well as influence the direct and subtle messages that fathers convey to their children about the value, achievability, and power associated with literacy and knowledge.

More recently, several works drawn from intervention and basic research in literacy have provided images of the types of relationships, potential instruction, and possible effects of father engagement. None of the studies is a large-scale effort; most are case studies, provide narrative accounts, or use qualitative approaches. Moulton and Holmes (1995) for example, use a case-study approach to explore the influence of a family's literacy interactions on all family members. The focus of their case is Len, a 47-year-old father and grandfather who had been learning to read. After he invited his family to participate in his reading activities, his reading improved and the frequency and nature of the family's interactions changed: some family members clipped relevant newspaper articles, Len participated more actively in oral reading during the family's religious evenings, Len's expectations for his son's reading increased, and Len and his children helped one another with their homework. The authors remind family literacy specialists that family literacy both strengthens and challenges relationships in families. For example, despite the success that Len experienced, the changes in Len's literacy and motivations to read affected the family, with the family sometimes interfering with and other times facilitating the learning process.

Hill (1998) provides a case study of a juvenile residential facility practitioner who worked to engage young fathers in a literacy classroom of peers, using literature from a range of genres. The author argues for the importance of stimulating an interest in reading and literature in young fathers if they are to identify with being readers, writers, and storytellers and if they are to pass along literacy to their children. Hill's article describes three themes of the program discussion and readings: the bully (meanness); embarrassing moments; and anxiety, competition, and fear. Each theme was taken from the participants' experiences as boys, was covered in relevant literature, and had relevance to the messages of survival and caring that the young fathers conveyed when reading and encouraging their children to read.

Edwards (1995) describes how a school-based program encouraged low-income mothers to share books with their children and encouraged other parents to do the same, even after the program developer was no longer involved. Phase 1 of the program entailed the development of a rapport between participants through group discussion. Phase 2 included book-reading practice with children. Participants helped to evaluate the impact of the program, and many became local advocates for literacy. Edwards found that families often do not know how to take part in theoretical and practical work for the benefit of their members' literacy and that the voices of parents add a critical dimension to researchers' and practitioners' understanding of the problems facing families, as well as the knowledge and skills families can contribute to a program. (See chapters 6 and 11 for descriptions of family literacy programs built on families' strengths.) Although the participants in this program were primarily women (33 mothers and 3 fathers), Edwards suggests that her model is as successful in engaging fathers as mothers.

Early childhood researchers and educators have taken a lead in examining the dimensions of father involvement in relation to the education of young children. Some researchers, such as Ortiz, Stile, and Brown (1999), provide early childhood educators with approaches and strategies to foster father-child literacy, with a particular focus on examining cultural differences and frames of reference to learn more about the children and fathers studied and served by programs. Ortiz and Stile (1996) examined the literacy activities of 47 father-child pairs over a two-year period in New Mexico. Fathers in the study reported using a range of reading activities, including book reading and engaging children in reading relevant, environmental print such as road signs, logos, and billboards. The researchers similarly explored father-child writing activities, such as spelling and defining words, coloring letters, spelling names, and tracing letters. The authors report that fathers' reasons for seeking literacy support related to two themes: ensuring that their children are prepared to face the demands of school and bonding with their children.

At NCOFF at the University of Pennsylvania, my colleagues and I have been examining a range of research questions on father involvement and initiating work on fathers and literacy. However, to our knowledge, there has been no coordinated effort in the field to explore this issue, although the National Center on Family Literacy and the National Institute for Literacy are beginning to examine issues related to fatherhood. As a result, studies on fathers are few in number and scattered in their focus and application. Research that extends the work of Durkin, Hiebert, and others to address more intensively the individual and collective interactions of fathers and mothers—as well as other studies that examine different dimensions of family literacy—are greatly needed; that is, there is a need for work that focuses on both fathers and mothers and that yields information on the effects of their interactions on children's literacy engagement and literacy learning. Such work might define the nature of father-child literacy interactions and identify the ways in which they are similar to or different than mother-child interactions. Social science fathering researchers as well as fathering practitioners would be particularly interested in how fathers' behaviors differ from those of mothers within an area such as literacy.

Literacy researchers increasingly will need to be concerned with whether and how the literacy behaviors of and support from both fathers and mothers (as well as other adults in a household) result in any difference in children's engagement and performance in reading. However, regardless of the research agendas, scholars by necessity will need to address the differential relationships that fathers have with their children, recognizing that unlike the mothers who are the focus of most parent–child literacy studies, fathers' residence, marital status, or availability may determine whether and how much they interact with children. It is equally important to address how fathers and mothers are situated within the larger family unit and how they collaborate with other family members to formulate their own self-assessments of their literacy, literacy practices, and the purposes of literacy learning both in relation to their roles as adult learners within families and to the literacy development of children within the family.

Informing an Expansive Framework for Family Literacy: Learning From the Lives of Young, Low-Income, African American Fathers

Literacy and other education and social science researchers are only at the very early stages of investigating and framing the problems and issues relating to fathers within family literacy. Much of what researchers and practitioners need to know can be provided aptly by fathers themselves, who offer critical information on the nature and role of literacy in their lives. In the text that follows, I provide an overview of discussions about a much highlighted subset of fathers: low-income, African American fathers in urban settings. Then, I present the commentaries of these fathers who discuss their expectations of literacy, their barriers to learning, and the social factors that minimize both their construction of and access to opportunities.

Most images of fathers in need of support, as presented by popular media and academics alike, are disproportionately of low-income, nonresident, noncustodial fathers who are African American or Latino and living in urban areas. These fathers were almost invisible prior to the passage of the Family Support Act in 1988. Low-income fathers and nonresident, noncustodial fathers had been invisible in the sense that neither researchers nor policymakers had considered seriously the limitations these fathers might face in fulfilling the responsibilities of child support and the fact that many never married the mothers of their children.

Two large demonstration projects contributed to researchers', practitioners', and policymakers' understandings of these fathers. Both were designed for low-income fathers and funded with a combination of U.S. federal and private support. The Young Unwed Fathers Project, coordinated by Public/Private Ventures in Philadelphia, Pennsylvania, focused on young fathers between the ages of 16 and 25, providing them with educational assistance, employment and training, fatherhood development activities, and case management. The Parents' Fair Share Demonstration, conducted by the Manpower Demonstration Research Corporation in New York City, focused on enhanced child support enforcement, employment and training, peer support and instruction in parenting skills, and mediation services. The two programs differed from most previous efforts in terms of their target group (low-income fathers), funding streams (a combination of public and private sources), and focus (capacity building to engage fathers in supporting their children). The projects, coupled with increasing U.S. national attention, prompted the federal government to act more directly on the interest in fathers that it had been developing for nearly a decade.

Both studies have yielded findings of considerable importance for crafting an agenda of support; both also have become more significant in light of subsequent welfare reform legislation. Two early reports emerging from the demonstrations (e.g., Achatz & MacAllum, 1994; Furstenberg, Sherwood, & Sullivan, 1992), as well as more recent studies (e.g., Doolittle & Lynn, 1998), provide a picture of the social and personal lives of low-income, urban, African American fathers. Although offering a rich context for understanding the issues these fathers face, the studies' findings often were consistent with the perception that many low-income, African American, urban fathers do not systematically provide for their children financially. What neither these nor other studies have supplied with sufficient breadth or depth is the answer to a simple question: If these fathers do not provide financially for their children, what is the reason?

In addition, researchers rarely ask urban fathers themselves about their perspectives or choices regarding fatherhood. The advantage of such inquiry is that it avoids simply blaming fathers for the problems of childrearing in low-income urban communities. For research to help fathers engage in proactive behavior that enables them to become more involved in their children's lives, researchers need greater knowledge about the challenges of urban fathering. That knowledge should come from the fathers' viewpoints and must address the ways in which their challenges shape their development as fathers.

Recent attention by policymakers and researchers alike to low-income, minority, nonresident, noncustodial fathers has been examined within the context of *urban fathers*, a euphemism for men who have limited resources and capabilities to support their children and families and whose relationship with their children and the children's mothers may vary significantly from the norms of Western culture. Recent research on these fathers is both impressive and limited. The research is important in that it creates new knowledge and understanding about the lives of these fathers and the conditions and circumstances that promote or interrupt their relationships with their children. On the other hand, it is limited in its conceptualization of the issues as being located primarily or solely within an urban context. For example, practitioners providing support for fathers in poor rural settings remind us that these fathers face similar issues, some of which are longstanding problems in rural areas. The research is similarly limited in the knowledge it provides about poor, white men or men in other social classes who display differential levels and kinds of engagement with their children (Brody, Stoneman, Flor, McCrary, Hastings, & Conyers, 1994; DeFrain, LeMasters & Schroff, 1991). Lastly, the studies on urban fathers and those on rural fathers tell us relatively little about poor men who do reside with their children. What these studies do enhance, however, is our knowledge of the range of issues faced by a subset of low-income men.

Two U.S. studies focus on low-income fathers in urban settings. The continuing National Study of Early Head Start, which involves a range of universities across the United States, is providing new information on how the fathers access early childhood education programs as well as family and fathering programs (see also the efforts of the National Association for the Education of Young Children). The Fragile Families Study (see Garfinkel & McLanahan, 2000), a multisite study throughout the U.S., has yielded considerable data on the lives of young fathers and the connections that they make with their children and the children's mothers. In a recent study, my colleagues and I (see Gadsden, Wortham, Ray, & Wojcik, 2000; Wortham & Gadsden, in press) completed narratives of a subset of 15 fathers participating in a larger study with low-income fathers in an urban fathering program in the midwestern United States. We drew from Anderson's (1999) three-part theoretical/conceptual framework, representing three distinct realms of urban life: (1) the street (a male-dominated context, a realm of self-presentation and sometimes of violence), (2) the home (a female-dominated context, a realm of childcare and relative safety from the street), and (3) the system (a white or at least middle-class context with laws and policies that shortchange and harass lower class, urban African Americans).

For those men who spent most of their time in the street realm, issues of their own schooling and the schooling of their children may become secondary to the daily acts of ensuring that they and their children survive. A difficult environment for young children, the street does not provide a supportive environment for fathers to care for their children, although some fathers did tell us that they interact with their children like peers, in ways partly drawn from the street. Some fathers also expressed that they tried to establish a home for their children in their own residences, but the effort was difficult. They said that it did not always fit with their identities as men or that they had not learned the necessary skills to care for children on their own. The system sometimes intervenes, by forcing fathers to support children financially but providing few supports for them to sustain their families and achieve self-sufficiency. As a result, these men responded with hostility toward the system, which they believed did little to encourage intrinsically motivated connections between fathers and their children. In short, low-income, urban, African American fathers face a difficult confluence of factors—race, income, environment, and a host of misunderstandings about their potential to contribute to children's health, safety, and well-being—that interfere with broader societal expectations of their roles as fathers.

Literacy, Fathers, and Children:
Fathers' Perspectives and Their Implications for Literacy Programs

I'm lost, I don't understand what reading and writing has [sic] to do with fathers and families. I understand that we have to be able to teach our children, but . . . . (Tony, a single father)

Tony was one of 30 participants in the Fathers and Literacy Study, a two-year project focused on low-income custodial and noncustodial fathers in an urban fathers program (Gadsden, Brooks, & Jackson, 1997). In an era of changing gender roles and parenting roles and responsibilities, this statement by one father clearly casts doubt on the relevance he sees in engaging in his children's reading and writing development. Family literacy programs, hoping to attract fathers, will most likely come across numerous fathers who similarly question how their own literacy achievements influence their children's literacy achievements. Without an understanding of fathers' viewpoints in this regard, family literacy programs may be unable to attract this essential family member to their interventions.

The fathers and literacy research team at NCOFF conducted an exploratory study of fathers participating in a series of family literacy seminars. My colleagues on the research team and I were interested in gaining insights into fathers' beliefs about the uses, value, and problems of literacy learning. We were particularly interested in fathers' perceptions, views, and concerns as young, mostly unmarried, low-income, African American fathers. In addition, the young fathers talked about their roles as fathers and their status as economically impoverished men wanting to support their children's literacy development. As we researchers learned about the ways that the fathers constructed definitions of fathering, literacy, learning, and persistence, we also were interested in the question, Do cultural or economic factors influence the likelihood that fathers will contribute, in direct ways, to their children's literacy development and academic achievement?

Fathers in the study were participating in a fathering program in Philadelphia with which staff members at the center had a longstanding relationship. At the time of the study, the program had been in existence for five years and was focused on enhancing the capacity of young, mostly unmarried fathers to become responsible and involved parents, wage earners, and providers of child support. All the fathers in the seminar had participated in the fathering program for at least one year. The program also included a variety of experiences and activities designed to enhance fathers' relationships with their children and to improve their communication with their children's mothers.

The study and seminar series drew from a larger group of 50 fathers who participated intermittently in individual seminars. For in-depth interviews conducted by my colleagues and me, we focused on seven fathers who attended all of the sessions. The fathers in the larger study ranged in age from 18 to 31, with an average of 10 years of formal schooling and one with a year of college. The participants identified themselves as low-income wage earners, and only one half were employed. Six of the seven men who were the focus of the case studies were unmarried. They each had fathered between one and three children, all of whom at the time of the study were under the age of 7. More than one half the participants were living with their children or were their children's primary custodians, and all the fathers characterized themselves as being deeply connected to their children's lives. They expressed concern over the conditions in which their children received care, although they realized that their children's mothers sometimes misinterpreted their intentions. In addition, the fathers reportedly made sustained efforts to spend regular time with their children.

The program's family literacy seminars, conducted by a small group of male and female facilitators, offered the participants support in workplace proficiency and self-advocacy, parenting skills, and literacy enhancement. By interweaving the three components of workplace, parenting, and literacy, the research team and I aimed to address the self-identified issues affecting how fathers interact with children around literacy and educational activities.

From the outset, the research team was aware that most fathers in the program were from father-absent homes and that, although many of the young fathers experienced literacy problems, they were uncomfortable with the idea of participating in a literacy program. The research team then decided that we would initiate the sessions with a topic that was perceived as being uncontroversial and helpful. We focused the discussion on parenting, beginning with fathers' reflections, interpretations, and applications of issues, as well as on the roles and responsibilities of fathers as expressed in Arbello's poem, "I Want To Be the Kind of Father My Mother Was" (Abdullah, 1993):

> I want to be the kind of father my mother was. I want to be the kind of father my mother was. I want that same power. I want to give you that sense that I ain't ever going to leave you, like my mother gave me as my father. I want to be the one who loves you. . . . Maybe one of my boys will say I want to be the kind of father my dad was because that is the way it is suppose to be. (p. 7)

Although the issues raised and problems and possibilities described in this poem do not have universal application, the poem itself does depict a range of parent–child relationships that the fathers in the study had imagined or felt had meaning—relationships both innumerable and typically unresearched. To the fathers in the program, the poem encompassed many fundamental qualities of strong parent–child relationships. As expected, it triggered the fathers' memories about their own fathers' involvement during the course of their development, recalling some fond memories and also invoking painful and emotionally charged issues that are still unresolved, as described by Jay, one of the fathers in the program:

> Like you said yourself, people are carrying around stuff for 25 years. I think it's a lot of guys in this program who might have problems with their fathers because I'm one of them. Now, we can sit here and talk about it, we can write it down, we can have someone come in and share, but that doesn't mean nothing, even though we're sharing what's inside of us. It takes a long time to get 25 years worth of anger or whatever the case may be—it takes a long time to get that anger out of you.

As researchers of father involvement, families, and fathering programs, as well as literacy specialists, my colleagues at NCOFF and I expected that these seminars would evoke childhood memories of participants' own absent fathers and rekindle past wounds. For many of the fathers, their past experiences and feelings influenced current beliefs about their own parenting roles and responsibilities.

In general, family literacy programs ultimately focus on the ways in which adults can facilitate children's literacy. However, through

NCOFF's work in the seminar series, it became apparent that, in order for family literacy programs to attend to the needs of multiple family members, they must consider the distinct needs of adults and children, along with approaches to promote parental and individual adult interactions around literacy and children's literacy achievement. If family literacy programs consider the contexts of families and literacy, they must attend to the perspectives and issues presented by those whom they intend to serve. These items may involve questions about the nature of interactions or emerge as a function of participants' and practitioners' shared or different ethnicities, cultures, classes, genders, or social experiences. Programs that aim to influence fathers must consider how to engage them as literacy learners and teachers for their children. Where to begin is a complicated matter, but a beginning should provide a context for the knowledge, experiences, literacy beliefs, and needs of the fathers, as they describe them. The commentaries of the fathers in the seminar provide a lens with which to conduct this contextualization as a pretext to formal program development. Eight themes, which my colleagues at NCOFF and I considered as *evolving themes* to denote the ongoing nature of their development, were identified.

Theme 1: Determining the needs of fathers in family literacy efforts requires that practitioners have multiple approaches; to gauge the fathers' formal and informal literacy skills, practitioners must establish a systematic approach that is not unduly intrusive or invasive. The fathers in the program were willing to complete basic literacy assessments, including the *Self-Perceptions Regarding Reading Scale* (Jacobs & Paris, 1987), comprehension measures, and interest scales. The assessments were administered early in the study to identify the fathers' definitions and expectations for literacy, family, and work. The fathers' willingness to complete the assessments may have been related to the research team's preseminar presence in the fathering program; my colleagues at NCOFF and I were familiar to them and were able to establish mutual respect and trust. In other words, the fathers expected that we would help them to improve some facet of their lives. The delicate nature of the issues around literacy, however, were clear for many of the men, who stated that they resented what they considered to be societal assumptions of "their illiteracy," a perception that they felt was based on cultural and economic stereotypes.

Theme 2: Fathers read and wrote for different purposes at home and work and engaged in literacy activities with their children. The fathers in the program indicated that they spent continuous periods of time reading to their children, helping them with their homework, and serving as advocates for them with teachers. One father, Jim, commented on his feelings about reading to his son:

> Well, I read to him, and I don't know how I would feel if I wasn't able to read to him or if I wasn't able to read it well. I have a friend who every time he picks up a book to read to his children, he read[s] the same thing. It's the same thing. And they know it's the same book, but he reads it wrong.

Often, as revealed in this father's comments, the men had definite understandings of what skills were essential to becoming good readers or writers and participated in reading activities with their children. They measured themselves and other fathers against clear standards and, as one father pointed out, realized the problems inherent in "having child[ren] and never expos[ing] them to reading and writing and put[ting] them in school and expect[ing] them to learn."

Theme 3: An exclusive focus on literacy as the initial activity or as an approach or method to engage fathers' interest and participation is potentially problematic and unproductive. The component of the seminars directly focusing on literacy enhancement with the fathers was initially problematic. Although the reasons were multifaceted, the fathers seemed to interpret literacy through a relatively narrow lens—as decoding, basic reading, and writing. This ambivalence and discomfort with literacy was reflected in the comments of Malik when the curriculum was explained during the introductory seminar. He remarked,

> I'm not understanding what our curriculum is for. What kind of studying material can we possibly use? There are probably a few people who may need some remedial tutoring, but for the most part, I think the guys in this program know how to read and write?

Malik's comment was especially important. The fathering program director and coordinator had assumed at the outset of their program that literacy was not a problem for the fathers. As the director indicated, "Most of these guys have a high school diploma, GED, or have completed several years of high school." The program administrators subsequently found that some fathers never completed several assignments in the program, did not follow up leads for employment, and did not achieve developmental activities with their children. The administrators surmised that the problem was not a problem of motivation but one of literacy.

One might argue that, although Malik felt he had reached a comfortable level of reading and writing attainment, he was less aware of the wide range of literacies and literate behaviors he could learn to aid in his children's literacy development or the needs of other fathers. Moreover, another father, Jay, had not considered whether his own reading and writing achievements were adequate goals for helping his children. He also may have believed literacy and illiteracy to be polar opposite terms, rather than literacy being a continuum of abilities and knowledge. He felt that since he was not what he referred to as "illiterate" (a term typically not used in literacy research and practice), he was the wrong candidate for a program focused in some way on literacy. Literacy for Jay meant reading and writing, rather than a more expansive view of literacy that also included problem-solving skills— the abilities that enable a struggling adult reader to survive within different family, community, and work contexts. Literacy and its associated programs were, in Jay's opinion, for the unfortunate, those with fewer skills and abilities than the men in the program possessed. To Jay, any implicit reference to his or the other fathers' need to enhance their literacy was equated with, in his words, "[being] at the bottom, lacking, deficient." Other fathers shared Jay's views, and none of the fathers wanted to be connected to an image they perceived as negative. One might say that all the men in the program were engaged in what Freirian ideology would consider "reading the world and the word" (Friere, 1970/2000), but, from the fathers' perspectives, they needed little from literacy programs. Yet the fathers attended sessions and persisted in the seminar series.

Theme 4: The fathers equated literacy with basic schooling activities. The fathers did not subscribe to a multiple-literacies construct, which would include ways in which they had to read social service agency policies to protect their rights as fathers, read legal service documents to challenge custody decisions or ensure visitations, or write applications and reports for work or for work-related benefits. Their definitions of literacy were grounded in relationships with texts alone, rather than socially constructed literacies grounded in pooled funds of knowledge and information. In many respects, because the men resisted assumptions about their own literacy, they exerted a stance of self-agency, self-definition, and self-control within the context of the seminar's instructional activities. Their provocative stance, demonstrated frequently, changed the dynamics of power and authority during the seminars and allowed the men to shape and expand their frame of reference to literacy within the program context while achieving the goals of the program itself.

Theme 5: Despite their stated commitment to be responsible fathers, fathers felt challenged by the notions and expectations attached to parenting roles. This theme was reflected initially in fathers' responses to survey questions and subsequently in their questions generated in the seminar, such as, What does the word *father* mean to you? What do you believe a father's responsibilities are or should be? Do you know someone who you believe is a good father? What makes this person a good father and how are you similar to and different from your own father or your mother? The general consensus among the fathers was that each one's primary role was breadwinner and that this role was crucial. Everything else, including engaging their children around literacy and other educational activities, was secondary. In some ways, this response distinguishes these fathers from middle-income men, who also see their role as breadwinners but who may accept more readily the financial contributions of their wives. Other work with practitioners (e.g., Kane, Gadsden, & Armorer, 1996) found that young, low-income fathers who are attempting to achieve perfect images of the family, formed early in life and via television, have goals that are more likely to approximate historical relationships between men and women (in which the father is breadwinner and the mother is responsible for children), even if in reality the gendered division of labor and expectation is not achieved.

Because the fathers placed such a heavy emphasis on the breadwinner role and relegated literacy and assisting children's literacy to an important but secondary status, we were curious about why they participated and persisted in the program. When asked what attracted them to the seminars, Jay explained,

> I think a lot of the guys in here are more concerned with getting their personal lives straight, like taking care of their families, financial issues, or co-parenting issues. They will come to this program if they think it will help them in any way.

For these young men, the line between helping their children and helping themselves is not always definitive or clearly demarcated. Often having been thrust into adult responsibility or exposed to severe forms of poverty, parenthood and fatherhood became substitutes for adulthood. Thus, as is true of fathers in many family literacy programs, the fathers in the study conducted by the research team had not only a desire to help their children learn literacy but also a personal need to receive attention that was compromised or forfeited as a result of early or adolescent fatherhood, withdrawal from school, or involvement in activities that complicated their developmental transition into adulthood.

Theme 6: Fathers with little income perceived their limited earnings to be the culprits to their economic and personal success, even though literacy was perceived to be a path to greater success. Limited income was reported to be the primary barrier to their involvement and their relationship with their children, not low literacy levels. The fathers described limited income as the most debilitating factor to their abilities to promote and ensure their literacy development and future educational achievements or to contribute to the literacy and academic achievements of their children. The fathers repeatedly expressed their interest in the economic well-being of their children and acted on this interest by providing food, shelter, and clothing whenever possible, regardless of whether they coresided with their children or were custodial parents. This abiding commitment to the provider role—along with the intersections of the provider and nurturer roles—served as both a source of pride and frustration. One participant, Cole, recalled,

> I have WIC [a U.S. federal grant program to provide nutritious foods, information on healthy eating, and health care referrals for women, infants, and children] for my daughter, and when I go to pick it up, people ask me what am I doing, and I tell them "I'm here to get my daughter's WIC," and a lot of women just look because they don't see men in there taking care of their children.

Jerry also described himself as caught between his desire to support his daughter and the harsh reality of his small paycheck, coupled with the mandates around child support. He stated,

> OK, you have a child, you're working and supporting yourself, but you're not doing enough. They don't want to go by "OK, how much do you make a week?" Well, my gross pay is $400; my net pay is $165. Then, they'll say, "OK, since your gross is $400, then you can afford to pay this much." That's not realistic because that's not what I'm coming home with on Fridays.

Although the fathers subscribed to parental social laws connecting the fathers to the breadwinning role, they were likewise frustrated when their caring was equated only with their ability to offer financial assistance, resulting in a shared analysis by the fathers that "Sometimes, we just can't do it!"

Overall, these comments are similar to those of other low-income families with whom I have worked—families who value literacy and the teaching and learning roles that they can serve but who are faced with preferencing the immediate needs of shelter, food, and money and who wrestle with the urgency to improve their literacy and become better prepared to support their children's literacy (see Gadsden, 1995).

Theme 7: Fathers' beliefs about their children's educational success and future possibilities were ambivalent, often contraindicated in their practices, and sometimes at odds with their self-perceptions of facilitating children's literacy achievement. All the fathers expressed the importance of their children receiving a good education. They believed that if their children could achieve the highest level of literacy, which they attributed to a college education, it would permit them to have choices and pursue opportunities rather than be trapped at what they called "a low level." The fathers accepted the notion that literacy had communal and cultural value and that it contributed to the social capital and culture of the family. As Larry stated, "Education enables you to give something back, to pool your resources with those in need."

However, although they seemingly accepted the idea that a child must get a better education to get ahead, the fathers perceived that this road had serious potholes and that achieving this goal was beyond their grasp as fathers. With limited exposure to good schools themselves, they were uncertain about their children's futures and vacillated between embracing a sense of hope and feeling distrustful of schools and the so-called system. For instance, despite his own limited schooling, Andy perceived inconsistencies regarding the available opportunities, the influence of personal agency on what is possible, and supports available from institutions intended to promote learning:

> It depends on how far you want to go. They keep saying the white man is holding us back; it's not the white man, it's you! We're allowed to go to college now, and public school is free, and they still won't go. In college there are loans and scholarships and anybody can go, black, white, Asian and whoever... My counselor had more than 350 kids. [Shadley] is the biggest school in the city... You must make your self present. He be there every day. I made myself present. I got awards. I didn't have to pay for any [college] application fees.

The everyday realities of Andy's life refute the sentiment in his commentary and raise questions regarding the ways young people learn to negotiate within institutional settings such as schools. Although the fathers recognized the importance of educational institutions, some also felt unfairly undermined by schools that deliberately created barriers to their full participation in society; some felt that schools were not places that prepared them for the literacy tasks that they ultimately were facing. In addition to expressing educational concerns, one man also spoke in both hopeful and despairing ways about other formidable barriers to navigating the demands of work and family and providing for their children's future successes:

> I hear people saying, "I can't get out the ghetto, I can't do this, I can't do that." It's where you want to be and where you want to go. If you want

to leave from down in the bottom, you can leave. This [the United States] is a free country. Now, you have to make the rules work for you. It's not the white man's rules, the white man's world. The rules work for you, if you make the rules work for you. (Parker, single father)

Other fathers mentioned the constraints of their economic conditions and struggled to be realistic about their children's chances for breaking out of cyclical poverty. For example, Larry said,

The same thing I saw when I was younger, I see today. The same people that sat on the steps all day and did nothing are still sitting on those same steps doing nothing.... In my neighborhood, I never saw any doctors or attorneys. I never saw anyone that I could look up to.

The fathers also denoted changing social norms and societal shifts, such as the shift from an industrial to a technological focus in the workplace. They demonstrated a basic understanding of the ways in which global economic restructuring had moved opportunities for employment to distant shores beyond their reach. They were able to count the shuttered factories in their neighborhoods and surrounding communities and attach meaning to these images in terms of their potential to earn livings.

Theme 8: Low-income, African American fathers are a diverse group, not only in their literate abilities, literacy experiences, literacy preparation, and goals for their children but also in their family relationships and family resources. The men in the seminars came from families who ranged from lower middle class to public-assistance recipients, from intact families to single-parent homes, from coresident families to habitation in group or foster homes. Despite the placement of their experiences along different points on the continuum of class and cultural assimilation, they all understood the ways in which systemic barriers operated to constrain their opportunities and those of their children. The men expressed the need to develop strategies that would help them dismantle these barriers on multiple levels and provide resources to pass on to their children. These issues became the content of literacy that, for them, would motivate their engagement as fathers and family members.

Reflecting on our experiences, my colleagues and I on the NCOFF research team recognized that the young fathers offered compelling insights for restructuring assumptions about effective classroom pedagogy and family literacy practices. Although not our intent, at first my colleagues and I narrowly perceived the reasons why fathers participate in literacy or educational activities with their children. It did not take long, however, for the participants to reveal their multiple purposes for seeking literacy support while denying their needs or the layers of issues and histories influencing their literacy and educational interactions with their children. The fathers' comments reinforced we researchers' sense of the variety of ways literate behaviors are intergenerationally learned, made valuable or not, and used in daily contexts. Long-standing traditions of parental gender-role behaviors, made even more complex with the addition of cultural and economic factors, are worth acknowledging. However, before offering family literacy prescriptions, it is essential that researchers and practitioners gather more background data and attempt to uncover more information about the inherent complexities and possibilities of involving fathers in family literacy programs.

Although the research team gained new information about what the content of programs focusing on fathers and family literacy could be, the full scope of options was not evident. Differences in gender roles and the ways in which social practices set expectations for masculinity, as well as the cultural frameworks that contribute to gender identity, are not small matters and require consideration. In the case of fathers—specifically of low-income, minority fathers in urban settings —one size definitely does not fit all.

However, one point became clear, both throughout the seminars and in my experiences with fathering programs and practitioners throughout the United States: Fathering programs headed by women often experience a range of problems related to an absence of male practitioners. In NCOFF's work, most of the facilitators were female; the gendered differences, while neither overwhelming nor significantly altering the nature of the interaction, were potentially reminiscent of the fathers' school experiences, in which most of the teachers were women. This limitation also restricted the research team's access to the most pressing issues and needs of the fathers. The learning community became a place where these men were making connections between their gendered roles and their communities and families. Inadvertently, we interrupted this process. Although the fathers appreciated the concerns and efforts of women engaged in this work, they resisted the ways in which the literacy sessions unwittingly perpetuated stereotypical depictions of literacy as a woman's domain and disrupted the learning community they had established with their male mentors. The fathers were very interested in learning from authentic lived experiences of men from minority groups who have negotiated social and educational systems more strategically and effectively than they had and who had achieved an element of personal and family success.

Conclusion

A U.S. federal policymaker recently asked a group of researchers to define the components of family literacy. The comments in the room were varied, with each followed by a sound rationale supporting a particular viewpoint. At that point, I made a mental distinction between how family literacy is confined in current discourse and what it could be. The field is still in the process of formation, and it is simply not possible to respond to this policymaker's question with a coherent framework that scholars would accept widely. (See chapter 1 for an overview of the frameworks on which family literacy programs are based.)

Family literacy both resembles other areas of study and diverges from them. Not unlike other fields of educational study, family literacy's definition depends on the specific interest of the specialist (e.g., early childhood education, adult literacy, or English as a second language) and may vary from one literacy specialist to another. However, most specialists (researchers and practitioners alike) would agree that there has been a recent increase in research studies and in practice and policy reports that address family literacy. Despite this attention, the numbers of family literacy studies constitute a relatively small subset of the larger research literature on reading, literacy, family development, and family studies. Areas fundamental to the strengthening of learning outcomes and the effective assessment of learning and language differences, such as teaching, pedagogy, assessment, and professional development, still receive limited attention compared to the structural programmatic issues of sustainability.

On the one hand, the field has begun to examine the multiple domains that connect literacy to other disciplines. Researchers have aimed to explore the potential and actual effects of literacy for different configurations of families and family members, although there are few data on program outcomes for participating children and families. On the other hand, several characteristics imply a persistently narrow focus of family literacy efforts. For example, many, though not all, discussions continue to be centered on the compensatory nature of family literacy and reducing intergenerational poverty or to be developed based on the notion that parents with low reading and writing literacies are unable to make meaningful contributions to their children's literacy development. Oddly, this rationale for family literacy serves an important function. It calls attention to the reading and writing problems that often plague families across different generations and the relation between restricted access to good schools and teaching and learners' limited access to jobs that can sustain them and their families (Hendrix, 2000).

However, this rationale is also restrictive, not only for learners but also for practitioners, researchers, policymakers, and for families themselves. Because family literacy has been highlighted primarily, if not entirely, as compensatory or remedial, the field has not positioned itself to understand how family units and individuals within a family—across different income levels and accepted modes of success—achieve, use, and transfer literacy. A significant portion of the work is either directly or indirectly based on assumptions that are concerned with the deficits of knowledge and functioning within families, rather than with the cognitive and social capacities, capabilities, and strengths within families as points of teaching and learning (Auerbach, 1995; see also, chapters 6 and 11). The perspective that low-income parents, typically the populations served by family literacy programs, bring little or nothing to the learning process renders insignificant and useless the cognitive and social abilities that parents and other family members contribute. They are abilities that researchers and practitioners have yet to capture, understand fully, interpret appropriately, or use effectively.

Early conceptualizations of family literacy were relatively simplistic in their focus and expectations. With an emphasis on literacy requiring little knowledge of families, researchers and practitioners have defined the field in a range of ways. However, they have begun with what is most feasible and practical—parents and children—perhaps in the hope that this work will lead to a larger focus on the implications of literacy for other family members. What has occurred in the field, nevertheless, is the reproduction of approaches from other domains of literacy research and practice. This adoption is no more apparent than in the continued focus on mother–child literacy as the primary area of work in family literacy. This approach, too, was a realistic starting point. Yet at this juncture in the field, opportunities exist for practitioners and researchers to take a more critical stance about their focus on other family members, while deepening their knowledge about mothers as well. From my perspective, attention to fathers and other family members who serve as protective factors for children is both a reasonable and highly well-positioned approach.

As is true in other areas of educational research, practice, and policy, efforts in the field of family literacy stand as stark reminders of both their promise to thread together the known literacy issues facing children and adults in reading, writing, and problem solving and the apparently inherent complexities in achieving these goals. It is essential that those of us involved in family literacy consider issues of content and assessment and be able to invoke appropriate methodological approaches. These issues are informed by a greater understanding of the field of fathers and families and by empirical work on fathering and on the populations who, based on current participants, are most likely to be adversely affected by poverty, racial discrimination, structural barriers, and poor schooling.

As an entry point into the discussion of fathers and family literacy, researchers should consider several questions regarding the focus and purpose of research, practice, and policy, not only within the domains of literacy and education but also within the context of family support:

- When fathers have limited literacy themselves, how can we realistically engage them in children's literacy, particularly in the case of young fathers and their children's early literacy? How can programs help fathers become effective evaluators of their children's literacy progress?
- How might we build on the historical relationships around play that fathers have with children to promote early literacy?

- How do family literacy programs prepare to serve fathers who are diverse in ethnicity, class, and relationships to their children and the children's mothers? Can programs and the field of family literacy configure a framework that investigates and responds to the different role patterns of and possibilities for these fathers?
- What role do family literacy programs and early childhood programs, such as Head Start, have in supporting a different kind of transition; that is, helping schools prepare for father involvement?
- Currently, concepts such as family literacy are integrated into a range of early childhood and school-based programs for parents and children through federally and state-funded programs such as Even Start. As research in the field emerges, how do researchers begin to separate the role of fathers as similar yet different from the role of mothers and build on the shared goals of fathers as parents?
- How do fathers contribute to the environmental and social development of early literacy learners or serve as protective factors that allow children to learn literacy? How do practitioners and researchers understand, use, and build on this knowledge?

Research on families and the development of literacy, with particular focus on and understanding of how literacy is situated within the larger social system and family culture, is essential for the field to expand. Family- or school-based literacy programs are sites of possibility in which learning and the exchange of knowledge might occur between a child and parent or between a child and another family member. These educational and school-based settings have served as the focus of most research on literacy and on instruction as well as learning. The study of family literacy learning within traditional school contexts has provided educators with rich sources of important information that help to shape and revise research paradigms and practice. However, deepening the work of family literacy and understanding father involvement within the context of family literacy, not unlike other areas such as family studies and early childhood education in which fathers have been integrated into the research, will be a complex task that requires moving beyond the typical boundaries of literacy research in schools and other school settings.

Author Note

The author expresses appreciation to the NCOFF research team who contributed in some way to the section on literacy, fathers, and children: Wanda Brooks, Lisa Gelzer, Jacqueline Jackson, and Wendy Lovell.

REFERENCES

Achatz, M., & MacAllum, C.A. (1994). *Young unwed fathers: Report from the field.* Philadelphia: Public/Private Ventures.

Amato, P.R., & Gilbreth, J.G. (1999). Nonresident fathers and children's well-being: A meta-analysis. *Journal of Marriage and the Family, 61,* 557–573.

Anderson, E. (1999). *Code of the street: Decency, violence, and moral life in the inner city.* New York: W.W. Norton.

Auerbach, E. (1995). Deconstructing the discourse of strengths in family literacy. *Journal of Reading Behavior, 27,* 643–661.

Bowman, P.J. (1995). Commentary: On family structure and the marginalization of black men. In M.B. Tucker & C. Mitchell-Kernan (Eds.), *The decline in marriage among African Americans: Causes, consequences, and policy implications.* New York: Russell Sage Foundation.

Brody, G.H., Stoneman, Z., Flor, D., McCrary, C., Hastings, L., & Conyers, O. (1994). Financial resources, parent psychological functioning, parent co-caregiving, and early adolescent competence in rural two-parent African American families. *Child Development, 65,* 590–605.

Cochran, D. (1997). African American fathers: A decade review. *Families in Society, 78*(4), 340–350.

Cohen, J. (1987). Parents as educational models and definers. *Journal of Marriage and the Family, 49,* 339–351.

Cohen, O. (1998). Parental narcissism and the disengagement of the non-custodial father after divorce. *Clinical Social Work, 26*(2), 195–215.

Coley, R., & Chase-Lansdale, P.L. (2000). Fathers' involvement with their children over time. *Poverty Research News, 4*(2), 12–14.

Davis, J.E., & Perkins, W.E. (1996). *Fathers care: A literature review.* Philadelphia: National Center on Fathers and Families.

DeFrain, J., LeMasters, E.E., & Schroff, J.A. (1991). Environment and fatherhood: Rural and urban influences. In F.W. Bozett & S. Hanson (Eds.), *Fatherhood and families in cultural context* (Vol. 6, pp. 162–186). New York: Springer-Verlag.

Doherty, W.J., Kouneski, E.F., & Erickson, M.F. (1998). Responsible fathering: An overview and conceptual framework. *Journal of Marriage and the Family, 60,* 277–292.

Doolittle, F., & Lynn, S. (1998). *Working with low-income cases: Lessons for the child support enforcement system from Parents' Fair Share.* New York: Manpower Demonstration Research Corporation.

Durkin, D. (1966). *Children who read early: Two longitudinal studies.* New York: Teachers College Press.

Edwards, P.A. (1995). Empowering low-income mothers and fathers to share books with young children. *The Reading Teacher, 48,* 558–564.

Erikson, E.H. (1969). Adult stage: Generativity versus stagnation. In R. Evans (Ed.), *Dialogue with Erik Erikson* (pp. 50–53). New York: Dutton.

Erikson, E.H., & Erikson, J.M. (1981). On generativity and identity. *Harvard Educational Review, 51*(2), 249–269.

Fagan, J., & Iglesias, A. (1999). Father involvement program effects on fathers, father figures, and their Head Start children: A quasi-experimental study. *Early Childhood Research Quarterly, 14,* 243–269.

Family Support Act of 1988, Pub. L. No. 100–485, §103b, (1988).

Freire, P. (2000). *Pedagogy of the oppressed* (M.B. Ramos, Trans.). New York: Continuum. (Original work published 1970)

Furstenberg, F.F., & Harris, K.M. (1993). When fathers matter/why fathers matter: The impact of paternal involvement on the offspring of adolescent mothers. In A. Lawson & D.L. Rhode (Eds.), *The politics of pregnancy: Adolescent sexuality and public policy* (pp. 189–215). New Haven: Yale University Press.

Furstenberg, F.F., Sherwood, K., & Sullivan, M.L. (1992). *Caring and paying: What fathers and mothers say about child support.* New York: Manpower Demonstration Research Corporation.

Furstenberg, F.F., & Weiss, C.C. (2000). Intergenerational transmission of fathering roles in at-risk families. *Marriage and Family Review, 29*(2–3), 181–201.

Gadsden, V.L. (1995). Literacy and African American youth: Legacy and struggle. In V.L. Gadsden & D.A. Wagner (Eds.), *Literacy among African American youth: Issues in learning, teaching, and schooling* (pp. 1–12). Cresskill, NJ: Hampton Press.

Gadsden, V.L. (1998). Family culture and literacy learning. In J. Osborn & F. Lehr (Eds.), *Literacy for all: Issues in teaching and learning* (pp. 32–50). New York: Guilford.

Gadsden, V.L., & Bowman, P. (1999). African American males and the struggle toward responsible fatherhood. In V. Polite & J. Davis (Eds.), *African American males in school and society: Practices and policies for effective education* (pp. 166–183). New York: Teachers College Press.

Gadsden, V.L., Brooks, W., & Jackson, J. (1997, March). *African American fathers, poverty and learning: Issues in supporting children in and out of school.* Paper presented at the annual meeting of the American Educational Research Association, Chicago, IL.

Gadsden, V.L., Fagan, J., Ray, A., & Davis, J. (in press). Fathering indicators for practice and evaluation: The fathering indicators framework. In R.R. Day & M.E. Lamb (Eds.), *Measuring father involvement in diverse settings.* Mahwah, NJ: Erlbaum.

Gadsden, V.L., & Ray, A. (2002). Engaging fathers: Issues and considerations for early childhood educators. *Young Children, 57*(6), 32–42.

Gadsden, V.L., Wortham, S., Ray, A., & Wojcik, T. (2000, April). *How urban fathers represent the transition to fathering: A discourse analysis of fathering narratives.* Paper presented at the annual meeting of the American Educational Research Association, Seattle, WA.

Garfinkel, I., & McLanahan, S. (2000). Fragile families and child well-being: A survey of parents. *Focus, 21,* 9–12.

Gary, L., Beatty, L., & Weaver, G. (1987). *Involvement of black fathers in Head Start* (Final report submitted to the Department of Health and Human Services, ACYF, Grant No. 90-CD-0509). Washington, DC: Howard University.

Grolnick, W.S., & Slowiaczek, M.L. (1994). Parents' involvement in children's schooling: A multidimensional conceptualization and motivational model. *Child Development, 65,* 237–252.

Hans, S. Ray, A., Bernstein, V., & Halpern, R. (1995). *Caregiving in the inner city* (A final report to the Carnegie Corporation of New York and the Charles Stewart Mott Foundation). Chicago: University of Chicago Press.

Hawkins, A.J., & Dollahite, D.C. (Eds.). (1997). *Generative fathering: Beyond deficit perspectives.* Thousand Oaks, CA: Sage.

Hendrix, S. (2000). Family literacy education: Panacea or false promise? *Journal of Adolescent & Adult Literacy, 43,* 338–346.

Hiebert, E., & Adams, C. (1987). Fathers' and mothers' perceptions of their preschool children's emergent literacy. *Journal of Experimental Child Psychology, 44,* 25–37.

Hill, M.H. (1998). Teen fathers learn the power of literacy for their children. *Journal of Adolescent & Adult Literacy, 42*, 196–202.

Hill, R. (1986). Life cycle stages for types of single parent families: On family development theory. *Family Relations, 35*, 19–29.

Hogan, D.P., Hao, L.X., & Parish, W.L. (1990). Race, kin networks and assistance to mother-headed families. *Social Forces, 68*, 797–812.

Hosley, C.A., & Montemayor, R. (1997). Fathers and adolescents. In M. Lamb (Ed.), *The role of the father in child development* (pp. 162–178). New York: Wiley.

Jacobs, J.E., & Paris, S.G. (1987). Children's metacognition about reading: Issues in definition, measurement, and instruction. *Educational Psychologist, 22*(3–4), 255–278.

Johnson, W.E. (1998). Paternal involvement in fragile African American families: Implications for clinical and social work practice. *Smith College Studies in Social Work, 68*(2), 215–232.

Kane, D., Gadsden, V.L., & Armorer, K. (1996). *The fathers and families core learnings: An update from the field.* Philadelphia: National Center on Fathers and Families, University of Pennsylvania.

Lamb, M.E. (1987). Introduction: The emergent father. In M.E. Lamb (Ed.), *The father's role: A cross-cultural perspective* (pp. 3–25). Hillsdale, NJ: Erlbaum.

Lamb, M.E. (2000). The history of research on father involvement: An overview. *Marriage and Family Review, 29*, 23–42.

Lamb, M.E., Pleck, J., Charnov, E., & Levine, J.A. (1985). A biosocial perspective on paternal behavior and involvement. In J. Lancaster, J. Altmann, A. Rossi, & L. Sherrod (Eds.), *Parenting across the lifespan: Biosocial dimensions* (pp. 111–142). New York: Aldine de Gruyter.

Lerman, R.I., & Ooms, T.J. (Eds.). (1993). *Young unwed fathers: Changing roles and emerging policies.* Philadelphia: Temple University Press.

Levine, J.A., & Pitt, E. (1996). *New expectations: Community strategies for responsible fatherhood.* New York: Families and Work Institute.

Luthar, S.S., & Zigler, E. (1991). Vulnerability and competence: A review of the research on resilience in childhood. *American Journal of Orthopsychiatry, 61*, 6–22.

McLanahan, S., & Sandefur, G. (1994). *Growing up with a single parent: What hurts, what helps.* Cambridge, MA: Harvard University Press.

McLanahan, S., & Teitler, J. (1998). The consequences of father absence. In M.E. Lamb (Ed.), *Parenting and child development in nontraditional families* (pp. 83–102). Mahwah, NJ: Erlbaum.

McLoyd, V. (1990). The impact of economic hardship on black families and children: Psychological distress, parenting, and socioemotional development. *Child Development, 61*, 311–346.

Mincy, R.B., & Dupree, A.T. (2000). *Can the next steps in welfare reform achieve PRWORA's fourth goal? Family formation in fragile families* (Working Paper No. 00-23-FF). Princeton, NJ: Princeton University Center for Child Well-Being.

Moulton, M., & Holmes, V.L. (1995). An adult learns to read: A family affair. *Journal of Adolescent & Adult Literacy, 38*, 542–549.

National Center on Fathers and Families. (1994). *The fathers and families core learnings.* Philadelphia: Author.

Nord, C.W., Brimhall, D., & West, J. (1997). *Fathers' involvement in their children's schools.* Washington, DC: U.S. Department of Education.

Ortiz, R.W., & Stile, S. (1996, April). *A preliminary study of fathers' reading activities with their preschool-age children from three academic programs: Head Start, developmentally delayed, and gifted.* Paper presented at the New Mexico Federation of the Council for Exceptional Children Conference, Albuquerque, NM.

Ortiz, R.W., Stile, S., & Brown, C. (1999). Early literacy activities of fathers: Reading and writing with young children. *Young Children, 54*(5), 16–18.

Palkovitz, R. (1997). Reconstructing "involvement": Expanding conceptualizations of men's caring in contemporary families. In A.J. Hawkins & D.C. Dollahite (Eds.), *Generative fathering: Beyond deficit perspectives*. Thousand Oaks, CA: Sage

Parke, R.D. (1996). *Fatherhood*. Cambridge, MA: Harvard University Press.

Parke, R.D. (2000). Father involvement: A developmental psychological perspective. *Marriage and Family Review, 29*, 43–58.

Phares, V. (1997). Psychological adjustment, maladjustment, and father–child relationships. In M.E. Lamb (Ed.), *The role of the father in child development* (3rd ed., pp. 261–283). New York: Wiley.

Pleck, J.H. (1997). Paternal involvement: Levels, sources, and consequences. In M.E. Lamb (Ed.), *The role of the father in child development* (pp. 66–104). New York: Wiley.

Pollack, W.S. (1995). A delicate balance: Fatherhood and psychological transformation. In J.L. Shapiro, M.J. Diamond, & M. Greenberg (Eds.), *Becoming a father. Contemporary, social, developmental, and clinical perspectives* (pp. 316–331). New York: Springer-Verlag.

Ray, A., & McLoyd, V. (1986). Fathers in hard times: The impact of unemployment and poverty on paternal and marital relations. In M.E. Lamb (Ed.), *The father's role: Applied perspectives* (pp. 339–383). New York: Wiley.

Seltzer, J. (1991). Relationships between fathers and children who live apart: The father's role after separation. *Journal of Marriage and the Family, 53*, 79–101.

Silverstein, L. (1996). Fathering is a feminist issue. *Psychology of Women Quarterly, 20*, 3–37.

Taylor, D. (1983). *Family literacy: Young children learning to read and write*. Portsmouth, NH: Heinemann.

Taylor, D. (1990). *Learning denied*. Portsmouth, NH. Heinemann.

Taylor, D., & Dorsey-Gaines, C. (1988). *Growing up literate: Learning from inner-city families*. Portsmouth, NH: Heinemann.

U.S. Bureau of Census. (1997). *My daddy takes care of me! Fathers as care providers* (Current Publication Rep. No. P70-59). Washington, DC: U.S. Government Printing Office.

Wakschlag, L.S., & Hans, S.L. (1999). Relation of maternal responsiveness during infancy to the development of behavior problems in high-risk youth. *Developmental Psychology, 2*, 569–579.

Wortham, S., & Gadsden, V.L. (in press). Urban fathers positioning themselves through narrative: An approach to narrative self-construction. In A. DeFina, D. Schiffrin, & M. Bamberg (Eds.), *Discursive construction of identities*. New York: Cambridge University Press.

LITERATURE CITED

Arbello, A. (1993). I wanna be the kinda father my mother was. In O. Abdullah (Ed.), *I wanna be the kinda father my mother was* (p. 7). New York: New Readers Press.

CHAPTER 6

Family Literacy in English Language Learning Communities: Issues Related to Program Development, Implementation, and Practice

Flora V. Rodríguez-Brown

National statistics show that English language learners (ELLs) represent a major segment of today's U.S. population. According to the census for the year 2000, one in eight people in the United States is of Hispanic origin (Therrien & Ramirez, 2000), and U.S. citizens of Hispanic origin are the fastest growing group in public schools (Sable & Stennett, 1998). According to the School Population Census from the Illinois State Board of Education (2001), in Chicago, Illinois, alone, over one third of the school-age children are Hispanic, and over 30% of these children come from homes in which English is not the primary language.

A report from the National Council of La Raza in 1990 states that 43% of the Hispanic population 19 years old and older—many of them ELLs—were not in school at the time of the report and lacked a high school diploma. In terms of functional literacy (defined as completion of 5 or more years of schooling), the report also stated that 12.5% of Hispanics 25 years old or older were not literate.

In regard to schooling, according to Applebee, Langer, and Mullis (1987), Hispanics at all grade levels lag far behind their non–Hispanic white counterparts in reading and writing achievement. According to Sable and Stennett (1998) this gap has narrowed over time. The problem of low achievement is complex, and it seems doubtful that either home-based or school-based efforts alone will be sufficient to meet the academic needs of the Hispanic children in the study. Some researchers (Cummins, 1986; Delgado-Gaitan, 1992; Goldenberg, 1987; Moll, 1998; Reese & Gallimore, 2000; Reyes, 1992; Serna & Huddelson, 1993) have shown that instruction that takes into account the social, cultural, and linguistic strengths of families, as well as programs that emphasize interactive meaningful experiences between parents and children, provide more support for children's learning both at home and at school. Furthermore, continuity between ways of learning at home and school supports children's learning and achievement (see chapter 13). Rogers (2001) has found that cultural learning models used in homes from minority populations are different from those of the mainstream population (white, middle-class, European Americans). Unless students fit mainstream models of learning, schools do not recognize the knowledge that culturally and linguistically different children acquire at home. However, Reese and Gallimore (2000) have shown that cultural learning models existing in new Hispanic immigrant families, although relevant and important to their everyday lives, are not static systems. Through interaction with teachers and other school personnel, parents learn to adapt to the beliefs and practices supported by teachers and schools except in cases in which parents see change as jeopardizing the traditional moral beliefs of the family. In addition, Reese and Gallimore believe that teachers telling parents to read to their children is not an effective way to change cultural model patterns. Also, they have learned that one-shot training sessions for parents on how to read to children have little effect in changing the literacy learning behaviors in these homes. Reese and Gallimore have found that, with new immigrant Hispanic parents, explicit demands from teachers about reading as part of homework seem to promote the desired effect on families.

Family literacy programs offer families a long-term commitment toward enhancing the understanding of the parent's role in early literacy learning. (See chapter 1 for an overview of family literacy instruction.) Some programs also support efforts for school personnel to learn about the cultural models of learning, primary discourses, and literacies that culturally different children bring from home (Paratore, 2001;

Rodríguez-Brown, 2001b). In turn, this type of program strengthens the connection between the home and the school and enhances the opportunities for children to succeed in school. Family literacy programs based in sociocultural knowledge about ways children learn at home accept these cultural models of learning (Rogers, 2001), primary discourses, and literacies (Gee, 1999; The New London Group, 1996), and as such, the programs create learning environments in which parents and children share literacy in meaningful ways. (See chapter 11 for a description of another family literacy program building families' cultural beliefs.) These programs also provide families with opportunities to learn about new and different ways to share literacy at home, which could be added to the families' own repertoire. This way, parents and children learn to share literacy at home in ways that provide for some continuity in learning between home and school. It is under this premise that Project FLAME (Family Literacy: Aprendiendo, Mejorando, Educando [Learning, Improving, Educating]) functions today. This family literacy program has provided me with a context for the discussion of issues related to program development and implementation, which will be described later in the chapter. Parents in Project FLAME have been an invaluable source of information to me in my goal of finding the best ways to support parents' needs in their roles as teachers for their young children.

Project FLAME as Context

The relevance of context in the development of family literacy programs does not become obvious until the program is implemented. Then, the understanding of the community and the program developers' interpretation of what the community needs and wants may enhance or hinder the success of the program. Issues related to context involve more than knowledge of the setting in which the program will take place. Context includes knowledge and understanding of the cultural and linguistic backgrounds of the population to be served and sociocultural issues that may have an impact in the program's implementation. To learn about the context requires the ability to listen, to share knowledge, and to recognize that the population to be served could make valuable contributions to the program. It is also important to see the program activities as sources of new information, which participants can add to their already existing repertoires and behaviors.

With these ideas in mind, I cooperated in the design of a family literacy program called Project FLAME. The program was created to support Hispanic parents' learning about the relevance of their role as teachers and to show them different ways to share literacy with their young children at home (Rodríguez-Brown & Shanahan, 1989). In creating the program, several assumptions were made in support of the program design. The assumptions include the understanding that a supportive home environment is essential to early literacy development, the belief that parents can have a positive effect on children's learning, and the knowledge that, if parents are confident and successful learners, they will be the most effective teachers to their children. We, the Project FLAME staff, also assumed that a successful family literacy program should take into account the sociocultural context of the family.

The original program design included two activity components: *parents as teachers* and *parents as learners*. The parents as teachers component included activities leading toward the enhancement of ways and opportunities to provide literacy opportunities at home, to model literacy at home and within the community, to interact with children while pursuing early literacy activities, and to enhance the home-school connection. The parents as learners component included instruction on English as a second language (ESL), the General Educational Development (GED) exam, and basic skills to enhance parents' literacy skills. From a program design perspective, the second component was to serve as a way for parents to become literacy learning models for their children, but it has also served as a recruitment tool.

Through the years, the basic design and focus of the program has been maintained. However, the way my colleagues at the University of Illinois at Chicago and I carry out the program, the organization and planning of the activities, has been changing according to the needs of the population served. In addition, my colleagues and I also have added two additional components to the program: *parents as trainers* and *parents as school volunteers*. The program, which was originally supported by U.S. federal funds, is currently supported through gifts from private foundations, and it serves families whose children attend eight different Chicago public schools.

Project FLAME is a community program based in the schools and managed by the university. Participant parents and University of Illinois at Chicago personnel work together and share knowledge about program activities. The collaboration has allowed parents to validate their primary discourses, literacies, and cultural models of learning (Gee, 1999; The New London Group, 1996; Rogers, 2001). The parents' perspective has provided the program with a sound theoretical/sociocultural framework to support the actual family literacy design and content. The program also has allowed participants to learn different ways to share literacy, which in turn has added to and enhanced the ways and opportunities for parents to share literacy with their children at home and in the community. An analysis of self-reported data, collected between 1999 and 2001 from 189 adult FLAME participants who provided pre- and postprogram data through a survey questionnaire, shows *significant changes* in parents uses of literacy-related behaviors at home. (See chapter 12 for discussion of a range of assessment strategies for family literacy programs.) The data from tests show *significant changes* in parents using environmental print in the community (e.g., the supermarket and street signs) for literacy learning purposes with their children ($t = 9.21$), checking children's books out from the library ($t = 9.79$), reading for pleasure at home in front of the children ($t = 8.53$), writing in front of children ($t = 7.59$), reading books to their children ($t = 3.16$), and talking with their children about books ($t = 3.69$). The parents also reported that they had increased their knowledge about how to teach the alphabet ($t = 8.83$) and about how to select books for their children ($t = 10.31$). They also reported significant changes in their interaction with the schools their children attended. The parents also reported knowing more about what their children were learning at school ($t = 4.77$), talking with their children's teachers more frequently ($t = 8.09$), and increasing their participation in their children's school activities ($t = 7.89$).

Although the program is not directed to children, data collected from 120 children 3 to 6 years old whose parents participated in Project FLAME show significant improvements in the children's early literacy behaviors and knowledge during the time their parents participated in the program. The data show significant gains (.001 level) in letter recognition (uppercase, $t = 11.73$ and lowercase, $t = 11.27$), concepts of print (Piedras/Stones Test, Clay [1979] [$t = 12.73$]), and cognitive concepts (pre–Boehm and Boehm Tests of Basic Concepts [1986], which were administered in both Spanish and English by age levels: 3–4-year-olds, pre–Boehm, Spanish $t = 9.81$, English $t = 7.84$; and 5–6-year-olds, Boehm, Spanish $t = 9.37$, English $t = 12.90$).

The primary focus of Project FLAME is on family literacy, but we provide instruction for adult participants in ESL, using an approach based on participatory communicative competence. We use ESL classes to support the parents' role as literacy models for their children. Language proficiency data collected from 172 adult participants in Project FLAME from 1999 to 2001 show significant gains (.01 level) in the total score ($t = 2.94$) in the Adult-Language Assessment Scales (De Avila & Duncan, 1993).

The data discussed above are relevant because they show that Project FLAME has an impact on the use of literacy behaviors at home, which indirectly benefits children's early literacy learning and cognitive development, even though children are not the main focus of the program. Also, although the parents have become learning models for their children, they have significantly improved their English proficiency, not only in oral language but in reading and writing as well.

(A further description of Project FLAME is beyond the scope of this chapter. More information about the program can be found in Li [2002]; Rodríguez-Brown [2001a, 2001b]; Rodríguez-Brown, Li, & Albom [1999]; Rodríguez-Brown & Meehan [1998]; Rodríguez-Brown & Mulhern [1993]; and Shanahan, Mulhern, & Rodríguez-Brown [1995]. Also see chapter 1 for a description of Project FLAME.)

This chapter focuses on a different and relevant type of learning that has occurred as a byproduct of Project FLAME. It involves the knowledge I have acquired through 14 years of work with mostly new immigrants in the Hispanic community in Chicago. Through these interactions with parents from Project FLAME, I have learned a great deal about ways in which family literacy programs can better address the needs of linguistically and culturally different families. For me, working with parents and children from the program has been a very enriching learning experience that could not be gained just by reading books. In working with Hispanic families, the understanding of the concept of *familia* (Abi-Nader, 1991) has been central in supporting the development and implementation of Project FLAME. *Familia* relates to the relevance of the family's needs over the individual family member's needs. In the following pages, I will discuss some issues that are critical to the success of programs directed to ELL populations, with an emphasis on new Hispanic immigrant populations.

Issues Related to Program Design, Development, and Implementation

TALKING TO HISPANIC PARENTS ABOUT THEIR ROLE AS TEACHERS

During the early years of Project FLAME implementation, I had the opportunity to discuss with groups of parents their role as teachers of their children. To my surprise, I discovered that they did not see themselves in that role. They explained that they were not or could not be teachers because they did not have much schooling and they did not know English. When I asked them whether there were things they thought they could teach their children, they talked about cooking, sewing, going to the store, reading labels, writing letters, and making lists. Suddenly, they realized that not all knowledge comes from schooling. They also realized that they did not need to use English in order to support their young children's literacy learning at home. Immediately, I sensed a change in attitude and increased self-efficacy. In other words, the parents realized that they were already teachers for their children. This experience led me to decide that an important requirement in working with culturally and linguistically different parents is the need to validate their language and knowledge to strengthen their belief in their role as the first and most important teachers of their young children.

LANGUAGE AND LEARNING: PARENTS' CONCERNS

Dealing with language differences did not work the same as our discussion about being teachers. The parents still thought that if they were in the United States, they should teach their children in English. This idea led to a discussion of how what matters in supporting the development of early literacy is more cognitive than language specific. However, I did not talk about cognition with the parents. Rather, I explained that they needed to help develop their children's brains (a concept they understood) and that whatever they taught their children in Spanish would help the children once they learned English at school. We also talked about the need to provide good language models in English in order for children to learn English well. From these conversations, the parents learned that they could and should share their knowledge with their children and that they could do it in the language they knew best—Spanish.

LANGUAGE AND CULTURE IN DEFINING PARENTS' ROLE AS TEACHERS

In spite of the parents' understanding of their role as their children's teachers, a dichotomy developed about teaching and supporting children's learning once they started school. At this point, parents differentiated between their roles in educating versus teaching their children. More specifically, in Spanish the words *educar* (to educate) and *enseñar* (to teach) have very distinct and specific meanings. As parents, they saw their role as one of *educating* their children. To the Hispanic parents, this term means that their role is to help their children become good people. They are supposed to teach morals, manners, and values. The school's role, on the other hand, is to *teach* math, reading, science, and other topics. As I was faced with this dichotomy and the parents' ambivalence about their role as teachers in support of their school-age children's learning, I later discovered that other researchers (Reese, Balzano, Gallimore, & Goldenberg, 1995; Valdes, 1996) had found the same distinction. Another issue faced by the parents when they saw themselves pressed to fulfill their role as teachers was related to the concept of *respeto*—a Spanish term whose closest, yet still inadequate, English equivalent is *respect*—which is discussed widely by Valdes (1996). Teachers are highly regarded in the Hispanic culture, and parents feel that they should not interfere or intrude with the teacher's role. Furthermore, the parents I have worked with in Project FLAME initially were not sure the teachers wanted them to help their children at home. Recent findings from a longitudinal study by Reese and Gallimore (2000) show that teachers' explicit demands for Hispanic parents to read to their children at home, as part of daily homework, positively affects the families' behaviors and their view of literacy development. The parents involved with Project FLAME were very compliant to teachers' wishes and instituted these helpful practices at home when asked to do so.

LEARNING FROM THE CONTEXT OF AND THE FAMILIES IN A FAMILY LITERACY PROGRAM

Project FLAME parents have been great teachers in my endeavors to support their needs as the most important teachers for their young children. This realization has made me understand the relevance of knowing the context in which the program will take place during the design and development phases of family literacy programs. I have learned that designing programs requires more than what I, as a literacy researcher and teacher, think these parents need to learn. Many programs that stay at this level, which I call *functional* (Rodríguez-Brown & Mulhern, 1993), disappear quickly unless the program design changes in order to better serve the needs of the families who participate in it. Family literacy programs need to change and adapt to the needs of the populations served, and flexibility should be a characteristic of the programs. That is not to say that the assumptions underlying the different program designs or their content have to change. The focus of the original program design may stay in place, but the implementation and delivery may change. I do not believe that a specific program exists that will fit all populations. That is why some U.S. national programs that mandate specific components for everyone show high rates of attrition and low attendance, despite the fact that funding is available. The reason for attrition and low attendance is not that parents do not want to participate or do not want to learn. These problems occur because some aspects of the programs are incongruent with the cultures of some populations who could benefit from such programs. With regard to Hispanics, for example, programs that require home visits may not be popular because fathers usually work during the day and do not want anyone visiting their homes unless they are present. As such, mothers may have to withdraw from programs that have home visits as a required activity of the program. Therefore, a culturally relevant program for Hispanic parents will take place in the school rather than in the home.

ISOLATION AND THE NEW IMMIGRANT HISPANIC FAMILY

While working in the Hispanic community, I learned about how isolated the new immigrant families are, even when they live in neighborhoods where their native language is spoken. This isolation is something you cannot foresee when planning a program. As you implement the program, you discover the value that networking has for these families. What that implies, in terms of implementation, is that program activities have to be very interactive, so as to allow families to learn from one another. The program also should allow participants to share experiences and knowledge. A program that focuses only on what the program developers think parents have to learn may not be successful in these communities. As discussed earlier, programs that validate the parents' language and knowledge enhance parents' sense of self-efficacy and involvement in their children's learning. Programs that rely on written instructions or short-term training are not very effective with the new immigrant Hispanic population (Reese & Gallimore, 2000). Program activities should allow parents to show examples and talk about what they do at home and in the community to support their children's early literacy learning. By allowing parents to bring homemade books to the class or to show alternative, cultural ways to interact with their children, programs validate parents' knowledge and accept their cultural models of learning (see chapter 11 for a good example of a program that follows this philosophy).

THE CONCEPT OF *FAMILIA* AND ITS RELEVANCE TO PROGRAM DEVELOPMENT AND IMPLEMENTATION

The concept of *familia* (Abi-Nader, 1991) is central to everyday life in Hispanic communities and is especially important to new immigrant families. In other words, whatever you do in everyday life should benefit not only the individual but also the family. For example, if mothers do something for themselves, such as attending classes to learn English, they think of ways to connect the activities with the good that they will bring to their families, particularly the children. This is one reason why I think family literacy programs are better alternatives to adult education programs in Hispanic communities.

Because of the fathers' role as breadwinners, mothers tend to be the ones that participate more regularly in family literacy program activities. However, that does not imply that the fathers are not involved. Project FLAME has activities that fathers attend and in which they participate actively. The activities include field trips; any activity involving money, such as the book fairs; special celebrations; and, of course, graduations. (See chapter 5 for more about father involvement.)

Every family literacy program's implementation should include activities for the whole family. Participation will depend on the type of activity and the scheduling. In Project FLAME, the participants, mostly mothers, have decided that they prefer to meet in the mornings when they bring their children to school. They feel more secure walking in the community at this time of day, and they feel safe in the schools. Also, their husbands do not mind that the mothers go to their children's schools.

As part of program development, the other Project FLAME staff and I have discussed the possibility of meeting in the evenings or on Saturdays in order to include fathers or other adults at home, but meeting at these times has not been feasible because of constraints with the daily lives of the families we serve. There are other programs that meet during the evening, such as the Intergenerational Literacy Program (ILP) (Paratore, 2001), and they are well-attended. Because of any potential conflicts, decision-making—even on issues of attendance—should include the voice of potential program participants, and it should take into account the lives of each participant's whole family.

These considerations have implications for enrollment and activity planning. Depending on the time of the day when the program activities take place, activities must be planned for those members of the family other than the parents who will also attend the program. In the case of Project FLAME, we know that the mothers will not attend unless they bring their preschool-age children with them. Because only a few activities in the program are intergenerational (e.g., shared readings), we offer child care for the young children who attend the program with their mothers.

Two important issues exist regarding child care with Hispanic parents. First, the parents have to trust the person doing the child care. It helps if the person is someone well-known in the community or is a mother with grown children. For some parents, it takes a while before they let the children go away for child care. These young children are surprisingly well-behaved if they stay with their mothers in class. They show a lot of *respeto* for the fact that their mothers are in school and learning. The second child-care issue relates to the need for organized child care. The mothers want their children involved in creative learning activities while in child care. In Project FLAME, my colleagues at the University of Illinois at Chicago and I provide training activities to the child-care givers. We also provide supplies so that the children, at different age levels, are involved in nonstructured, age-appropriate learning activities while the mothers attend FLAME activities. During summers, we offer activities for parents that go beyond literacy, and we call these activities "leadership institutes." In these institutes, we cover topics relevant to Hispanic parents such as parental rights, discipline, and immigration issues. All the children in the participants' families come to the program, and we plan activities for school-age children.

When planning activities for parents, family literacy workers have to accommodate the whole family. This effort will enhance attendance and retention of parents as participants in a program. When the parents feel that the program is for the whole family, they are likely to attend the program more regularly.

Defining Family for Program Activity Purposes

When my colleagues at the University of Illinois at Chicago and I started the implementation of Project FLAME in 1989, the Amnesty Program (a now-defunct program that allowed undocumented individuals to receive U.S. visas to work) required that applicants attend ESL classes to improve their English skills. In Hispanic communities at the time, it was hard to enroll in ESL classes, and when we provided ESL classes through FLAME, we had more people than we expected attending our classes. At that point, we had to start asking questions about how the people attending the program were related to the Project FLAME families. It was then that we had to deal with issues of extended family in the Hispanic culture, which would include first, second, and third cousins, as well as their cousins and friends. For the program to be effective, we defined family members as being parents, children, and grandparents enrolled in the program. It was also important to clarify that FLAME was a program directed to parents of children ages 3 to 9, and that it was a family literacy program rather than ESL instruction. Through the years, we have kept this definition of family in trying to identify participants for Project FLAME. We also make it clear to prospective FLAME participants that the program is for family literacy rather than for ESL instruction and participants have to participate in both components.

RECRUITMENT AND RETENTION ISSUES

As explained before, Project FLAME is a community program based in the public schools. Through the years, the other Project FLAME staff and I have moved some programs to park–district facilities because of a lack of space at the schools. In the park–district settings, we have served several public schools at one site. No matter where the program activities take place, the school connection is very important for recruitment purposes. Over the years, we have learned that neither mailings nor the phone are good sources for recruitment. Many times, families do not receive mail because they do not have mailboxes or their names are not on tenant lists. In regard to phone calls, my colleagues and I have found that many families cannot afford a phone. Furthermore, this demographic group tends to change phone numbers often. Thus, the best source for recruitment has been bilingual notes, which teachers send home through the students, requesting information from interested families and inviting parents to participate in the program. The Project FLAME facilitators ask parents to respond by returning a form to their children's teachers. Once we have this information, we invite the families to an organizational meeting to explain the program. Other sources of recruitment have been community organizations and word of mouth from previous program participants.

For recruitment and retention purposes, my colleagues and I have found it useful to have community liaisons at each site. These liaisons are usually people who are known and respected by the school and the parents, and they are instrumental in facilitating the university personnel entrance into the community and in assessing the needs for the specific program in their school setting. Usually the liaisons are bilingual, and culturally speaking, it is better that they are females because Hispanic husbands prefer that their wives deal with female—rather than male—teachers or staff members. The liaisons serve as a link between the families, the schools, and the university. These liaisons are able to identify the people with the most need and/or who are new in the community. In addition, liaisons talk to family members if the family patterns of attendance change, and they inform program personnel about problems that may be addressed at this level. As a result, the liaisons have been an asset to Project FLAME in scheduling activities at the school and in contacting families when needed.

SUPPLEMENTAL SERVICES THAT ENHANCE PROGRAM PARTICIPATION AND SUCCESS

Besides child-care services for young children and possibly for older children, Project FLAME offers other services to program participants that enhance the successful implementation of the program. For instance, some families may need transportation service, particularly in cases where children are bussed to school and the parents may not live in the community where the school is located. Often, we teach parents to use public transportation, and we give them bus passes to attend classes. Parents who own cars can bring other parents to the program. In return, we pay each of them a weekly fee for that service.

Occasionally, we also help parents fill out job applications and, at times, this has been a topic for an ESL class. Moreover, as parents become friends with project staff, they begin asking questions related to issues such as parental rights, child abuse, discipline, and the use of services at hospitals and banks. To fulfill the parents' need for this information, we have created a Summer Leadership Institute. For the institutes, we invite speakers to talk to the parents about issues of interest to them that are not related to literacy. For this activity, we bring all the parents to one site, usually a park-district facility. To enhance parents' participation in the institutes, we offer free transportation from each school and provide lunch. The summer institute allows for networking opportunities and sharing of knowledge among participants from different Project FLAME sites and has created a sense of community among all FLAME participants.

Teachers' Role in Program Planning and Implementation

As previously explained, schools are ideal settings for family literacy programs or at least for making the connection with families. Enhancing the understanding and relations between home and school must be handled in a sensitive manner. More specifically, it is important that parents be able to show the school what they teach their children at home and demonstrate their involvement in their children's education without feeling that the school will misunderstand their intentions. This type of interaction is especially important when working in communities where people believe that the school is the setting in which children learn literacy.

As my colleagues at the University of Illinois at Chicago and I started talking to schools about Project FLAME in 1989, the school principals were excited about having family literacy programs in their buildings. Their only concern, however, was that we not use teachers' time. My colleagues and I accepted those conditions and agreed to their concerns, but as the year went on, teachers started asking Project FLAME personnel about the program. Teachers noticed that Project FLAME parents were more involved with school activities, responded promptly to teachers' requests, and often sent teachers a list of library books that their school-age children had read in a given week.

Because part of the original design of Project FLAME included a home-school connection and some teachers were aware of the program benefits to participant families, they agreed to volunteer for sessions related to the home-school connection by the time we did workshops with parents. The teachers agreed to allow parents to observe in their classrooms, and they also agreed to meet with the parents afterward to answer their questions, deal with their concerns, and share expectations. Through these experiences, teachers learned how much parents want to understand what happens in classrooms in the United States. The teachers also learned that these new immigrant Hispanic parents have very high expectations for their children. Parents talked not only about their children learning English and doing well in school but also their desire for their children to become, among other professions, lawyers, doctors, and teachers. In discussing information and ideas, the teachers were able to share with the parents their expectations for their children to succeed in school. The teachers who volunteered in these activities did not receive pay but were given a gift of books for their classroom. These sessions lowered the anxiety that parents previously may have had when talking to teachers, and the teachers learned about the families and their expectations for their children.

Since then, we have teachers volunteer every year for these activities. We usually pay for substitute teachers to attend the classrooms while the teachers meet with the parents. The principals have been supportive of the teachers' involvement as volunteers in Project FLAME.

THE LENGTH OF FAMILIES' PARTICIPATION IN THE PROGRAM

When my colleagues at the University of Illinois at Chicago and I originally started working with families, we did not foresee a need to define a length of service to the families. Eventually, we learned that two years are needed to develop parents' self-efficacy in supporting literacy learning at home. For example, emergent writing is a difficult concept for the parents to understand and accept. Most of the Hispanic parents in our program define writing in terms of copying, and they want their children to trace the words written by the parents very clearly and neatly. It is not until the second year in the program that they start bringing samples of their children's emerging writing to show and discuss with their Project FLAME classmates. The parents also need two years to understand the need to ask different types of questions while sharing books with their children.

Those parents who stayed over two years started telling us that they were bored and wanted different activities, such as crafts, as part of the program. It was then that we had to explain to them that the focus of the program was on early literacy and that they needed to graduate. Convincing the parents of the need to finish the program was not an easy task because the parents had developed networks, which they wanted to keep, but that was beyond the scope of our program.

ADDRESSING THE NEEDS OF GRADUATING PARENTS

It is very hard to have been involved with a group of families for two years and then graduate them. The families who participate in family literacy programs may have the expectation that the program leaders should tell them what to do next, and these leaders may feel some obligation to support the families' needs. In the case of Project FLAME, my colleagues and I directed the majority of parents to community organizations that offered ESL, technology, or sewing classes. We were fortunate that the communities in which we worked had all kinds of organizations, as well as very strong library and park-district systems able to support Project FLAME graduates. Some parents also started discussion groups on various issues and met in different families' homes. For example, one discussion group was based on discussion of movies that they watched together. Some Project FLAME personnel were invited to these activities and kept in contact with these families on their own.

Through the years, facilitators also have created new program components that involve some graduating parents. The first was the *training of trainers* component. We created this component to develop a capability within the community to continue the program once the University of Illinois at Chicago is no longer involved. To this effect, two or three graduating parents per school are invited each year to become trainers of other parents. Within this two-year program, the trainers in training meet with the university staff to plan literacy sessions with activities that are relevant and specific to their schools and communities. The first year, most trainers serve as teachers' aides to the program. By the second year of training, they present the workshops with the help of program staff. These parents are paid for the planning and their teaching. Some of the parents who have graduated from this training of trainers component have been hired as family literacy teachers at schools that have adopted the Project FLAME model, while others have been hired by parent-oriented organizations for community leadership positions such as parent trainers or community organization officers.

Many Project FLAME parents like to spend their free time volunteering in the schools, and they find themselves in the classrooms, helping teachers. Teachers sometimes like their help but do not have time to tell them what to do. Because of this, we have developed a *parents-as-school-volunteers* component as part of Project FLAME. We train parents on specific tasks to carry out in classrooms, at the request of a school principal or an individual teacher. This component has been very successful in a school in which teachers gave the Project FLAME staff the specific objectives and activities to train the parents before they go into the classroom.

Although we do not consider the training of child-care personnel a Project FLAME component, we usually hire and train graduating parents as caregivers. They also are paid to provide this service.

In working with parents, it is very important for them to realize that teachers value their knowledge and want to support their goals beyond those related to their participation in the program. Educators have to make parents aware that as they graduate, the program can open the doors to new families who will benefit from the program as much as their own families have.

Issues of Change and Ethics in Family Literacy

My work with families through Project FLAME has opened my eyes to issues of change in families as parents, mostly mothers, develop self-efficacy in their role as teachers for their children. Mothers who have participated in the program talk about how they now plan activities for their children rather than watch television. They talk about their home literacy center and the books that the children borrow from the library. They also talk about the fact that they have to share the room where children do homework with the fathers who are watching television. Sometimes, the mothers feel that their husbands should get more involved in their children's learning and sometimes find ways to involve the father in home literacy activities. Other times, the father prefers that they move the literacy activities to another room while he watches television. Situations such as this one have created some tensions in the families. Some of these issues have been brought up in group discussions. Together, Project FLAME facilitators and participants try to find possible solutions, but it is important to find ways to deal with these issues without disturbing families' lives. The mothers are changing—they have more friends, they have networks of support, and they tend to spend more time outside their homes. How are these changes affecting their family lives? How does participation in a family literacy program affect the family? These are very important questions that need to be addressed by people working in family literacy.

Once change occurs in any community or a group, the issue of the ethics of change comes into play. Change for what? Who changes? How does change affect people and communities? These questions should not be overlooked by people working in the family literacy field.

Conclusion

This chapter shows that successful family literacy programs need theoretical/sociocultural frameworks in support of the program objectives and design. Unless the program addresses the context and cultural concerns of the participants, it may become irrelevant to the population it is trying to serve. Community-based programs should be planned with an understanding of the context and culture of the prospective participants in the program. In deciding the content of these programs, developers need to recognize and respect the cultural models of learning used by the participants. Also, it is important to validate participants' knowledge and language. Family literacy programs should add to—rather than change—the repertoires of behaviors and practices used by parents to support their children's learning at home.

My experience with Project FLAME has shown that flexibility in scheduling, attendance, and planned activities are some of the main characteristics of successful programs. A need also exists for adaptation of the program to the participants' needs, which does not mean that the content, design, and focus of the program changes, but that input from the participants is used to make the program more relevant to their needs. Connecting new knowledge to what the participants bring into the program is also necessary for a successful program. Families that feel their voices are heard by program staff take ownership of the program, and, as such, become more involved in all program activities. Opportunities for sharing knowledge and networking among participants enhance both attendance and active participation in training sessions. According to Reese and Gallimore (2000), being explicit in content and practice encourages the Hispanic families' willingness to support their children's learning at home. Allowing participants to discuss with one another ways in which they share literacy within the family will demonstrate to program staff how the program content is affecting the families' literacy practices.

Because the concept of *familia* (Abi-Nader, 1991) is central to the lives of Hispanics, a successful and relevant program for this population should plan activities and services that serve the needs of different family members (e.g., children and grandparents), who in some capacity may participate in the program. In some situations, the program needs to define who qualifies as family because this definition relates to program activities.

The issues discussed in this chapter are not issues that were taken into account from the beginning of the development and implementation of Project FLAME. Program participants have been the best teachers in transforming a functional family literacy program (see Rodríguez-Brown & Mulhern, 1993) into a program that the participants own and use critically. The Project FLAME staff owes the participants *respeto* and gratitude.

REFERENCES

Abi-Nader, J. (1991, April). *Family values and the motivation of Hispanic youth.* Paper presented at the annual meeting of the American Educational Research Association, Chicago, IL.

Applebee, A., Langer, J.A., & Mullis, I. (1987). *Learning to be literate in America.* Princeton, NJ: Educational Testing Service.

Boehm A.E. (1986). *Boehm Test of Basic Concepts, revised.* San Antonio, TX: The Psychological Corporation/Harcourt.

Clay, M.M. (1979). *Stones: The concepts about print test.* Portsmouth, NH: Heinemann.

Cummins, J. (1986). Empowering minority students: A framework for intervention. *Harvard Educational Review, 55,* 18–36.

De Avila, E., & Duncan, S.E. (1993). *The Adult-Language Assessment Scales (A-LAS).* New York: McGraw-Hill.

Delgado-Gaitan, C. (1992). School matters in the Mexican-American home: Socializing children to education. *American Educational Research Journal, 29,* 495–513.

Gee, J.P. (1999). *An introduction to discourse analysis: Theory and method.* New York: Routledge.

Goldenberg, C. (1987). Low-income Hispanic parents' contributions to their first-grade children's word recognition skills. *Anthropology of Education Quarterly, 18,* 149–179.

Illinois State Board of Education. (2001). *School population census.* Unpublished manuscript.

Li, R.F. (2002). *Final evaluation report for FLAME: Academic excellence project (1997–2002).* Unpublished manuscript, University of Illinois at Chicago.

Moll, L.C. (1998). Turning to the world: Bilingual schooling, literacy, and the cultural mediation of thinking. In T. Shanahan, F.V. Rodríguez-Brown, C. Wortham, J.C. Burnison, & A. Cheung (Eds.), *47th yearbook of the National Reading Conference* (pp. 59–75). Chicago: National Reading Conference.

National Council of La Raza. (1990). *Hispanic education: A statistical portrait.* Washington, DC: Author.

The New London Group. (1996). A pedagogy of multiliteracies: Designing social futures. *Harvard Educational Review, 66*(1), 60–62.

Paratore, J.R. (2001). *Opening doors, opening opportunities: Family literacy in an urban community.* Boston: Allyn & Bacon.

Reese, L., Balzano, S., Gallimore, R., & Goldenberg, C. (1995). The concept of educación: Latino family values and American schooling. *International Journal of Educational Research, 23*(1), 57–81.

Reese, L., & Gallimore, R. (2000). Immigrant Latinos' cultural model of literacy development: An alternative perspective on home-school discontinuities. *American Journal of Education, 108*(2), 103–134.

Reyes, M. de la Luz. (1992). Challenging venerable assumptions: Literacy instruction for linguistically different students. *Harvard Educational Review, 62*(4), 427–446.

Rodríguez-Brown, F.V. (2001a). Home-school collaboration: Successful models in the Hispanic community. In P. Mosenthal & P. Schmitt (Eds.), *Reconceptualizing literacy in the new age of pluralism and multiculturalism: Advances in reading and language research* (pp. 273–288). Greenwich, CT: Information Age Publishing.

Rodríguez-Brown, F.V. (2001b). Home-school connections in a community where English is the second language: Project FLAME. In V.J. Risko & K. Bromley (Eds.), *Collaboration for diverse learners: Viewpoints and practices* (pp. 273–288). Newark, DE: International Reading Association.

Rodríguez-Brown, F.V., Li, R.F., & Albom, J.A. (1999). Hispanic parents' awareness and use of literacy-rich environments at home and in the community. *Education and Urban Society, 32*, 41–57.

Rodríguez-Brown, F.V., & Meehan, M.A. (1998). Family literacy and adult education: Project FLAME. In M.C. Smith (Ed.), *Literacy for the twenty-first century: Research, policy, practices, and the national adult literacy survey* (pp. 176–193). Westport, CT: Praeger

Rodríguez-Brown, F.V., & Mulhern, M.M. (1993). Fostering critical literacy through family literacy: A study of families in a Mexican-immigrant community. *Bilingual Research Journal, 17*(3–4), 1–16.

Rodríguez-Brown, F.V., & Shanahan, T. (1989). *Literacy for the limited English proficient child: A family approach.* Proposal funded by OBEMLA/USDE under the Title VII ESEA Family Literacy Program. Unpublished manuscript, University of Illinois at Chicago.

Rogers, R. (2001). Family literacy and cultural models. In J. Hoffman, D. Schallert, C. Fairbanks, J. Worthy, & B. Maloch (Eds.), *50th yearbook of the National Reading Conference* (pp. 96–114). Chicago: National Reading Conference.

Sable, J., & Stennett, J. (1998). The educational progress of Hispanic students. In National Center for Education Statistics (Ed.), *The condition of education 1998* (pp. 11–19). Washington, DC: U.S. Department of Education.

Serna, I., & Huddelson, S. (1993). Becoming a writer of Spanish and English. *Quarterly of the National Writing Project and the Center for the Study of Writing and Literacy, 15*(1), 1–5.

Shanahan, T., Mulhern, M., & Rodríguez-Brown, F.V. (1995). Project FLAME: Lessons learned from a family literacy program for linguistic minority families. *The Reading Teacher, 48*, 586–593.

Therrien, M., & Ramirez, R.R. (2000). *The Hispanic population in the United States* (Current Population Reports No. P20-535). Washington, DC: U.S. Census Bureau.

Valdes, G. (1996). *Con respeto: Bridging the differences between culturally diverse families and schools.* New York: Teachers College Press.

CHAPTER 7

Family Literacy and Local Understanding: Literate Citizenship for Children With Disabilities

Christopher Kliewer

In an ethnographic interview, Sheila Jordan told me about her son's early instruction professional with a sigh and shrug: "She'd show up with these boxes of electronic gizmo toys. Push a button and all these bells would go off." Jordan continued, "I don't like electronics—Nintendo things. I don't like TV. I like imagination." The youngest of Jordan's three children, Samuel, was born with cerebral palsy. Now a 4-year-old, Samuel has extremely limited physical motion and uses a wheelchair for mobility outside the home. He primarily communicates through rigid right-arm movement, head shakes, and expressions that shine through his wonderfully handsome face and bright, brown eyes. Recently, preschool personnel have begun experimenting with a voice-output computer system to aid his expression.

Professional early intervention disability services began soon after birth for Samuel and his mother. "At first I was so confused and here was people with all this stuff—experts to talk to," Jordan said. (All quotes are presented as they were spoken. I have not altered grammar for any quote.) Over time, however, her feelings toward the home-based instructors became increasingly ambivalent. "I read to Samuel all the time," Jordan explained to me while Samuel was in school. "He loves books. Always loved books, the Bible, kids' Bible stories, and I thought, 'Well, this has got to be good. This means something.' But they [the home-based instructors] didn't seem very interested. It was all,

'Do this hand clap with him. Have him sit like this. Have him push this button, and 'Oh look! The toy does everything by itself!'"

Jordan recognized that stories from books fascinated her child, even in his infancy. She presumed he had symbolic capacities—the ability to understand and use symbols. Based on this presumption, she created a context—mother and child with book in hand—that allowed for his expression of those capacities. (See chapters 3 and 9 for discussion of parent-child literacy activities with young children.) Jordan felt, however, that Samuel's home-based instructors were surprisingly disinterested in his engagement with pictures and printed language, choosing to focus instead on skills thought to precede demonstrations of symbolic or abstract understanding. One of Samuel's home-based instructors, interviewed following his transition into preschool, recalled,

> Those first couple years, he really wasn't doing much. We just had to get him moving. He had no motivation, and there was this feeling that we weren't getting anywhere. I remember we resorted to putting M & Ms in front of him, trying to get him to reach out, move a bit.

Supporting any child's mobility is clearly a necessary goal, and for Samuel, its importance is heightened because of the physical dilemmas he faces. In addition to those concerns, however, Jordan alone interpreted her child as having the capacity to engage and understand symbols—vital now that school personnel had begun promoting his use of a communication system requiring symbol and print recognition.

In a separate in-depth interview conducted in a town 500 miles from Jordan's, Mr. and Mrs. Clemente describe a similar encounter with special education professionals who appear disinterested in their child's reading and writing development. The youngest of the Clemente children, Paulo, Jr., is a bright-eyed 5-year-old with a love for firefighters and—because of his older brother's exploits on the football field—a passion for all things related to football. He was born with Down syndrome and has been labeled by early childhood professionals as cognitively disabled. "They wanted him to be in the 'moderate room,'" Paulo Clemente, Sr., explained in a recent research interview. He was referring to school district personnel who had tried to steer the Clemente family toward placing the younger Paulo in a primary-grade special education program segregated for children with disabilities. Paulo, Jr., had previously spent two years in an inclusive preschool, which taught children with and without disabilities together.

"They had nothing for him there," Mrs. Clemente interjected, referring to the "moderate room"—the room's moniker actually used by education personnel. "At his preschool, they had books, play, dress-up. Not there [in the moderate room]." Had the Clementes given in to professional pressure and agreed to place him in the moderate room, young Paulo would have found himself in a classroom nearly devoid of materials and activities commonly associated with kindergarten and primary education, including books and opportunities to play and learn to read.

Denying Literacy

The parents of Samuel and Paulo view their children as literate and naturally involve them in their various forms of family literacy. These activities include reading books and providing opportunities for play and dress-up—all critical to any child's development of a symbolic presence. Special education professionals, however, have demonstrated what the parents consider to be severe disinterest in their children's literacy. Such dismissals of family literacy concerns stem from a general professional disbelief in the very relevance of literacy to the lives of youth with significant disabilities. As Erickson and Koppenhaver (1995) note,

> It's not easy trying to learn to read and write if you're a child with severe disabilities in U.S. public schools today.... Your preschool teachers are unlikely to be aware of emergent literacy research or to include written language activities in your early intervention program. Many of the teachers you encounter across your public school career do not view you as capable of learning to read and write and consequently provide you with few opportunities to learn written language. (p. 676)

Current, predominant assumptions on the development of literacy in children dismiss parent knowledge on the literacy skills of their children with significant disabilities as provincial and naive. This attitude belies a professional dismissal of what may be termed a family sense of literacy in which children are naturally included in daily literacy events, whether that be grocery shopping from a list, ordering food from a drive-through menu, or visiting the public library in the evening (Biklen, 1992). Professionals deny literacy for children with significant disabilities based on a rigid adherence to a fixed, technological meaning of the notions underlying what is believed to be the organic emergence of symbolic and written language capacities. Hence, if one's organic presence is considered to be disordered (e.g., presents a disability), then developmental trajectories (e.g., literacy) thought to be based on a foundationally sound, organic presence also are implicated as disordered.

A fixed, technological definition of literacy most often describes it as the sequenced and combined subskills associated with decoding and encoding printed language. Put another way, it is the mechanics of "reading and writing alphabetic texts" (Whitehurst & Lonigan, 2001, p. 11). Within this framework, the literate citizen is ultimately one who has—primarily through the course of formal instruction—mastered and combined sets of presumably essential, orthographic subskills in a linear fashion and at a normative pace associated with efficient movement through the educational grades (see Adams, 2001; Adams, Foorman, Lundberg, & Beeler, 1997).

Elsewhere, I associate this linear, subskill model with a metaphoric ladder to literacy (Kliewer & Biklen, 2001). Each rung of the ladder constitutes increasingly complex, normative subskills, primarily letter and phonemic in nature, as identified in school-based reading programs. Children are thought to begin the rigidly sequenced climb at young ages. Individual cognitive mastery at each step, or rung, is considered a requirement before further movement up the ladder. Ascension ultimately leading to citizenship in the literate community is thought to be an individualistic effort. Adams (2001), for example, likens learning to read to an individual child's bodily kinesthetic maturation. "In any complex endeavor," she writes, "children must learn to walk before they run. Learning [to read] must start somewhere: if not with letters and phonemes [considered the base subskill focus], then where?" (p. 68). The image of a child naturally, or biologically, unfolding—from walker to runner, from preliterate to literate—is clear.

Shannon (1995) critically explains that teachers and schools have all children's specific literacy development "completely mapped out from kindergarten through sixth grade" (p. 42), prior to any child's entry into school, and, he notes, "They would use the same map for all students" (p. 42). He describes this standard map as beginning with kindergarten-based efforts on the part of teachers to focus children on specific letter recognition and recreation skills followed by

> the teaching of how to recognize and draw other letters, to recognize the sounds associated with letters, to blend those letter sounds to syllables and words, to place those words in grammatical phrases and sentences, to combine those sentences into paragraphs, and finally to arrange and interpret paragraphs into stories, essays, and the like. This additive process would be followed for both reading and writing and would ensure that all students would receive the same skills if they can work their way through the sequence *from letters to meaning* [italics added] in a timely fashion. This approach is designed so that the school "products" will have standard equipment, if they make it all the way to the end of the assembly line. (p. 42)

The metaphor of a singular ladder to literacy—or, in Shannon's words (1995), a rigid map or assembly line—works pretty well for many people (or, at the least, does not visibly damage them) in that they successfully become readers and writers in a manner demanded by both school-based reading programs and cultural definitions of literate citizenship. This prominent model, however, in its demand that a subskill be mastered and added to another subskill to be mastered and so on until the simple sum of parts mechanically accumulates into a demarcation of literate citizenship clearly leaves many children out of reach of a citizenship goal.

For children judged to have developmental-intellectual deficits, including Samuel and Paulo, eventual citizenship in the literate community by following the ladder to literacy model is an intellectual improbability. The metaphor of incremental ascension to the privileged height of competent readers or writers supports the removal of these students to other locations. It is, so the logic goes, in their own interest. They are steered onto stepladders with fewer rungs that lead to functional or life-skills reading and writing, if they are allowed to engage the printed word at all (Kliewer & Landis, 1999). Literacy as a process of critical thinking, interaction, or abstract communication is never considered attainable for them. A further essentialist logic then follows: Denial of the opportunity—indeed segregation from the opportunity—to access written language is considered wholly logical, or essential, when planning for the instruction of individuals with severe intellectual disabilities (Kliewer & Biklen, 2001).

This logic of denial and segregation sharply contrasts with the approach many parents take toward the literacy development of their children with disabilities. Around the world, children with significant disabilities have come to demonstrate symbolic literacy capacities. Their expression of competence, generally within the family relationship, demands a reconstitution of segregated educational traditions that are aligned with the metaphor of an invariant ladder to literacy.

Local Understanding and Symbolic Expression: Supporting Literacy

Sheila Jordan has recognized Samuel as a literate being, although professionals have not. In her approach to Samuel, Jordan demonstrates what researchers have termed *local understanding* (Kliewer & Landis, 1999): a radically deep, intimate knowledge of another human being. Local understanding of people with so-called severe intellectual disabilities comes from caring, interactive, and interdependent relationships in which both participants confer valued capacities and competence on the other.

The intimacy of the relationship is important because it allows those in positions of relative authority to see idiosyncratic behavior demonstrations of understanding that more distant observers otherwise dismiss or disregard. For instance, in the case of Jordan with her son Samuel, what others might interpret as a meaningless head nod, as Samuel "not getting anywhere," his mother understands as a signal of her child's interest and engagement with a part of a story or a picture in a book. Such a situated, concrete signal then flows into a more abstract sense of Samuel as a smart little boy, which in turn leads to further situations that support his involvement with books and so on.

Intimacy, however, strikes at the very heart of scientific detachment and construed objectivity from which special education practices purportedly emerged (Kliewer & Biklen, 2000). Yet local understanding of the sort shown by Jordan in interaction with Samuel, constructed on a deeply intimate relationship, appears in our observational studies to promote the symbolic and literate capacities of individuals clinically labeled severely impaired (Kliewer, 1998; Kliewer & Biklen, 2001; Kliewer & Landis, 1999). The following dimensions have emerged from studying families and excellent teachers as important situated components when ascribing abstract competence on those who are culturally dismissed as intrinsically incompetent.

SEEING THE SYMBOLIC: THE SOCIAL GENERATION OF COMPETENCE

Christy Brown's (1970) autobiographical novel, *Down All the Days*, depicts the character of the father stumbling drunkenly through Dublin, Ireland's dark alleyways. A young woman walking in the night helps the father past a police officer when the father stops to vomit. The two begin talking, and in the stream-of-consciousness dialogue, she tells him,

> "Twelve of us my Ma had by the time the eldest was twenty. She died last year giving birth to the last. A little boy. He lived, but he's all twisted and deformed. Can't walk or talk, can't feed or dress himself. Dribbles all the time. They say he's mental. They want to put him in a home. But I won't let them. I know he's not soft in the head. I just know. In here." She laid her index finger gently on her left breast. "He speaks to me with his eyes. I won't let them take him away from me. By God I won't!" Her voice was suddenly defiant, strong, the voice of a woman facing the world, defying the world in defense of something she loved. The face she now turned toward him was charged by that strength and that love. It was luminous, transparent, fired from within. (p. 166)

As an internationally acclaimed author, Brown knows well the extreme necessity of intimacy when defining (thus generating) as competent those whom the world otherwise shuns. Brown was born with cerebral palsy. The movie *My Left Foot*, based on his autobiography by the same name (Brown, 1989), depicts his life story. For years, he was considered severely intellectually impaired by all around him except his mother.

In a similar vein, Carol Schroeder also sees possibility where most others find only impairment. A respite care provider and a self-described advocate who works for a disability service agency in a medium-sized city in the midwestern United States, Carol spends approximately 20 hours a week supporting the community participation of 4 children and young adults. One of her participants, Steven, is 16 years old, labeled autistic, and attending a school segregated for students with disabilities. Schroeder and Steven are extremely close. Steven's mother is frequently hospitalized, and during those periods, Steven leaves his home to stay with Carol. "Except for his grandma, I'm the only one he's ever agreed to stay with," Carol noted.

"Steven knows everything there is to know about butterflies," Carol explained in an interview in which Steven also took part. He interjected, "Monarch butterflies. Would you like to see?" Steven had with him his ever-present notebook filled with tattered pages of his own detailed drawings of various types of butterflies and cocoons. "Pupa or chrysalis," he corrected. "Steven's read everything there is in the library on butterflies," Carol noted. Indeed, he had with him, as always, several different public library books, all related to butterflies and insects. He laid three of the books open on the floor, then centered himself among them, glancing at each of the exposed pages. He then flipped to the next page of each book and repeated the process. Carol shrugged, "That's how he reads. I tried to get him to do it one book at a time, but it wasn't worth the battle—didn't I, Steven?" Immersed in his reading, Steven appeared not to hear the question.

Not everyone in Steven's life has believed that he is able to read library books or that he is able to read at all. In a separate interview, Carol explained that Steven's mother, Nikki, had shown her Steven's individualized education plan (IEP) from his school. "I wanted to know what stuff they were working on," Carol said, but she was shocked while flipping through the document. "There was nothing in it about stuff you'd think—his reading, writing, art. There was, like, all these things on getting him into the swimming pool. Steven hates swimming, but they sure are going to get him in the pool. That's useful," Carol noted.

Steven's mother agreed to have Carol join her at Steven's subsequent IEP meeting in which school personnel, including the head administrator, explained to Nikki the purpose of each present goal. Carol said, "I finally got up the courage to say, like, 'Uh, excuse me but what about his reading and writing?' Something like that, and there was this real silence, and his teacher says, 'Steven's not a reader yet.' I'm like— [Carol's expression was one of extreme bewilderment]—but Nikki, she just sat there and didn't say anything." When the two left the meeting, Carol remembered asking Nikki, "What was that all about?" In response, Nikki told Carol, "Oh, he doesn't do reading at school."

In an interview at Steven's home that included both Carol and Nikki, Nikki was asked about the perception of school personnel toward her son's reading and writing abilities. "School's not really a place for reading," Nikki confirmed. "We've always done that at home, and you [Carol] with the library." "But they don't even think he's able to read," Carol interjected, "They told us he might 'decode, but doesn't process'—or something. How do they explain his stuff with butterflies?" "Butterflies aren't really a part of school," Nikki said, her calmness standing in stark contrast to Carol's exasperation.

On entering and leaving Nikki's home, we had to carefully step around a large, apparently fragile structure made of refuse held together with duct tape. "That's Steven's creation," Nikki apologized. Most days, on arriving home from school, Steven works for several hours gathering trash from his neighborhood and turning it into family room sculptures that he will eventually demolish and begin again. "He's got so much creative energy," Carol remarked.

Carol has been intimately involved in Steven's life for almost two years. On first meeting him, she did not think to question or challenge Nikki's private efforts to surround Steven with books. Learning from Nikki, Carol simply assumed Steven's symbolic competence and opened new and expanded opportunities for him to read, write, and draw about his favorite topic. The library presents Steven with a whole new range of books his mother cannot afford. This local understanding, built up from Steven in intimate, social relationships, generates a deep sense of his symbolic and creative presence. In contrast, Steven is radically redefined each day when he steps off the short, yellow bus at school. Here, in the midst of methods and procedures, if his interest in butterflies is acknowledged at all, it is to dismiss it as a perseveration, an obsession. Reading as a way into understanding is denied to him, and Steven's artistic being does not exist.

SOCIAL INTERACTION DRIVES SYMBOLIC DEVELOPMENT

The metaphor of the ladder to literacy belies a cultural determination that the use of written language and symbols as social tools is predicated on subskill mastery, which is itself, preceded by cognitive development. Thus, people defined as severely retarded are commonly stalled at a readiness stage in which proof of intellect is demanded—an exceedingly difficult task when symbol use is profoundly restricted. In contrast to convention, our studies suggest that parents who effectively support the development of symbolic capacities in individuals with disabilities act on an often subconscious recognition that social engagement drives the development of internalized symbolic capacities (Kliewer & Biklen, 2001).

"I was concerned—we all were," said teacher LeeAnn Foster, recalling her initial impression of Rebecca, a student in her fifth-grade classroom, "I hate to say that—I mean, honestly, she—she posed some challenges," Foster explained, picking her words with care. She is a public school teacher credentialed in both regular and special education, and she has over 20 years of teaching experience. The last 10 have been as lead teacher in inclusive elementary classrooms ranging from first through fifth grades. Despite the experience and a reputation as a master teacher, Foster expressed an initial nervousness at the prospect of Rebecca joining her class.

Rebecca is 11 years old. Her family moved into the district at the beginning of the school year from a different community precisely because of the inclusion opportunities offered by Foster's school. Until her current placement, Rebecca had attended segregated public school classrooms for students considered to be severely disabled. At age 3, she was diagnosed as autistic by personnel at a university hospital. At 10 years of age, when Foster first met her, Rebecca was considered severely mentally retarded, preliterate (and nonsymbolic), primarily nonspeaking, and, based on certain developmental assessments, was said to function at so-called infant to toddler stages. She also exhibited aggressive behaviors, most often directed at herself in the form of scratching or biting. Rebecca's parents, however, saw their daughter in a very different light than professionals did. They considered her a worthy member of the community—someone who did not require segregation. Further, her parents considered Rebecca a child able to learn, whose symbolic presence deserved a chance to grow within an accepting, tolerant community. "We never doubted that she had a lot to offer,"

Rebecca's father told me. Such an attitude however, required a will to resist expert interpretations neatly maintained in Rebecca's school's files.

Following several meetings with the family, the teaching team—comprising Foster, therapists, and classroom associates—agreed that its initial, primary responsibility was, as Foster expressed it, "to make [Rebecca] a part of this [classroom] community." Years earlier, Foster had instituted a schoolwide, classroom level program she termed "Circle of Friends," based in spirit on advocacy procedures described by Perske (1989) and Forest and Pearpoint (1992). "We got the circle started right away," Foster explained, "Letting the kids know we have this new kid—child—just moved in, and how to think about her, make her comfortable." Foster divided her students into small groups, or circles, assigned to brainstorm ways to include Rebecca at different times of the day. "One of the groups—Jess, Shelly—it was all girls. They were brainstorming ways that friends talked to one another, and thought of notes" (the personal type passed from student to student). Foster said,

> Jessie was like, "Well, Rebecca doesn't really talk so maybe we should do notes with her." I'm thinking to myself, "Hmm, [the students are] not quite getting it," but it would be nice for her to be part of the clique.... So they start writing her these notes, and they fold them up like they do, and then of course, they unfold them for her and read them to her. It was really funny.

This interaction was funny and profound. Foster said that, among other classroom efforts, "That was really how it all got started." She and her teaching team noticed the intensity with which Rebecca focused on the note reader with "total eye contact. No stimming [self-stimulation]." Often, the notes included boxes to check such as, "Do you like James? Yes? No?" Foster noted, "So whoever wrote the note would be like, 'Do you?' Just waiting for an answer, and Rebecca would answer with a look. Sort of a head nod [she widened her eyes and slightly nodded in demonstration], and the kid would scream out, 'You do!'" Foster admits that initially the difference between Rebecca's expression of yes and no was difficult to interpret, "I think most of the time the kids just guessed at whatever they wanted her to say, but they would laugh and Rebecca was laughing and she was a part of it all. So we had the idea of yes and no," Foster continued, "It was the kids who did it." Foster and Rebecca's language therapist made up a small *Yes/No* board. "She needed facilitation, a lot more than now," Foster said, meaning that an adult would physically support, but refrain from guiding, Rebecca's hand as she reached out to indicate a positive or negative response. As the school year progressed, the note passing remained an important part of Rebecca's interaction with her peers. For one of many of her activities, the language therapist created a set of symbols from which Rebecca could choose in order to "write" notes back to friends. "It's become a jealousy thing," Foster said, "Kids get upset when another kid gets a note from Rebecca."

Within the course of a single school year, Rebecca has gone from being perceived as nonsymbolic to constructing symbolic interactions with her classroom friends. Rather than requiring proof of symbolic competence prior to the development of relationships, Foster has turned the traditional equation on its head: Entrance into interaction constitutes the terrain on which symbol literacy is recognized. In this sense, social engagement in specific, localized situations precedes demonstrations of intellectual competence and a more abstract definition of Rebecca as a thoughtful, engaged, and engaging human being.

Certainly, no one can know if Rebecca had full symbolic understanding locked within her prior to her inclusion in Foster's class. In essence, then, it could be said that Foster simply turned the correct key—which is itself a wonderful idea. A similar situation, however, further suggests the emergence of internalized symbolic literacy only after one enters into the social realm that demands abstract expression. When pondering how psychologists could have construed her intelligence quotient to be 24, the disability rights advocate, author, and college student, Sue Rubin, responds simply, "I was retarded. I had no thoughts, couldn't speak, read, write, or point to pictures" (1995b, p. 1). Only after joining the transactional dance of language does Rubin recall the emergence of her own thoughts (see Rubin, 1995a, 1998).

THE WRITTEN WORD AS CONVERSATION

The development of skills with printed language for people with severe disabilities appears to proceed from the individuals' social engagement and often takes the form of localized conversation. Although seemingly a mundane observation, it should be emphasized that conversation is a *reciprocal* form of communication in which each person involved is recognized as having something to say. For people viewed as severely mentally retarded, the recognition of having something to say may be anything but mundane. Such a path to symbolic competence is found in an all-but-forgotten, out-of-print diary published in the early 1960s (Seagoe, 1964). The introduction to Paul Scott's diary notes that he was born with Down syndrome in 1917. His wealthy parents were immediately told that their infant was uneducable and should be institutionalized. For some years, it appeared the clinical prophecy would prove to be correct. When he was 4 years old and unable to speak, Paul's parents placed him in a "reputable private residential school for mentally retarded children" (p. 6). Paul quickly lost weight, appeared dirty and unkempt, and, on his father's visits, would cling to him "sobbing and weeping" (p. 7).

Paul's father, Clinton Scott, removed him from the institution. When Paul turned 6, his father took him to the University of California in Los Angeles, where Helen Bass Keller taught in the campus training school. Keller had gained some level of recognition from her successful work teaching reading to children who failed in school. She described her approach as the kinesthetic method, based on her belief that "movement and touch constitute an essential part of learning a word" (Seagoe, p. 10). On first meeting Paul, however, Keller's prognosis was less than optimistic. After all, the child had been diagnosed as uneducable by psychologists at Johns Hopkins, the University of Chicago, and the University of California at Berkeley, and

> He spoke no intelligible words or sentences and asked no questions. He made incoherent sounds as he played, pulling out the drawers of [Keller's] desk, taking the chalk and erasers from the blackboard and laughing with joy as he threw them at the ceiling. (p. 12)

Keller explained to the elder Scott that "children like Paul" (p. 12) could not learn. "What do you mean, 'Children like Paul'?" Scott responded, "Paul can learn. He does not belong with mentally retarded children; he is not mentally retarded" (p. 12). Against her better judgment, Keller agreed to attempt teaching Paul. She proceeded on two bases: (1) development of motor control and (2) development of writing skills that would then lead to reading.

In terms of the former goal, Keller immediately involved Paul in games such as ball tossing that required concentration and agility. For the latter, Keller created an interactional, conversational teaching structure. From Scott, Keller learned some of Paul's favorite activities. With Paul watching, she drew pictures showing Paul in these situations and printed labels and brief stories beneath the pictures. Soon after instruction began, Keller had Paul printing single-word descriptions of his actions: *run, jump, hide, play*, and so on. In silence, she wrote commands to him that he was then expected to read and correctly carry out (e.g., "Give me two pieces of chalk" [Seagoe, p. 12].). She wrote questions to him such as, "Can a house roll?" and asked him to read and respond. (His response to that specific question was "No," but he later changed his answer after seeing a house being moved [p. 16].)

Keller imposed printed language in Paul's life as a mode of communication. She worked from certain basic principles: "Give him concrete experiences as background for everything you try to teach; base reading and writing on play and travel and events that interest him; teach him to write words as a key to reading them" (p. 31). After just seven months of instruction, Paul, the 6-year-old deemed uneducable, was creating spontaneous written sentences on his own initiative. At the completion of one session, Paul wrote to his teacher, "I love you. Will see you soon. Paul Scott" (p. 16).

Some months into his instruction, Keller showed Paul a typewriter. At first, "he pounded all the keys at once until prevented from doing so, then gradually learned to type his name. That was the beginning of his self-taught use of the typewriter, a consuming interest and an indispensable tool" (p. 16). The typewriter proved indispensable because, despite Keller's efforts, Paul's hand dexterity remained awkward and clumsy. Typing allowed him to focus on the actual written message, not on the act of writing itself. Typing then facilitated his efforts to begin a journal that he maintained from age 12 to age 43, 4 years before his death. The journal provided three decades worth of Paul's insight on U.S. and international political events, his travels, theological notions, and friendships. Although in diary form, Paul's writing often directly addressed those closest to him. It was, in fact, a set of letters that kept him symbolically connected with his family and those who shared his everyday life. He also learned Spanish by translating certain diary entries from English to Spanish.

At the age of 43, with his loving father dead, Paul was committed by his sister to an institution. One of his final letters, written to his sister, was a plea to once again escape a "private school for the retarded" (Seagoe, p. 205). It read, in part,

> I do not like to be at school. I had enough of this school. What is the matter with Alida [his sister] to take Mr. Paul Scott here. I do not like many gentlemen here including the teachers.... My father, Mr. Clinton Scott [at this point deceased], wants Mr. Paul not to live my rotten life in school in the country. I want to live with you.... This morning I am homesick. Sunday night I cried so hard and prayed so earnest to Jesus Christ. (p. 206)

Sadly, Paul Scott would die two years later but not without leaving behind a legacy initiated by his family that revealed literate possibilities for people with disabilities.

UNIQUE SUPPORTS

The descriptions I have presented thus far demonstrate insight into competence generated from intimate relationships. Created from this local understanding, then, are situations and contexts that support and extend symbolic expression. As the vignettes make clear, the supports enacted for people with perceived severe intellectual disabilities often stray from conventions that fall along the ladder to literacy. The author-playwright, Christy Brown, for instance, first demonstrated literacy skills by writing with his foot—not an endeavor often encountered in school.

Carol Schroeder, the respite care provider who worked with Steven, Nikki's son, noted her own initial discomfort with the child's reading style: opening several books at once, then moving from book to book before flipping to the next pages in *all* of them. When asked why she had attempted to force Steven to read just one book at a time, Carol responded simply, "Because it would be normal." She explained that she had given up on the effort because of Steven's resistance, "He just got all agitated. I would take his books and be like, 'OK, just this one,' and you just know when he's upset, and he'd just walk away."

Carol believed there was value to Steven performing in what she described as *normal* ways, but she saw a greater good in supporting his reading in whatever manner it took. She said, "You know, I've heard [President] Clinton reads a bunch of books at once. Maybe not exactly at once, but—hey—maybe Steven's just the next step. Maybe he'll be president? I hope not—for his sake!"

The deeply ensconced image of a ladder to literacy reflects, and also furthers, a rigid cultural sense of how one's symbolic presence emerges. (See chapter 6 for discussion of the role of culture in family literacy interactions.) The expectation is set that readers all do basically what everyone else does in their climb to printed language competence. Our studies, however, in combination with certain of the (often forgotten or disregarded) literature suggest that those families and teachers who have successfully supported the valued abilities of people with severe disabilities have done so by stepping beyond the demand for strict adherence to notions of normal performance (Kliewer, 1998; Kliewer & Biklen, 2001; Kliewer & Landis, 1999).

THE PRINCIPLE OF UNCERTAINTY

In conjunction with providing unique supports for persons with intellectual disabilities, emerges an interesting, albeit tacit, challenge posed to those parents and teachers who make use of local understanding: To what ends will these and others of my efforts lead? Although sets of procedures based on more distant or institutionalized understanding commonly come complete with objectives detailed for the consumer audience (hence, success is [ostensibly] easily judged), Jordan with her son Samuel; the Clementes with their youngest son, Paulo; Paul Scott's father; and others previously described, proceeded on a terrain of tacit uncertainty.

No one can predict where early efforts with print will lead. The principle of uncertainty, however, as tacitly present as it was, appears not to hinder such engagement. Local understanding is, after all, captured in the image of a parent's relationship with his or her child. Good parents do not specify an explicit course of development and achievement for their children. Love, nutrition, warmth, access to the library, curfews, and so on are contexts constructed in recognition of the always unknowable possibilities presented by all children.

RECOGNIZING MULTIPLE MODES OF VALUED EXPRESSION

Carol was earlier quoted as recognizing Steven's "creative energy"—a sense of Steven she had learned from Nikki, Steven's mother. His fine-lined, detailed drawings of butterflies and his "creations," the mass sculptures made from trash and duct tape, demonstrate what should be recognized as valued ways of connecting with the surrounding community. Art is, after all, both an emotional and intellectual statement.

Carol and Nikki do realize the power and seeming necessity of art in Steven's life, but few others appear interested. His pictures are constantly with him, and he enjoys showing and discussing them. He does not, however, discuss his sculptures, although they dominate the living area of his home and take hours of his time. "Nope, doesn't explain them," Nikki said, "They're his private thoughts." She laughed as she surveyed the cramped quarters of their home.

I recognize that not everyone will be equally adept at using printed language to connect with others and to demonstrate understanding. Clearly, some people will struggle with this culturally valued tool for expression and thought. In contrast, many people, including Steven, not only engage written language to varying degrees of effectiveness but also have at their disposal other modes of expression. In either case, the research my colleagues and I have conducted suggests that people who effectively support the symbolic presence of individuals construed to be severely intellectually disabled seek out and engage multiple modalities for human connection—what Gardner (1991) has referred to as domains of literacy.

Conclusion

The themes associated here with local understanding grow directly out of family literacy and inform professional practice. The themes demonstrate that people viewed as severely intellectually disabled do demonstrate a symbolic and literate presence when effectively supported by those with whom they share an intimate relationship. I will briefly discuss two major implications arising out of this realization.

RECONSTITUTING THE LADDER TO LITERACY

The metaphor of a rigid ladder to literacy demanding conformity in one's ascension leads to the common exclusion of people defined as having severe intellectual disabilities from opportunities to engage the written word. Based on the range of family literacies and the experiences of research participants with whom my colleagues and I have worked, however, we suggest a new imagery for conceptualizing the social generation of an individual's symbolic presence: that of a web of relationships that forms a family and a community (Kliewer, 1998; Kliewer & Biklen, 2001; Kliewer & Landis, 1999). Written language and other symbolic tools constitute fibers in the strands that make up the web.

The shift in metaphor, from rigid climb to encompassing web, better captures the multiple social paths on which an individual's symbolic presence is generated. By so stating the way to literacy, I depart from traditions that assume individual human development is primarily a biologically driven, intrinsic process of natural unfolding. Rather, unique individuals are constructed in interaction with others on the terrain of family and community. Some of the research participants with whom my colleagues and I have worked are defined into an existence of intrinsic defect by certain surrounding people in positions of authority (Kliewer & Biklen, 2001). In contrasting relationships, these same participants are understood through interaction to be competent, symbolic, literate people.

TOWARD A LOCAL UNDERSTANDING

The person as defective and the person as competent are both social constructions. People who have the power to define the capacities of other human beings are making moral decisions. On what basis, then, should such decision making proceed?

In our studies, it appears that those most intimately connected to the individual with disabilities assume that person's place in the web of relationships and work to connect him or her in ever-more valued ways (Kliewer, 1998; Kliewer & Biklen, 2001; Kliewer & Landis, 1999). The social performances of people with severe disabilities do not necessarily conform to culturally valued patterns associated with normality; still, intimate partners who deeply value the person are able to interpret in idiosyncratic behavior some signs of engagement with the social world. This local understanding results in the creation of contexts that further support signs of competence and so on. Parents, through family literacy efforts, are the people who can foster the development of local understanding for professionals interested in the literacy development of individuals with significant disabilities.

REFERENCES

Adams, M.J. (2001). Alphabetic anxiety and explicit, systematic phonics instruction: A cognitive science perspective. In S.B. Neuman & D.K. Dickinson (Eds.), *Handbook of early literacy research* (pp. 66–80). New York: Guilford.

Adams, M.J., Foorman, B.R., Lundberg, I., & Beeler, T. (1997). *Phonemic awareness in young children: A classroom curriculum.* Baltimore: Brookes.

Biklen, D. (1992). *Schooling without labels: Parents, educators, and inclusive schooling.* Philadelphia: Temple University Press.

Erickson, K.A., & Koppenhaver, D.A. (1995). Developing a literacy program for children with severe disabilities. *The Reading Teacher, 48,* 676–684.

Forest, M., & Pearpoint, J. (1992). Everyone belongs: Building the vision with MAPS–the McGill Action Planning System. In D. Wetherow (Ed.), *The whole community catalogue: Welcoming people with disabilities into the heart of community life* (pp. 95–99). Manchester, CT: Communitas.

Gardner, H. (1991). *The unschooled mind: How children think and how schools should teach.* New York: Basic Books.

Kliewer, C. (1998). Citizenship in the literate community: An ethnography of children with Down syndrome and the written word. *Exceptional Children, 64,* 167–180.

Kliewer, C., & Biklen, D. (2000). Democratizing disability inquiry. *Journal of Disability Policy Studies, 26,* 1–12.

Kliewer, C., & Biklen, D. (2001). "School's not really a place for reading": A research synthesis of the literate lives of students with severe disabilities. *Journal of the Association for Persons With Severe Handicaps, 26,* 1–12.

Kliewer, C., & Landis, D. (1999). Individualizing literacy instruction for young children with moderate to severe disabilities. *Exceptional Children, 66,* 85–100.

Perske, R. (1989). *Circle of friends.* Nashville, TN: Abingdon Press.

Rubin, S. (1995a, June 12). Battling for the disabled with Cesar Chavez in mind. *Los Angeles Times,* p. B5.

Rubin, S. (1995b, April). On doing one's homework. *Facilitated Communication Digest: Newsletter of the Facilitated Communication Institute, Syracuse University, 4*(1), 1.

Rubin, S. (1998, December). Invited keynote address at the annual conference of the Association for Persons With Severe Handicaps, Seattle, WA.

Seagoe, M.V. (1964). *Yesterday was Tuesday, all day and all night: The story of a unique education.* Boston: Little, Brown.

Shannon, P. (1995). *Text, lies, and video tape.* Portsmouth, NH: Heinemann.

Whitehurst, G.J., & Lonigan, C.J. (2001). Emergent literacy: Development from prereaders to readers. In S.B. Neuman & D.K. Dickinson (Eds.), *Handbook of early literacy research* (pp. 11–29). New York: Guilford.

LITERATURE CITED

Brown, C. (1970). *Down all the days.* London: Mandarin.

Brown, C. (1989). *My left foot.* New York: Simon & Schuster.

SECTION III

A Close Look at Diverse Family Literacy Programs

CHAPTER 8

Exploring Even Start and Head Start Family Literacy Programs

Rebecca K. Edmiaston and Linda May Fitzgerald

Recognition of the critical significance of facilitating literacy development before children start elementary school has led to U.S. federally sponsored family literacy initiatives. (See chapter 1 for an overview of frameworks guiding family literacy program initiatives.) The U.S. government funds such initiatives to improve the educational opportunities of both children and adults in low-income families and to help break the cycle of poverty experienced by many families. Federal legislation currently mandates funding for a number of two-generation, or intergenerational, programs, to provide not only direct services to young children but also services for their families. In this chapter, we will present a theoretical orientation for viewing U.S. federally sponsored family literacy programs, a brief overview of the two major federally sponsored family literacy programs (Even Start Family and Head Start), and examples from each of these programs. The chapter will conclude with a discussion of current issues that challenge U.S. federally sponsored family literacy programs.

The William F. Goodling Even Start Family Literacy programs (ESEA, Part B, Subpart 3, 2001) are described as follows in the U.S. federal legislation:

> It is the purpose of this part to help break the cycle of poverty and illiteracy by improving the educational opportunities of the Nation's low-income families by integrating early childhood education, adult literacy or adult basic education, and parenting education into a unified family literacy program, to be referred to as "Even Start." The program shall—

(1) be implemented through cooperative projects that build on high quality existing community resources to create a new range of services;

(2) promote the academic achievement of children and adults;

(3) assist children and adults from low-income families to achieve to [sic] challenging State content standards and challenging State student performance standards; and

(4) use instructional programs based on scientifically based reading research (as defined in section 2252) and the prevention of reading difficulties for children and adults, to the extent such research is available. (p. 4)

The current reauthorization of the Head Start Act (1998) describes the purpose of Head Start programs as follows:

To promote school readiness by enhancing the social and cognitive development of low-income children through the provision, to low-income children and their families, of health, educational, nutritional, social, and other services that are determined, based on family needs assessments, to be necessary. (p. 2)

The overviews of these programs provide the context of the more specific programs described in this chapter.

Theoretical Orientation

Researchers who have studied developmental risk factors in children have identified poverty and low levels of parental educational attainment as a set of variables predictive of children's difficulties in school and subsequent low-income status as adults (Bredekamp & Copple, 1997; National Commission on Children, 1993; Natriello, McDill, & Pallas, 1990). Federally sponsored U.S. family literacy programs subscribe to the belief that "two-generation programs have a stronger capacity to improve long-term outcomes for children than many traditional early childhood interventions" (Smith & Zaslow, 1995, p. 2). Two-generation programming addresses educational needs of both parent and child.

The current federal definition of family literacy reflects the assumptions underlying intergenerational programming. Cited in the reauthorization of the Head Start Act in 1998, family literacy services are defined as

> services that are of sufficient intensity in terms of hours, and of sufficient duration, to make sustainable changes in a family, and that integrate all of the following four activities: (a) interactive literacy activities between parents and their children, (b) training for parents regarding how to be the primary teacher for their children and full partners in the education of their children, (c) parent literacy training that leads to economic self-sufficiency, and (d) an age-appropriate education to prepare children for success in school and life experiences. (ACYF-IM-HS-00-25)

This definition was adopted in the 2001 reauthorization of the Elementary and Secondary Education Act (ESEA) of 1965 and applied to the Even Start statute and the Literacy Involves Families Together (LIFT) Act (P.L. 106–554, 2001). Three other laws governing U.S. family literacy programs also share this definition: Reading Excellence Act (P.S. 105–277, 1998), Workforce Investment Act (adult education) (P.L. 105–220, 1998), and the Community Services Block Grant Act (P.L. 105–285, 1998).

Although federally sponsored U.S. literacy programs operate under the definition described above regarding program activities, the nature of the family–school relationship in these programs is less clear. Implementation of a family literacy program centers on the relationships forged between family literacy program staff and family members. These relationships fall on a continuum ranging from a deficit model—in which families and children are viewed solely as clients to be fixed or candidates for remediation—to a full partnership between families and program staff. In the deficit model, parents are passive recipients of parent education, whereas with the full partnership model, parents are active partners in program governance and community change. Only with a partnership model are there multidirectional participatory learning relationships, a two-way flow of information (Auerbach, 1995; Ceglowski, 2002; Fitzgerald & Goncu, 1993; Quintero, 1999; Zigler & Muenchow, 1992). (See chapters 6 and 11 for descriptions of family literacy programs based on such learning partnerships.)

Programs may subscribe to multiple interpretations of family participation, some of which are contradictory. For example, U.S. program standards for Head Start encourage families to join local policy councils and acknowledge their competence to participate in program governance, ostensibly in full partnership with the program leaders. However, local Head Start programs also may base family education programs on the belief that parents are deficient in their abilities to make sound educational decisions for their families, following a deficit model. In her discussion of family literacy programs as intervention or empowerment experiences, Auerbach (1995) states, "We need to reverse the 'from the school to the family' model and allow what happens in families and communities to inform schooling" (p. 23).

Drawing from her work with Head Start, Quintero (1999) calls for authentic and meaningful parent involvement in a nonthreatening environment that will lead to or enhance multidirectional participatory learning as a context in which "learning not only is transmitted from teacher to students (whether we are speaking about children or their families), but teachers learn from students, and students learn from each other" (p. 475). Examination of the two primary federally sponsored U.S. family literacy programs—Even Start and Head Start—reveals the full continuum of family-program relationships, ranging from interventionist approaches to authentic participatory involvements. However, before providing specific examples of practices within Even Start and Head Start, a brief overview of each program is needed.

Overview of Even Start and Head Start

Convinced of the important role that families play in their children's development, policymakers have allocated and continue to allocate substantial funds for the design and implementation of family literacy programs. Among a wide variety of such programs, Even Start and Head Start receive the largest amount of public funding and are the most widespread across the nation (see Morrow, Tracey, & Maxwell, 1995). These two programs alone are listed as contacts for family literacy programs in the brochure—*What Is Family Literacy? Getting Involved in Your Child's Literacy Learning* (2001)—written by the International Reading Association's Family Literacy Committee for parents and guardians. Even Start, administered by the U.S. Department of Education, is an educational program; Head Start, administered by the U.S. Department of Health and Human Services, focuses on the whole child. A brief overview of each program follows.

EVEN START

As Paratore argues in chapter 1 of this book, Even Start "has the most ambitious goal" of any federally sponsored U.S. family literacy program. Unlike Head Start, which is the oldest federally sponsored two-generation program, Even Start (initiated in 1989) has the primary charge to fight poverty by improving academic achievement of children and their families, particularly in the area of reading. Even Start provides educational services for families so children will have opportunities to experience high-quality early education and so parents and guardians will be able to support children's development and be more likely to have to have good jobs themselves. Former Republican congressman of Pennsylvania William Goodling (1994), who sponsored the program legislation, characterizes Even Start as a program that "supplies parents with the training to be their child's first teacher; allows them to gain needed literacy skills and to complete their formal education; and provides a preschool program for children" (p. 24). Participation in Even Start requires an adult within the family who is eligible for an adult basic education program under the Adult Education and Family Literacy Act (1998) or who is within the state's compulsory school attendance age range and a child under age 8 from birth through age 7. In addition, the family must live in the attendance area of an elementary school that receives federal Title I monies. St. Pierre and Swartz (1995) describe Even Start as a family-focused program with the following three interrelated goals:

- to help parents become full partners in the education of their children
- to assist children in reaching their full potential as learners; and
- to provide literacy training for their parents. (pp. 38–39)

Federal legislation (ESEA, Title I, Part B, Subpart 3, 2001), requires Even Start programs to make available the following four core components first developed by the Kenan Trust and most commonly known as the Kenan Trust model (Barbara Bush Foundation for Family Literacy, 1989; Darling, 1992): (1) an early childhood education program for children from birth to age 8; (2) an adult education program that helps adults develop basic educational and literacy skills, including basic or secondary adult education, English as a second language (ESL), or preparation for a General Education Development (GED) certificate; (3) a parent education program to enhance parent–child interactions and parents' support of their children's growth and development, and (4) interactive literacy activities between parents and their children. Even Start is predicated on the belief that all four services are necessary to effect lasting change and improve children's achievement in school. Families must participate in each of the four components.

Despite these mandates, individualized grantee agencies in a particular locale still have significant flexibility in designing Even Start programs to best address their own community needs. A variety of program designs result from mandated collaboration with existing community programs such as instructional programs, transportation, and child care. Such collaboration simultaneously eliminates duplication of services within a community and fulfills Even Start program requirements.

Even Start also can target certain characteristics within the population of children and families to receive program services. Although projects are encouraged to serve children from birth through age 7, they are only required to provide services for a minimum 3-year age range of children. For example, one Even Start program might only serve children from birth to age 3 who have teenage parents. Another program might target children ages 3 through 5 with parents identified to be most ready to complete a GED. In some programs, a local Head Start might provide the child development component, or a community college might provide adult education.

HEAD START

Head Start (initiated in 1965) provides the primary model for involving families in the education of their children. Washington and Bailey (1995) describe Head Start as "a trailblazer" (p. 11) in helping to focus our country's attention on the needs of young children. Head Start receives U.S. and international recognition as the most successful and enduring antipoverty program in the United States. Although evaluation studies throughout its nearly four-decade existence are not all in agreement, many researchers would concur with Mills (1998) that Head Start is "arguably the best investment America has ever made in its youngest citizens" (p. 2). However imperfectly implemented it has been, Head

Start also presents the most recognizable model of a two-generation program, which offers education and services not only to the children but also to the adults in low-income families (Parker, Piotrkowski, Horn, & Greene, 1995; Smith, 1995; Washington & Bailey, 1995; Zigler & Muenchow, 1992).

Since the inception of the program, a strong emphasis on family involvement and support of family self-sufficiency also has set Head Start apart from other early childhood intervention programs. Harmon and Hanley (1979) credit Head Start with launching the trend of family-school partnerships within the educational community. From the beginning of Head Start, family involvement has been a key element of the program. Head Start performance standards mandate that grantees recognize parents and guardians as the children's primary educators and plan experiences and activities that will support families in carrying out this role. Specific roles for families are mandated in Section 70.2 of the Head Start Performance Standards. In addition, Head Start has supported and continues to support career training opportunities and employment opportunities for families. For example, Washington and Bailey (1995) report that 30% of Head Start staff members are former or current Head Start families. According to Sissel (2000),

> Head Start has always been a preschool program for children, a provider of adult education for parents, a site of workplace and on-the-job training, and an agent of the state that develops, prescribes, funds and implements educational policy and curricula. (p. 7)

Head Start has a long history of work in the area of family literacy that spans the full continuum of involving families passively or actively in the program. Initially, Head Start addressed foundations of literacy by preparing young children for elementary school and by indirectly and directly supporting parental literacy training, both in preparing families for economic self-sufficiency and improving parenting skills. Research on early literacy and clearer delineation of the role of families in literacy development (e.g., Teale & Sulzby, 1986) has provided an impetus for a more explicit focus on family literacy than Head Start's whole-child and whole-family approach and has resulted in several U.S. federally sponsored Head Start family literacy initiatives. For example, in 1989, The Head Start–Library of Congress Partnership Project assisted local Head Start programs in working with their community libraries to increase parent involvement in their children's literacy development. In 1990, Head Start Family Service Centers were established to focus on family issues and help ensure that family needs were being addressed. In the 1998 reauthorization of Head Start, family literacy was one of three need areas—along with substance abuse and unemployment—that were identified for Head Start Family Service Centers to address. In the following year, every Head Start grantee had the opportunity to apply for additional monies to fund family literacy efforts. The emphasis on family literacy continues today. In 2000, the National Center for Family Literacy committed to a five-year cooperative agreement with Head Start to provide training and technical assistance for Head Start grantees in the implementation of comprehensive family literacy services to document effective family literacy services in Head Start programs across the United States. Family literacy has indeed become a major component of current Head Start programs. The following section provides some specific examples of both Even Start and Head Start family literacy practices.

Program Examples

Programs differ in their orientations toward families, particularly in regard to educating parents and guardians to be their children's first teachers or developing full partnerships in the education of their children. The strengths that Even Start and Head Start contribute to family literacy fall into different arenas. With its educational perspective, Even Start focuses on research-based literacy practices. Head Start, on the other hand, views the child as its primary focus and works with parents primarily to support their children's development. (Given the flexibility that local grantee agencies have, any one Even Start or Head Start program can have unique characteristics.)

Four programs demonstrate services at different points across the continuum of family participation models. The first, an Even Start program, represents for the most part a one-way flow from school to families in which families are viewed within a deficit model. The second, a Head Start program, demonstrates components across the continuum. The third and fourth programs, an Even Start Program collaboration with a variety of programs funded by local, state, and federal sources, and a Head Start collaboration with university faculty, respectively, strive to maximize the two-way flow of information characterizing the full-partnership model.

An Even Start program that addresses families' deficits and is located in the upper midwestern United States serves a group of immigrant women and their children. The low-income adult participants are primarily mothers who do not use English as a first language, have not obtained high school diplomas, and are not able to manage financially without receiving government assistance. Children participate in preschool classes four days a week while their mothers attend adult education and parenting classes. The family education component addresses parental deficits in language (emphasizing ESL programs), job training, and skills for parents as teachers of their children. Day classes are held for the women and their children at three elementary schools. The program collaborated with the Job Training Partnership Act Program (1996) to provide training for these women in self-sufficiency and academic needs. Child care is provided for siblings who are too young to enroll in the preschool program, and adults join their preschool children for about two and a half hours per week in classroom activities and in observing the teacher model reading aloud to children. Although one full-time bilingual aide facilitates communication between staff and families, the communication barrier between these groups limits opportunities for more participatory governance by the families. Recognizing the limitations of this model, the staff acknowledges the need to develop more authentic and meaningful participation within the family academic and parenting component. However, as the program was originally implemented, the focus was on supplying what the adults lacked.

A midwestern Head Start program, serving rural and urban families who are ethnically and racially diverse, lies along the continuum of school-family partnerships rather than at one extreme or the other. This program participates in a statewide staff development literacy initiative that provides training in best practices for facilitating literacy development of young children. The program uses this curriculum to deliver training to both staff and families. Although this family education component reflects a prescriptive approach to parent education, as teachers and families become more knowledgeable about literacy development in general, individual partnerships between teachers and families are becoming increasingly participatory, as the following examples show.

Local Head Start teachers also recognize the significant impact that families' literacy levels and activities can have on children's emerging literacy skills. The university with the largest teacher education program in the state provides inservice sessions for Head Start teachers with ideas for family literacy projects and also places preservice teachers in local Head Start classes for practicum experiences. The students have brought writing suitcases—portable containers filled with literacy tools such as writing instruments, materials to write on, and stories in print and electronic media—to share with the Head Start students and their families (Rich, 1985). One of the Head Start teachers recognized the idea when she read a similar article in a later issue of *Young Children* about a book backpack program (Cohen, 1997; see chapter 3 for a discussion on this topic) and took the initiative to adapt the program to meet the needs of the children and families she served. As a veteran Head Start teacher, she had noticed that her children's parents were much younger than participants from previous years and did not seem well informed about how to facilitate their children's literacy development. Because they were participating in employment preparation programs, the parents were also unable to come into the classroom to observe or volunteer. This teacher agrees with Cohen's (1997) belief that it is important to increase parents' or guardians' time with their children, get good books into homes, and help families develop their children's love of books.

Starting with books from her own home, the teacher piloted the project in her classroom. She individualized a backpack for each child to address the child's unique goals and strengths. The Book Backpack program was so successful that she submitted a proposal to the Head Start administrators to implement it and subsequently received funding to purchase the books and other necessary materials. Her program inspired a colleague in the local Head Start program to implement the program as well. Both instructors have used the program as a way of informing families about the curricula and activities that children experience in the classroom. A feedback sheet included in the backpacks gives the parent or guardian an opportunity to share ideas and suggestions for improvement, thus opening the door for more partnership in deciding what and how the children should learn.

A second collaboration in the same grantee agency brought together another local Head Start teacher and a professor in early childhood and literacy education (Rebecca K. Edmiaston). The two educators worked together to build rapport between Head Start staff and families so families would feel more comfortable sharing important events in their lives. Edmiaston and the Head Start teacher implemented a shared-writing experience in this classroom to facilitate children's literacy development and to increase communication between staff and families. During activity time, they took photos of children's participation in physical knowledge activities (early science experiences). One of them then spoke with each child about the pictures and the child's actions. Next, the child selected photos to place in a book, sequenced the photos, and composed text about the activities. After the child shared the book at group time, the teachers made copies of the book. Each child took a copy home, and the other copies were placed in the classroom library.

This type of collaboration provides an open invitation for families to record and share what children are doing at home with the books their children have made, thus establishing a spirit of partnership between the Head Start program and the children's families. Some families particularly appreciate this activity because it provides the only photographs they have of their children. The informal sharing of the children's activity books provides teachers with valuable information about children's experiences at home and demonstrates mutual respect for the families by seeing them as capable of reporting on and extending classroom activities. More important, the sharing creates a context for multidirectional learning between the Head Start program staff and the participating families.

The third example, an Even Start Program, is part of a learning community, a comprehensive program that seamlessly integrates the services of a variety of U.S. federally and state-funded programs. A major factor contributing to the learning community's success has been its commitment to acknowledging and accepting each family's assets and abilities and then respectfully supporting families in realizing their goals and dreams. Major components of the learning community include Even Start, Early Head Start and Head Start, the School Readiness Program, adult education, employment services, community education, K–12 education services, and other family-centered services. Because of the dual enrollment of adults and children, Even Start is the pivotal program that has allowed the learning community to become a truly integrated service model.

Each year, this Even Start program typically serves 40 diverse families of highest financial need and families who have children with disabilities, regardless of income, targeting families with children entering kindergarten. The program goals match the Even Start philosophy of parent as learner, child as learner, and parent as teacher. Under each of these goals are three measurable outcomes chosen from the following list: literacy, career development and job training, parenting, child development, and development of independence and self-reliance. Within four semesters, the teachers evaluate participant progress through a unique curriculum with two major components:

1. literacy connection with an experiential/home focus in which home visitors learn about how families use literacy in their homes and instruct the families in a culturally sensitive manner while in this nonthreatening environment, and

2. literacy connection with a skill-based/school focus that has adults and children in a school setting in which teachers model what goes on in classrooms and provide skill-based literacy instruction and support.

Throughout their enrollment in the program, adults are encouraged to pursue higher formal education, job training (if needed), and involvement in their children's classrooms. The program is designed to provide a diminishing continuum of support over time, leading away from dependence on the program and toward individual and family self-sufficiency, empowering parents and guardians to act as advocates for themselves, their children, and education in general.

The final example comes from the study Quintero (1999) conducted on the Family Initiative for English Literacy (Project FIEL), which is a collaborative project among Head Start staff; university faculty; and Mexican, Mexican American, and Chicano parents and their children in

El Paso, Texas. Quintero describes this family literacy project as one that exemplifies authentic family involvement in a culturally and linguistically diverse community. Project FIEL is designed so parents and children can work together in a bilingual setting around a curriculum that reflects their prior knowledge and sociocultural background. Parents and children participate in intergenerational activities after school once a week for about one hour with approximately five to seven other families. According to Quintero (1999), learner-generated thematic lessons are carried out through the following five experiences:

> Initial Inquiry—an oral language activity which encouraged group dialogue
>
> Learning Activity—a concrete, hands-on experience activity done in family teams
>
> Language Experience Approach Activity—a writing activity done in family teams
>
> Storybook Demonstration—storytime that encouraged interaction
>
> Home Activity Suggestions—activities for the whole family to do at home (p. 481)

As teachers and families learn from one another, changes are made in instructional practices and the preschool curriculum to reflect the sociocultural context of the children and parents being served.

These four program examples illustrate different points on the continuum regarding the degree of family participation within a child's educational program. Although all federal programs require family involvement, not all programs demonstrate full parent partnership. Individual Even Start and Head Start programs must strive to define and implement programs.

Conclusion

Family literacy programs remain a priority of the current federal administration in the United States. However, these programs face a number of challenges. We will conclude by examining some of the following challenges: (a) employing well-trained program staff to work with children and parents, (b) the changing demographics within the population of the United States, and (c) current societal forces.

One challenge in implementing effective family literacy programs is the employment of program staff well versed in current research regarding children's literacy acquisition and the practices that best facilitate children's literacy development. Recent U.S. federal literacy initiatives address literacy needs for both families and program staff. The U.S. Congress recently established two new reading initiatives to support literacy efforts—Early Reading First and Reading First. Both initiatives support professional development of early childhood and elementary program staff in effective research-based literacy instruction practices.

A second challenge faced by federally sponsored literacy programs is the increasingly diverse population of children and parents requiring services. Demographics of the U.S. population are rapidly changing. Increasing numbers of families have a home language that differs from the school language (Quintero, 1999). Communication barriers between staff and families can negatively affect outcomes of family literacy programs. Programs may require translators in many different languages for both children and parents.

Third, a more recent form of language that also has an impact on family literacy programs is technology. As one of many changing societal forces, the expansion of technology in both the workplace and the classroom has significant implications for family literacy programs. Low technology literacy and the digital divide further limit adults in obtaining self-sufficiency and serving as their children's first teachers.

Another changing societal force affects family literacy programs. Rising costs in the U.S. economy may reduce the amount of time available for parents or guardians to share literacy activities with children at home and may make it increasingly difficult for families to spend time outside of the home in family education programs. For example, in single-parent homes, one adult bears sole responsibility for the family and may be required to work more than one job to meet financial obligations, thus limiting the time this parent can spend with his or her children. Even in many two-parent households, today's economic conditions require that both parents be employed. In addition, welfare reform requires significant changes in family literacy programs because adult education classes, parenting education, and working in a classroom with one's child no longer count as work activities. Because of these factors, the time at which family programs are offered needs to be flexible to coordinate with families' availability.

The challenges posed for family literacy programs vary across the United States. The changing needs of families require continuing modification of program practices and curricula. Local communities must design family literacy programs to address the needs of the adults and children in their neighborhoods. (See chapters 5 and 6 for discussion of the importance of building on community needs.) Existing U.S. federal programs provide local communities with a wide range of choices. Head Start and Even Start are not one-size-fits-all programs. Local programs can choose whether to provide deficit remediation or to develop partnerships with families in which staff and families share strengths and program staff learn about culturally appropriate curricula and other funds of knowledge, even from parents with limited literacy. With their collaboration facilitated by federally sponsored family literacy programs, families and teachers use current research and theory to design the most effective practices to serve both the children and their adult caregivers both at home and at school.

REFERENCES

Auerbach, E.R. (1995). Which way for family literacy: Intervention or empowerment? In L.M. Morrow (Ed.), *Family literacy connections in schools and communities* (pp. 11–28). Newark, DE: International Reading Association.

Bredekamp, S., & Copple, C. (1997). *Developmentally appropriate practices* (Rev. ed.). Washington, DC: National Association for the Education of Young Children.

Ceglowski, D. (2002). [Review of the book *Critical perspectives on Project Head Start: Revisioning the hope and challenge*]. *Early Childhood Research Quarterly, 17*(1), 140–144.

Cohen, L.E. (1997). How I developed my kindergarten book backpack program. *Young Children, 52*(2), 69–71.

Family Literacy Committee of the International Reading Association. (2001). *What is family literacy? Getting involved in your child's literacy learning*. Newark, DE: International Reading Association.

Fitzgerald, L.M., & Goncu, A. (1993). Parent involvement in urban early childhood education: A Vygotskian approach. In S. Reifel (Ed.), *Advances in early education and day care: A research annual* (pp. 197–212). London: JAI Press.

Goodling, W.F. (1994). Giving kids an even start. *Principal, 74*(1), 24–25.

Harmon, C., & Hanley, E. (1979). Administrative aspects of Head Start. In E. Zigler & J. Valentine (Eds.), *Project Head Start: A legacy of the war on poverty* (pp. 379–398). New York: Free Press.

Head Start Act, 42 U.S.C. 9831 § 635 *et seq.* (1998).

Head Start Performance Standards, Title 45 C.F.R., Parts 1301–1311. (1998).

Mills, K. (1998). *Something better for my children: The history and people of Head Start*. New York: Dutton.

Morrow, L.M., Tracey, D.H., & Maxwell, C.M. (Eds.). (1995). *A survey of family literacy in the United States*. Newark, DE: International Reading Association.

National Commission on Children. (1993). *Increasing educational attainment*. Washington, DC: Author.

Natriello, G., McDill, E., & Pallas, A. (1990). *Schooling disadvantaged children: Racing against catastrophe*. New York: Teachers College Press.

Parker, F.L., Piotrkowski, C.S., Horn, W.F., & Greene, S.M. (1995). The challenge for Head Start: Realizing its vision as a two-generation program. In S. Smith (Ed.), *Two generation programs for families in poverty: A new intervention strategy* (pp. 135–159). Westport, CT: Ablex.

Quintero, E. (1999). The new faces of Head Start: Learning from culturally diverse families. *Early Education & Development, 10*(4), 475–497.

Rich, S.J. (1985). The writing suitcase. *Young Children, 40*(5), 42–43.

Sissel, P.A. (2000). *Staff, parent, and politics in Head Start: A case study in unequal power, knowledge and material resources*. London: Falmer.

Smith, S. (Ed.). (1995). *Two generation programs for families in poverty: A new intervention strategy*. Westport, CT: Ablex.

Smith, S., & Zaslow, M. (1995). Rational and policy context for two-generation interventions. In S. Smith (Ed.), *Two generation programs for families in poverty: A new intervention strategy* (pp. 1–36). Westport, CT: Ablex.

St. Pierre, R.G., & Swartz, J.P. (1995). The Even Start family literacy program. In S. Smith (Ed.), *Two generation programs for families in poverty: A new intervention strategy* (pp. 37–66). Westport, CT: Ablex.

Teale, W.H., & Sulzby, E. (Eds.). (1986). *Emergent literacy: Writing and reading*. Westport, CT: Ablex.

Washington, V., & Bailey, U. (1995). *Project Head Start: Models and strategies for the twenty-first century*. New York: Garland.

William F. Goodling Even Start Family Literacy Programs, Elementary and Secondary Education Act (ESEA), 20 U.S.C. § 1231 (2001).

Zigler, E., & Muenchow, S. (1992). *Head Start: The inside story of America's most successful educational experiment*. New York: Basic Books.

CHAPTER 9

Read to Me: A Family Literacy Program for Young Mothers and Their Babies

Susan Straub

Although reading to a baby can be an extraordinary tool in both language development and parent-child bonding, parents and guardians first need to learn about and trust the richness of books in order to understand how they and their children can experience books in positive, playful ways. Many parents were not read to as children themselves (Straub & DeBruin-Parecki, 2002). Parents' school experiences may not have been rewarding or successful, or they may have attended school in another culture that did not emphasize storybook reading. Some parents wonder why anyone would read to a baby. Babies do not know how to read, and they do not understand the words being read aloud. Further, most new mothers are exhausted and far too busy with other, more pressing needs to even think about extra activities, such as reading. However, reading to a baby may be the single most valuable behavior a new family can develop.

The Importance of Parent-Child Reading

Increasingly, research supports long-standing anecdotal and observed evidence of the positive results of reading to all children, including newborns. A growing portion of literacy research focuses on the prereading skills and practices of preschool-age children. This research suggests that, rather than beginning with formal school-based reading instruction, literacy is a developmental progression that has its origins in a child's exposure to written and spoken language from birth onward (Whitehurst & Lonigan, 2001). (See chapter 2 for discussion of early literacy.) One example of such exposure is joint book reading, in which an adult caregiver reads to a child. (See chapter 14 for more on parent-child reading.) A number of studies have found that reading aloud to preschool children has been associated with increased vocabulary; school-age reading achievement scales; and early literacy skills, such as letter and name identification and phoneme blending (see Bus, van IJzendoorn, & Pellegrini [1995] for a meta-analysis and discussion of these studies). Reading interactions with older and younger preschoolers, however, differ from those with infants and toddlers. Infants and toddlers often interact with books as objects of play, while older preschoolers attend more to the stories being read (Bus, van IJzendoorn, & Pelligrini, 1995). Research has shown that the earlier the onset of regular joint reading activities, the stronger children's gains in language skills are (DeBaryshe, 1993). This information suggests that regular book reading to children—beginning in infancy—would result in significantly better early literacy skills at the start of a child's regular schooling.

This hypothesis has support from intervention studies, which demonstrate that an increase in joint reading activities results in significant and stable gains in language achievement. For example, Whitehurst and colleagues (1988) have found that 21- to 35-month-old children whose parents are given explicit instruction in shared reading interactions have significantly higher expressive language measures and a longer mean length of utterance than children in a control group. These significant differences remained when the children were retested six months later.

Arnold, Lonigan, Whitehurst, and Epstein (1994) use a videotape intervention to teach parents how to use dialogic reading techniques when reading to their preschoolers. These techniques encourage parents to move beyond merely reading the text to asking their children increasingly sophisticated questions about the story, with the goal being a reversal of roles as the children become the storytellers. The researchers' results showed that 24- to 34-month-old children whose parents are taught to use dialogic reading techniques scored significantly higher on standardized language measures than children whose parents followed a more traditional adult-centered reading style. Another study with teenage mothers showed that embedding read-alouds into home-based activities designed to foster preliteracy skills in 3-year-olds resulted in significantly higher receptive language scores for these children, as well as significantly more interactions with literacy-based activities (Neuman & Gallagher, 1994). Teaching read-aloud techniques and promoting joint reading activities are related to stronger early literacy skills.

Other evidence indicates that the cognitive effects of reading aloud to very young children may be mediated by the quality of the adult-child relationship. Joint book reading can be considered a socially created activity between two participants (Bus, 2001). This perspective suggests that the better the relationship between the adult and the child, the more effective the joint reading interaction. Bus and van IJzendoorn (1997) have found a negative relation between mother-child attachment and the quality of book reading interactions with infants averaging 12 months of age. Infants with secure emotional attachments to their mothers are more attentive to the books and more likely to respond to the story content and pictures than infants with insecure emotional attachments to their mothers. Mothers of insecurely attached infants are more restrictive during the interaction, often restraining their children or placing the book beyond the children's grasp. Another study with 18-month-old toddlers has found that parents of children insecurely attached to them are less likely to make the book reading an age-appropriate activity (Bus, Belsky, van IJzendoorn, & Crnik, 1997). Rather than interacting with their child by using the words and images in the book for a starting point, these parents more often simply read the text verbatim in a directive manner, regardless of their children's verbal comprehension abilities.

These few examples of parent-child reading studies suggest two directions for early literacy programs. First, such programs should begin as early as possible in children's lives. Parents should be made aware of the benefits of reading to even the youngest infants and should be given specific age-appropriate strategies for using the book and its accompanying text to encourage more open discussion and interaction with their children. Second, programs emphasizing shared reading should include methods for promoting a more secure relationship between the adult and child.

Overview of the Read to Me Program

The Read to Me program began in 1989 as a pilot program in an alternative high school parenting classroom in New York City, with the goal of encouraging teen mothers to enjoy and use picture books with their babies. Working in close collaboration with the classroom teacher, who was simultaneously exploring the resourcefulness of children's picture books with her high school students, I brought in a published author-illustrator and colleagues from the New York Public Library and developed and refined the classroom sessions into a series of workshops. In 1990, Read to Me gained the support of the Teachers & Writers Collaborative, a nonprofit arts education organization, and the program eventually secured funding from foundation grants and fees. Subsequently, the program expanded into all the schools managed by the Pregnant and Parenting Teen Services of the New York City Board of Education and their many Learning for Young Families Through Education (LYFE) day-care centers citywide. Additionally, inservice professional development workshops ran intermittently for staff working in the LYFE centers. Two demonstration workshops were offered: one in a Chicago, Illinois, public high school uniquely serving parenting teens and the other in Charlottesville, Virginia, under the auspices of the University of Virginia's Under Fives Study Center, which specializes in understanding the mental and emotional development of children under 5 years of age. An additional Read to Me program was initiated by a Boston, Massachusetts, junior high school art teacher in collaboration with a high school English teacher and a social worker as an after-school program for teen mothers.

The overall goals of Read to Me are

- to offer reading as a resource to young mothers for pleasure, parenting tips, and psychological insights;
- to stimulate imaginations and initiate early literacy education; and
- to improve the potential for healthy parent-child relationships.

The following section offers an overview of Read to Me program activities that guide teen parents to read with their babies. Although the entire program offers a variety of approaches into the world of picture books for children (see Figure 9.1 for a description of program activities), the focus in this chapter will be on modeling these skills for the young mothers as they begin reading pictures and then texts.

Figure 9.1
Read to Me Program Sessions

Session	Activities	Suggested Books
Introductory: Reading faces and wordless books	• Take pictures of faces to *read* (eye, nose, mouth) • Have some parents share in reading wordless books	Wordless (or foreign-language) books by authors such as Mercer Mayer, John S. Goodall, Tomie diPaola, Jan Omerod, Fernando Krahn, and Taro Gomi
Playful board and peekaboo books	Playfully try out and play with variety of board books, oven-glove puppets, and lift-the-flap or pop-up books	Books by Debby Slier, Rachel Isadora, Rosemary Wells, Martha Alexander, and Eric Carle
Picture books	Organize an array of books to read and think about by themes or random sampling: • Classics • Families • Language • Separation and loss • Problems	Books by • John Steptoe, Margaret Wise Brown, Maurice Sendak, Dorothy Kunhardt, Vera B. Williams, and Majorie Flack • Charlotte Zolotow, Angela Johnson • Dr. Seuss, Ruth Krauss, Richard Scarry, and Bill Martin Jr • P.D. Eastman, Ezra Jack Keats, Pat Cummings, and Charlotte Zolotow • Kevin Henkes, Bernard Waber, and Shirley Hughes
Library	Visit local public children's library to meet librarian and to enjoy • lap-sit and/or toddler demonstration • reissuing of library cards to parents	Check with librarian for Trelease's *Read Aloud Handbook*, Mem Fox's *Reading Magic*, and/or other guide books for choices
Creative	Have parents write or make a luggage tag or handcrafted book for children	Check local office and art supply stores, and trust your imagination to use old magazines, scissors, markers, and either cardboard, file cards, or luggage tags to create a book or tag
Guest writer–illustrator	Have the guest • model and support reading to babies • describe creative process • autograph gift books for participants	Check local bookstore, art school, or library for suggestions or use Pat Cummings's *Talking With Artists* series, published by Simon & Schuster, Clarion, and Bradbury Books

Description of the Read to Me Program Activities

The Read to Me program consists of a series of six basic sessions. Each session focuses on creating a new path into the world of books for very young children and offering strategies that support parents in reading with their babies and toddlers. Both the order and number of the sessions can be expanded or contracted to accommodate the demands of a particular curriculum or the circumstances of participant families. Just like reading a picture book, the Read to Me program can be stretched out or economically trimmed to fit the time available. The goal is to offer the young parents a variety of different approaches to reading that are pleasurable, useful, and positive. My colleagues and I want to ensure that the mothers and mothers-to-be believe that reading with their babies merits their time and effort. Importantly, the activities conducted with mothers include essential practice in read-aloud time with their babies and toddlers. Because the targeted population of teen mothers is often considered at-risk, attendance may be a problem and any session a mother attends may be her only session. This reality makes it imperative that any one session offers a meaningful learning experience that enhances the possibility that the mother will actually adopt the activity for use with her baby at home on a routine basis.

The following sections describe four Read to Me program activities that guide teen parents to read with their babies. Read to Me tries to make reading pleasurable on the simple premise that if it is fun and seems worth the effort, inexperienced readers will more readily adopt this invaluable habit. These specific sessions exemplify nondidactic techniques for dialogic reading and decidedly promote healthier mother-child attachments.

ACTIVITY I: POLAROIDS AND WORDLESS BOOKS

Reading begins with looking at faces. Using a Polaroid camera, the Read to Me leader takes a snapshot of each participant—awake or not, well-groomed or not, eager or not—in the first few minutes of the program's initial session. Not only is this activity a strategic icebreaker, introducing the leader to each participant in the room, but, using the rationale that a mother's face is the first book a baby reads, this project also gives the participants their first book to use with their babies. Once the complaints and giggles subside a bit, the group "reads" the photographs. Pretending to be their babies, the moms name something they observe in their photographs. Moving from the particulars of "What do you see?" (mouth, nose, teeth, earring, bangs), they shift to colors (red lips, yellow sweater, black eyebrow, gold earring) and then deeper still into the realm of feelings (grumpy, happy, sleepy, interested, annoyed).

The participants are all interested now. They have something to look at, think about, talk about, imagine, and put into words. They are reading. Usually, a lot of laughter fills the room. The simple snapshots often trigger deeper comments: "I need to cut my hair." "I look so fat." "I look just like my mother." "I never smile in pictures." The comments reveal beginning dialogic reading techniques. The leaders ask the participants to go beyond the obvious; the mothers reminisce, compare, contrast, and enjoy. Showing their snapshots to other group members allows for comparisons and the occasional nice comment about someone's good features. More important, however, this introductory exercise heralds a start in thinking about the power of books and the images in them. The instructors and participants have launched literary discussions.

One simple photograph is actually quite complex. It gives each reader a point of reference. For some readers, viewing the photograph triggers memories, comparisons, and insights. For others, it merely initiates ideas to keep for future reference. It may encourage the mother to take and keep photos of her baby as the infant grows. It may also make the mother feel special because she has a unique photograph of herself to show off, keep, and value. Also, the photo goes home. Maybe it goes in a photo album, maybe it even gets stuck to the fridge with a magnet, or perhaps it gets shown to the baby or the extended family. Hopefully, it serves as a reminder of the fun the mother had reading "books" in the Read to Me program and prompts newly acquired reading skills for her and her infant.

From reading photos, the group moves on to reading wordless books. A large and varied supply of wordless books have been published for children, and most are completely enchanting. The illustrators' gifts are fully engaged, and the books are so packed with visual narratives that words are really unnecessary. Program instructors and participants can read and tell their own stories based on these picture prompts, and the participants are invited to read these books with a partner. Partnering increases the fun and removes any sense of isolation or noninvolvement for the moms. (See Figure 9.2 for a list of suggested wordless books.)

Wordless books can provide a great bridge from individual snapshots to the printed page. One favorite, a laminated board book that pulls out like an accordion, is Wattenberg's *Mrs. Mustard's Baby Faces* (1989). One side of the strip shows seven beaming baby faces: several are bald and toothless, all have open mouths, and none show necks or bodies. Each face is uniquely different, but each is centered in the middle of a page against jazzy background patterns. The flip side is indeed the flip side. All the same infants now show cranky, crabby, crying, miserable little faces. Babies and parents alike appreciate this curious book, and they wonder why there are so few books that show crying or negative emotional states.

One master of the wordless picture book genre is Goodall, who draws small format stories with the added intrigue of a half-page flap that both encourages the reader to guess the next step and advances the story. Although these books have old-world English settings, contemporary readers have no difficulty identifying with their plots. One of Goodall's wordless books, *The Adventures of Paddy Pork* (1968), mirrors the thrill, as well as the possible dangers, of a toddler's first venture into

---

Figure 9.2
Suggested Wordless Picture Books

Anno, M. (1986). *Anno's counting book.* New York: HarperTrophy.
Briggs, R. (1989). *The snowman.* New York: Random House.
Carle, E. (1971). *Do you want to be my friend?* New York: Philomel.
Crews, D. (1997). *Truck* [board book]. New York: Tupelo.
dePaola, T. (1978). *Pancakes for breakfast.* New York: Harcourt Brace.
Goodall, J.S. (1968). *The adventures of Paddy Pork.* New York: Harcourt Brace.
Hoban, T. (1993). *Black on white* [board book]. New York: Greenwillow.
Hoban, T. (1993). *White on black* [board book]. New York: Greenwillow.
Hutchins, P. (1973). *Changes, changes.* New York: Macmillan.
Hutchins, P. (1998). *Rosie's walk.* New York: Little Simon.
Mayer, M. (1969). *Frog, where are you?* New York: Puffin.
Oxenbury, H. (1971). *Dressing.* New York: Little Simon.
Wattenberg, J. (1989). *Mrs. Mustard's baby faces* [board book]. San Francisco: Chronicle.

---

the wider world away from mother and home. Similar to a fairy tale in atmosphere, this book follows a piglet named Paddy as he escapes a boring shopping trip with his mother to follow his own path. Being separated from his mother inevitably leads the piglet to anxieties, which are expressed in confusion, bruises, tears, and bewilderment. Drawn deeper into the woods, he gets lost, and similar to his more famous pig ancestors, he encounters a seemingly kind wolf. Paddy is at first relieved to be cared for in his moment of fear. In fact, he is so comforted by the wolf's apparent caregiving that he lets down his guard and falls asleep in a chair by the roaring fireplace in which a large iron pot is heating up. The predatory wolf lunges to attack his dozing prey, but Paddy escapes and heads for the circus. Trying to fit in with a family of acrobat bears, he is hopelessly clumsy and departs in tears. Luckily, Paddy's distress at being lost and having failed is overheard by a kindly mouse, who directs him home to his mother's open arms.

These little books are fun, and their entertainment value is high. The parallels between the main characters and young children are clear. Paddy goes away from home and has adventures, as many young children want to do. Like a young toddler, Paddy is observant and persistent, he tests his newfound independence, and he gets into trouble. Goodall's half-page turns allow readers—even prompt them—to guess what will happen next. They push readers to anticipate actions and to become more involved in the unfolding story. These turns are examples of dialogic reading techniques, although they occur in the realm of wordless picture books.

Read to Me encourages its participating mothers to read these wordless books to their babies, trusting that by repeating the process at home the mothers will enhance their attachments to their babies. The reading slows down a bit to accommodate two sensibilities as each reader discovers new narrative details in the illustrations. The half-page, liftable flaps that advance Goodall's marvelous black-and-white illustrations not only add to the developing tension but also actively involve the readers, regardless of ages or reading abilities. Everyone in the Read to Me groups (whether community parent trainees for a day-care center with varying languages, adolescent mothers, social workers, or administrators working with pregnant and parenting teens) has consistently laughed, named, and pointed when given these small, gripping tales to read aloud with a partner. No one stops reading these books before they finish. Each reader tells the story as he or she sees it, in his or her own words, building and releasing tension and hurrying or slowing down according to new details observed on the pages.

During a specially organized inservice training session for community parents working in one of Manhattan's Lower East Side day-care centers, a Chinese speaker and a native speaker of English read one of these little books to each other in both Mandarin and English, respectively. Neither mother could speak or read the other's language, yet both chattered along happily, pointing at things and telling the other person about them in her native tongue. They laughed together, and each understood the story. Both thoroughly enjoyed reading and being read to in two languages.

ACTIVITY II: USING NON–ENGLISH BOOKS IN THE READ TO ME PROGRAM

As a next step, program leaders are encouraged to add books with text that are written in a non–English language. I include some books that are written in Japanese. So far, no Read to Me participant has been able to read the vertical Japanese sentences. Consequently, these charming books remain wordless books—eccentric ones at that because some are read not only from right to left but also back to front and in vertical columns. Because no one in the sessions has been able to read Japanese, the Read to Me moms who read these books are essentially in a preliterate condition, much like their babies who are mostly still preverbal.

One Japanese book that is particularly wonderful to use is *Mr. Finger* (1977) by Gomi, a famous Japanese children's author who is also well known in the United States for his book *Everyone Poops* (1983). *Mr. Finger* is the story of a child's index finger with a face painted on it. This finger-face companionably lives through a day with his child: they wake up, get dressed, eat breakfast, play in the toy box, shoot marbles, paint and wash up, tie shoelaces, explore the garden, and get a slight injury. This book combines several elements that are especially important in stories for very young children: playmates, adventures, a list of actual activities, and finally a moment of injury and tears. The blood and tears bring emotional drama to the storybook character, and the readers empathize with him, perhaps letting out audible gasps when the finger-face suffers his accident.

Although the painted finger-face is easy to locate in the focused pictures, his expression changes to reflect his emotional conditions. For example, the finger-face screams with a wide-open mouth and tightly shuts his eyes as he is nearly strangled by a shoelace his owner is attempting to tie. In another situation, the perplexed, frustrated, frowning finger-face tries to fit a camel-shaped jigsaw puzzle piece into a fairly obvious place in the puzzle frame. Each picture provides sufficient information to invite the reader either to name objects or elaborate on the story, perhaps even developing a dialogue between the child and his finger-friend. All readers delight in finding the finger-face in each image and empathizing with his efforts. It feels natural for readers to enter into the drama and tell what they see. Afterward, the readers can tell their families that they read a book in Japanese. More important, inexperienced readers feel emboldened and more assured of their abilities to read to their babies by using picture prompts. Although participants have been reading books with only pictures or non–English text up to this point in the program, the young mothers are reading and enjoying the novel experience.

ACTIVITY III: MOVING INTO ENGLISH

Adding English language text moves the Read to Me participants into the more usual realm of children's books that marry pictures with words. By now, the young moms in the program have confidence in their abilities to read aloud picture books and are enjoying the practice.

Well-written children's books provide readers with opportunities to experience language's ability to evoke emotion, to create a sense of place, and to usher the reader into that place. All utterances in these books attract attention, and some are gathered purposefully to inform and inspire. Each written line is an enticing promise of something to follow. Each rhythmic call sets up the readers' expectations. Will they be frustrated or satisfied? Either way, they have to wait for the resolution, the unfolding. Their interest is caught and aroused, and an adventure is begun, loaded with sensory, emotional, and imaginative possibilities. A successful children's book likely has several key ingredients in addition to the author's creativity: rhythm, repetition, and carefully chosen words in a narrative context.

Twist With a Burger (1995) by Lowery, for example, has a catchy musicality. The rhythm is insistently lilting and nearly irresistible. The story suggests all kinds of dances and rhythmic movements that readers can perform. An excerpt offers a taste of these suggestions:

> Boogie in the bathtub
> Hula–hula dance, rumba if you wanna in your underpants. (n.p.)

Teen parents at a high school in New York City attended to a reading of this book with rapt interest. Some got up and danced to the beat. In the discussion that followed, the parents said that this would be a fun book to read with a child of almost any age. Even if the child did not understand the words, they added, he or she would love the rhythm. They guessed that most babies would move and bounce in time to the beat. The parents were right, of course. Lowery's musical writing is an excellent example of language as pure entertainment. Using a recurring rhythm to amuse and delight, Lowery reaches into a place deep within readers, engaging children and adult's alike.

An even more popular and irresistible rhyming chant is *Chicka Chicka Boom Boom* (1989), a clever alphabet book written by Bill Martin Jr and John Archambault and illustrated by Lois Ehlert. The book follows the antics of an animated alphabet climbing a coconut tree. Indeed, only the stiffest human being could miss the lilting rhythm:

> A told B, and B told C, "I'll meet you at the top of the coconut tree." (n.p)

Each alphabet letter joins in the climb up the coconut tree. Suddenly, Ehlert's colorful tree is overburdened by all 26 alphabet characters, plus a few round, brown coconuts predictably falling. As the tree bends, the text captures the climax of this oddly dramatic moment with wonderfully exuberant skat syllables—"skit skat skoodle doot" (n.p.)—and the extended community of the letters' families come running to help. Yes, similar to human children jumping rope at the playground or playing some language game, these letters have families.

At the end of the tumble, the sun goes down. Is this a finale—the end of the adventure of climbing up and falling down the alphabet tree? No, not yet. "A is out of bed" (n.p.), daring readers to start it all again. The drama may be over, but the possibility of more fun remains. A book this pleasurable bears repeated readings. Part of the joy is the repetitious language. Rhyming a word twice and repeating it again later adds punch and a pattern of playfulness. The story unfolds in catching rhythms and rhymes, so readers are entertained on several levels. (See chapter 3 for further discussion of parent–child literacy interactions.)

What is the effect of rhythm and motion on babies? All mothers know that infants and small children respond instinctively to sound and motion. Rhythm is as natural to language as it is to music. Therefore, if babies are exposed to elaborated, rhythmic stories, so much the better. Rhythmic and rhyming books are so much fun that both mothers and babies want to read them again. Repeated reading leads to better shared experiences and closer, mutually satisfying relationships that continue to encourage reading.

ACTIVITY IV: READING BOOKS BY THEMES

At least one Read to Me session focuses entirely on reading piles of books organized by themes, such as families, siblings, friends, humor, and real problems for babies and toddlers. The following example will focus on the theme of families.

Families are universal. They are curious and dynamic, reassuring and irritating, and enriching and agonizing. Each new addition, subtraction, or exchange creates new and different configurations of characters and emotions. Likewise, no two children are born into the exact same family because each new child alters the overall family dynamics. Perhaps for this reason, books about family relations abound, as more than a browse in a library or bookstore will attest. Books that address the problems of being a child in a family, especially those books told from the child's viewpoint, can reduce the child reader's sense of isolation. Children can identify and empathize with picture book characters as they grapple with difficult feelings in their families. Similarly, these books enable parents to anticipate their children's feelings and reactions so parents can learn new ways to respond sympathetically.

Babies are powerful: They command center stage much of the time, often to the exclusion of other people and details. It is lucky for them that they do, for as we know, they are pretty helpless without adult attention. Books can encourage new parents to enter imaginatively into the minds of their new babies and begin to think about the world from the babies' viewpoints. Schwartz's book, *A Teeny Tiny Baby* (1994), describes the world as it appears to a new baby, born into a doting family of two parents and one grandmother within a supportive neighborhood with many shops and playgrounds. The writer gets inside the baby's world and notes the preferred *actions* ("jiggled or tickled or patted or burped" [n.p.]), and desired responses from the adoring family ("I like to be exclaimed over and 'oohed' over and 'aahed' over, or fed or changed, or sometimes I just want to be left to my own devices" [n.p.].) As is evident in the author–illustrator's narrative artwork, this baby receives a great deal of well-meaning attention and yet is as confused as his parents about what he wants *now*. This is, of course, the difficulty because a newborn baby is an incoherent mass of conflicting, unexpected, and often puzzling demands that parents do not yet know how to interpret or "read." How, for example, can one tell whether a baby wants to be jiggled or left alone in those first few weeks following birth? Luckily, for this newborn, his parents are willing to introduce him to his world and neighborhood (the deli, the cleaners, the drugstore, and the park), and luckily for readers, this fictional baby tells them how newborns act and what his parents do in response. By reading this fictional baby's account of whom he meets and what he sees, new parents can anticipate and think about their own babies.

Some parents would like to have a book of instructions delivered with their new child. What *does* a baby do? Ormerod, who has obviously observed babies closely, records their actions in her classic book, *101 Things to Do With a Baby* (1984). One-hundred-and-one numbered and labeled activities provide a random sampling from a day in the life of a 6-month-old baby and his family. An older sister, about age 4, is a great help, and, of course, the baby is included in the family's activities, including doing laundry and exercising. Sister and baby also watch television together until he is bored, and she gives him a book to read but not to chew or tear. Of course, when baby does chew or tear the book, the big sister shouts at him and makes him cry. Each activity begs for renewed connections to the reader's life at home with his or her baby and helps the reader enjoy these everyday activities in a fresh way.

The Read to Me program brings books into the workshops that address a real problem: Babies are not always fun, and sibling rivalry is an old and powerful emotion. Sometimes a book's art gets to the heart of the matter and allows readers to consider the problem. Henkes's book *Julius, the Baby of the World* (1990), is a humorous, well-illustrated tale of sibling love temporarily gone sour. The protagonist, Lilly, is a small mouse with a big adjustment problem. She initially likes the *idea* of a baby brother, but after her doting parents pronounce this disgusting new creature "the baby of the world" (n.p.), she experiences a radical change of heart:

> And she yelled insulting comments into his crib. "I am the queen," said Lilly. "And I hate Julius" (n.p.).

Henkes's illustrations show malevolent jealousy as exhibited by Lilly. Everything about her parents' reactions to the newborn disgusts her, especially their demands that she change her behaviors to accommodate the interloper. Despite her parents' efforts to raise her self-esteem, Lilly has her own ideas. She spends "more time than usual in the uncooperative chair" (n.p.). Even the inevitable praise, the plums thrown to her because she is the elder child, are washed away by Lilly's comparisons to her brother. Julius's bubbles are praised, although hers are reprimanded as unmannerly. His screams are amazing, indicative of great lung capacity, but Lilly's are unwelcome. Even Lilly's storytelling falls sway to her hateful feelings and earns her 10 minutes in the uncooperative chair. Lilly's parents demand her self-control. The desperate measures escalate as Lilly tells everyone how dreadful babies are, runs away several times one morning, excludes Julius from her activities, and dreams about his awfulness. Lilly refuses all her parents' efforts to change her mind, and Julius remains disgusting to her.

Inevitably, the much-hoped-for denouement comes: A visiting cousin pronounces Lilly's younger brother disgusting. Lilly, the queen, turns in a flash on her cousin and finally becomes the proud older sister of Julius, the baby of the world. When this member of her family is threatened, Lilly defends her family attachment. This disgusting creature, she realizes, is in fact hers and a permanent part of her nuclear family.

The hilarious artwork in *Julius, the Baby of the World* inventively supports the story. Lilly, habitually adorned in a golden crown befitting her royal status, revels in her fanciful costumes, masks, and cowgirl boots. She is at once creative and dramatic, an emotionally accurate portrait of a preschool child struggling to accommodate the birth of a baby brother.

Books such as *Julius, the Baby of the World*, and too many more to feature in this chapter, are suffused with pleasurably rendered real-life feelings in the characters and stories. These entertaining books should be used for several reasons. Initially, the more fun a reader has reading, the more likely he or she will repeat the experience. Most Read to Me program participants enjoy and chat about the book characters (e.g., readily connecting their own circumstances and problems with those of Lilly and her baby brother). Some of the connections are upsetting. During a program in a large New York City high school, a pregnant 16-year-old student told a worrisome story about her 3-year-old nephew. The nephew shouted at this teen mother that he hated her baby and wished it were dead. As the program participants talked about this terrible drama for both aunt and nephew, it became clear that the aunt understood how attached the nephew felt to her and how excluded he felt because of her new baby. The student had at one time been living in the same house with her nephew and had been a key person in his life and a baby sitter for him. Although she knew he was feeling terribly jealous, she was also a little bit afraid of his pronounced wish to kill her baby. She was able to talk about how she might confirm her nephew's hostile feelings and reassure him that there would still be room in her heart for him and that she could love him and the new baby, too. The student would also value his big-boy status and perhaps read picture books with him, pointing out that this was their special time together and not for the baby at all. It is possible that by reading about a mouse family in *Julius, the Baby of the World*, this mother was able to think about her own difficult situation at home. This advice could come straight out of several picture books, embedded in humorous or entertaining stories and artful drawings.

THE REST OF THE READ TO ME PROGRAM

Because this chapter has focused on actual reading activities, Figure 9.1 contains no description of the other activities noted within it, but these other activities are essential to the fun and success of the Read to Me program. Together, participants and program leaders make books for the babies, visit the local library, and have a celebratory visit from a published children's author or book illustrator. Each activity is another avenue into the realm of reading and using picture books for children, and the activities further connect young families to the world of books and enhance the possibility that the families will find books fun and useful for raising their children. The hope is that the families will have positive experiences to help them know and trust books so they can make books an important part of their young children's lives.

Conclusion

Reading to babies is a challenge for parents unaccustomed to having books in their lives. Because most parents want the best for their children, including wanting to raise them to be good in school, something needs to be done to help them begin reading to their babies as soon after birth as possible. (See chapter 10 for a description of a program that provides books to babies.) The Read to Me program has organized activities that demystify reading and encourage parents to begin to playfully enjoy inventing stories and reading illustrations as well as simple text with their babies.

REFERENCES

Arnold, D.H., Lonigan, C.J., Whitehurst, G.J., & Epstein, J.N. (1994). Accelerating language development through picture book reading: Replication and extension to a videotape training format. *Journal of Educational Psychology, 86*(2), 235–243.

Bus, A.G. (2001). Joint caregiver-child storybook reading: A route to literacy development. In S.B. Neuman & D.K. Dickinson (Eds.), *Handbook of early literacy research* (pp. 179–191). New York: Guilford.

Bus, A.G., Belsky, J., van IJzendoorn, M.H., & Crnik, K. (1997). Attachment and bookreading patterns: A study of mothers, fathers, and their toddlers. *Early Childhood Research Quarterly, 12*(1), 81–98.

Bus, A.G., & van IJzendoorn, M.H. (1997). Affective dimension of mother-infant picture-book reading. *Journal of School Psychology, 35*(1), 47–60.

Bus, A.G., van IJzendoorn, M.H., & Pelligrini, A.D. (1995). Joint book reading makes for success in learning to read: A meta-analysis on intergenerational transmission of literacy. *Review of Educational Research, 65*(1), 1–21.

DeBaryshe, B.D. (1993). Joint picture-book reading correlates of early oral language skill. *Journal of Child Language, 20*(2), 455–461.

Neuman, S.B., & Gallagher, P. (1994). Joining together in literacy learning: Teenage mothers and children. *Reading Research Quarterly, 29*, 383–401.

Straub, S.B., & DeBruin-Parecki, A. (2002, May). *Read to Me: A unique high school program linking teenage mothers, their babies and books.* Paper presented at the 47th Annual Convention of the International Reading Association, San Francisco, CA.

Whitehurst, G.J., Falco, F.L., Lonigan, C.J., Fischel, J.E., DeBaryshe, B.D., Valdez-Menchaca, M.C., et al. (1988). Accelerating language development through picture-book reading. *Developmental Psychology, 24(5)*, 552–558.

Whitehurst, G. J., & Lonigan, C.J. (2001). Emergent literacy: Development from prereaders to readers. In S.B. Neuman & D.K. Dickinson (Eds.), *Handbook of early literacy research*, (pp. 11–29). New York: Guilford.

LITERATURE CITED

Goodall, J.S. (1968). *The adventures of Paddy Pork*. San Diego: Harcourt.

Gomi, T. (1977). *Finger*. Tokyo, Japan: Iwakaki Shoten.

Gomi, T. (1983). *Everyone poops*. La Jolla, CA: Kane/Miller.

Henkes, K. (1990). *Julius, the baby of the world*. New York: Greenwillow.

Lowery, L. (1995). *Twist with a burger*. Boston: Houghton Mifflin.

Martin, B., Jr., & Archambault, J. (1989). *Chicka chicka boom boom*. Ill. L. Ehlert. New York: Simon & Schuster.

Ormerod, J. (1984). *101 things to do with a baby*. New York: Lothrop, Lee & Shepard.

Schwartz, A. (1994). *A teeny tiny baby*. Danbury, CT: Orchard Books.

Wattenberg, J. (1989). *Mrs. Mustard's baby faces*. San Francisco: Chronicle.

CHAPTER 10

The United Kingdom's Boots
Books for Babies Project:
A Case Study

Mary Bailey

This chapter describes the United Kingdom's Boots Books for Babies project and presents the case study that forms the qualitative strand of the independent evaluation of the project (Bailey, Harrison, & Brooks, 2000). The project is the result of a collaboration among The Boots Company—a leading U.K. retail chemist (drugstore) chain—the Nottingham City Council, the Nottinghamshire County Council, and Nottinghamshire Health Visitors (public health nursing workers who visit the homes of community members). The project's stated aims are to deliver book packs to the parents or caregivers of babies to increase the adults' awareness of the importance of sharing books with babies and to increase both the registration of babies with local libraries and the use of the library service. The packs are delivered to babies when they attend hearing checks at their local health centers, usually around 9 months old. This chapter sets the Boots Books for Babies project in the contexts of both general family literacy research and initiatives and the increasing prevalence of books for babies projects in the United Kingdom. The chapter describes the distinctive features of this particular project and interprets interviews with key participants in the case study area, situated in Nottingham.

Books for Babies Projects and Family Literacy

Much research has shown how families provide rich and varied contexts for children's literacy development, and some of these contexts are more strongly embedded in the cultures of print and books that are congruent with school curricula (Auerbach, 1989; Hannon, 1995; Heath, 1983; Morrow, 1995; Neuman & Celano, 2001; Taylor & Dorsey-Gaines, 1988). Such work helps literacy researchers counter the "discourse of family inadequacy" (Auerbach, 1995, p. 22) within which many large-scale literacy initiatives have been promoted at a political level in the United States (Auerbach, 1995), the United Kingdom (Bentley, Cook, & Harrison, 1995), and Australia (Cairney & Munsie, 1992). Clearly, certain kinds of literacy experiences in the home—shared reading, read-alouds, and the availability of books and other print materials—have a significant effect on children's literacy learning and provide an educational advantage to children (see Morrow, 1995). Providing books for babies has emerged as the most widespread early literacy initiative strategy in the United Kingdom, a strategy that, we would argue, need not imply a deficit model. Indeed, most of these projects are targeted at the general population within a fairly large area, rather than solely at socioeconomically disadvantaged groups. Here exists an interesting contrast to the United States, where books for babies projects are rare. In Morrow, Traccy, and Maxwell's (1995) survey of family literacy programs in the United States, only one such project is listed—the Gift Book Program in Pittsburgh, Pennsylvania— which is specifically directed toward low-income families. (See chapter 9 for another example of a books for babies program.)

At the start of the evaluation that we report on later in this chapter, the National Literacy Trust database (National Literacy Trust, 1999) lists 42 literacy initiatives in the United Kingdom that specifically mention babies. Nearly all these initiatives acknowledge a debt to the Birmingham Bookstart project (Wade & Moore, 1993), which provides books for babies. By 1997, at least 26 further local books for babies projects had been initiated in the United Kingdom, and in 1999, Sainsburys plc (a major supermarket chain) became a national books for babies sponsor, and participation became widespread. In most projects, as in Bookstart, a book pack—typically containing at least one book, booklists, and information about the project and libraries—is distributed by health visitors to each child who attends the local health clinic for his or her hearing test at age 7 to 9 months. About half the programs provide a library membership card, usually for the child. In almost all schemes, the interventions have been, first, the provision of the pack, and second, the mediation or support for using the pack provided to parents by various professionals, usually health visitors.

Research conducted into Bookstart (Wade & Moore, 1993, 1996a, 1996b, 1998a, 1998b) shows that early contact with books is associated with a substantial increase in parents' and children's awareness of books, the sharing of books between parents and children, parent enrollment of babies in libraries, and the joining of book clubs and family use of books. At primary school age, Birmingham Bookstart children performed better than their peers in the baseline (school entry) attainment data. Wade and Moore (1998b) have been able to trace 41 Bookstart children to school entry at around 5 years old and compare their assessment data with a group of children matched for age, gender, home language, ethnic group, and nursery experience. They have found that Bookstart children scored significantly higher than the comparison group in reading, numbers, English total, mathematics total, and the baseline total, but not in speaking and listening, writing, using and applying mathematics, and shape, space, and measurement. The pattern of results indicates that these differences in scores are due to specific highly significant differences in reading and number abilities (Bailey, Harrison, & Brooks, 2002). Wade and Moore (1998b) argue that the interesting, and unexpected, difference in scores may be because many early reading books introduce numbers and counting. Health visitors and librarians involved in Bookstart also praise the scheme (National Centre for Research in Children's Literature, 2001). (See Bailey, Harrison, & Brooks [2002] for a fuller discussion of the research on Bookstart.)

Clearly, the early impact of books for babies packs depends on the packs being simple (although not necessarily cheap) to put together and on effective delivery. Wade and Moore (1998a) write that

> partnership arrangements, particularly with health visitors, were viewed as essential by all projects [meaning all 27 projects that responded to their 1997 appeal for information].... Nursery nurses shared the general view that it was extremely important to explain the contents of the Bookstart pack to ensure parents were given the required message.... Project staff argued that the essential components of the pack need to be carefully selected and purchased. (p. 33)

In a review of research on books for babies projects in the United Kingdom, presented in the Boots Books for Babies evaluation report, my colleagues and I propose that the evidence suggests the following sequence of events, which forms the rationale for books for babies projects:

> Parents who are enthused by the pack into immediate increases in literacy-related behaviour seem to continue to enhance the sharing of books with their children. This apparently increases the children's interest in books, and all this in turn may well mean that they enter school better prepared in reading and number[s] than their peers who have not had the benefit of these early experiences. (Bailey et al., 2000, p. 10)

The Boots Books for Babies Project

The Boots Company, which originated in Nottingham in the mid-nineteenth century, is the United Kingdom's leading commercial provider of healthcare products and services. The chain stores sell many products aimed at the parents of babies and young children, including prenatal healthcare products, baby and child healthcare products, store-brand baby and child clothing, toys (mostly store-brand, educational toys), and picture books. The company includes Boots Healthcare International, a global pharmaceuticals company, concentrating on over-the-counter medicines. Annually, Boots invests approximately £6 million (equivalent to about US$9.5 million) in community projects in the United Kingdom, focusing on health and education. The company is a major employer in Nottingham, and much of this community investment takes place in and around the city. Boots Books for Babies is one such project.

All four previously mentioned partners in this project are represented on the Boots Books for Babies advisory group, along with representatives of the education department, colleges, other books for babies projects, the Early Years Unit, and social services. The project employs a part-time coordinator. The Boots Company initially provided more than £150,000 (approximately US$240,000) sponsorship for a three-year pilot rolling program, with special packs being delivered in each area of the city and county each year. The packs are distributed in a canvas book bag printed with the Boots Books for Babies logo. Packs included two board books, two laminated cards with advice on literacy development and library use on one side and nursery rhymes on the other, and a poster and information about local library and community services. Dual language books and rhyme cards are available. Typically, the health visitor, or healthcare assistant, gives the parent the pack at the end of the hearing test administered at age 9 months. The health visitor generally provides the gift of a pack along with a brief explanation of the pack's contents and the importance of books and reading for young babies. Pack distributions started in the first city and county health center areas in October 1998, and the initial plan was that the pilot would end in the final designated areas in December 2001.

Distinctive features of the Boots Books for Babies pilot project are the launch party held in the main local library each time the project rolls out to a new area and the range of further support activities provided. These activities included brief presentations from Boots Company staff, a representative of the library service or of Boots Books for Babies, and a guest, such as a local politician. Refreshments were provided for parents and caregivers, and there was usually some form of entertainment for babies, such as a puppet show or nursery rhyme singing, before the official launch of the project, at which time a cake was cut and distributed.

Other support activities for participants in the project included

- representation at local events
- talks to mother and baby groups
- follow-up coffee mornings
- distribution of materials to child caregivers
- special events for target groups
- partnership with preschool gymnastics sessions
- supplying toys for use in libraries

The Boots Books for Babies Evaluation Strategy

The Boots Company wrote to education departments in several universities in the East Midlands region inviting them to submit a bid for the £6,000 (US$9,500) evaluation project. The University of Nottingham

Centre for Literacy Studies' bid, in which my colleagues and I proposed an evaluation strategy that combined quantitative and qualitative methods, was successful.

The evaluation team shares the view of the Boots Books for Babies project steering group that the benefit of sharing books with babies from an early age is uncontestable, and the evaluation, therefore, concentrates on the project delivery and impact. The goals of the evaluation were to

- identify and recognize the achievements of the Boots Books for Babies project and to report on the range of activities undertaken as part of the project;

- evaluate the project's impact on parents, especially in relation to their book usage and confidence in relation to literacy issues;

- monitor library-related activity, especially membership and borrowing; and

- make recommendations for further improving the effectiveness of the project's activity.

Two fundamental beliefs underpin the methodology used in the evaluation. The first is that the evaluation should be *responsive* in the ways described by Stake (1979) and developed in relation to reading assessment by the University of Nottingham team (Harrison, Bailey, & Dewar, 1998). That is, it should make use of a variety of methodologies, as negotiated with key participants and end users. The second is that the evaluation should aim to work from the principle that parents are not problems in literacy development but most crucial resources, and that, as Hannon (1995) argues, the vast majority of parents are very keen to provide worthwhile and fulfilling support for their children's literacy development. All the proposed activities were discussed in advance with appropriate personnel and end users of the Boots Books for Babies evaluation in accordance with the principles of responsive evaluation. The evaluation contains both a qualitative, case-study strand, and a quantitative strand.

The qualitative strand, which is the focus of this chapter, involves semistructured interviews with librarians, health visitors, and parents and was carried out within a single target community corresponding to the area served by a particular health center. The quantitative strand of the evaluation analyzes county library service statistical data on baby library registration and baby book loans in 28 libraries. The Boots Books for Babies project had rolled out to 21 of these libraries by the end of our evaluation, enabling us to make some important comparisons based on baby registrations during 1998 and 1999. I summarize the results of these analyses in the conclusions of this chapter, but my colleagues and I report in detail elsewhere (Bailey et al., 2002).

My colleagues and I decided at the start of the evaluation, and following conversations with the project's sponsors, to focus on one health center area as a case study, interviewing health visitor teams, library staff, and parents in this area. Several criteria were relevant to choosing the area. First, the area had to be several months into the project. My colleagues and I also wanted an area where a sufficiently large number of babies had received packs. After consultation with several people and approval by the advisory group, Sneinton was chosen as the target area.

In March 1999, Boots Books for Babies was launched in Sneinton, an area on the edge of the city of Nottingham in which families attending the health center included some from neighboring suburban areas. We thought that it would be worthwhile to look at the impact of the project in an area that included families from a range of income levels and ethnic backgrounds; however, the majority of families in Sneinton itself are in low-income households, and the area has been identified by the city council as a priority for economic and social regeneration. Approximately 20% of Sneinton residents are from minority ethnic groups, compared to about 11% in the city of Nottingham as a whole and approximately 6.5% nationally (Nottingham City Council, 2001).

At this stage, the evaluation team and steering group decided that I would be the member of the team to conduct interviews with key participants. My own children were 1 and 3 years old at the time, and the team members thought that my having young children would be helpful when I talked to parents who had received Boots Books for Babies packs.

Health Visitors and Health Center Staff

I carried out interviews with two health visitors, a healthcare assistant, and a nursery nurse in the health center in Sneinton.

Despite the fact that delivery of the packs involved extra work and an extra 10 minutes or so in the hearing test appointment, as other books for babies evaluations have reported, members of the healthcare team have not found this additional effort burdensome. This fact in itself indicates a positive attitude to the project because, clearly, the extra work is seen as worthwhile and compatible with the health visitor role.

The usual practice in this health center is that the person assisting the health visitor with the hearing test, generally the nursery nurse or one of the healthcare assistants, one of whom is bilingual (Panjabi and Urdu speaking), gives the pack to the parent and explains what it is. The healthcare worker performs this action while the parent is dressing the child after weighing. The nursery nurse explained,

> My patter is "We've got this lovely pack of books here and all we ask is that you take a library card and maybe use the library," and no one says no. Then you tell them everything like "It doesn't matter if they chew the book."... It's promoted as a good bedtime routine: bottle, book, bed; milk, bath, book, bed. The routine of reading a book in a dim room, it's something I've done with the postnatal group, so it fits in very well.

In this part of the city of Nottingham, the role of the bilingual healthcare assistant is clearly crucial in delivering packs to parents who are not confident English speakers. One health visitor noted,

> Non-English-speaking parents are made aware of the importance of books.... The bilingual health care assistant has an important role in giving out the packs. She explains the content of the packs after the hearing test. She says that without a doubt it's very much appreciated.

All health center staff reported a positive response to the packs, noting that no parents or caregivers refused the packs or the library registration. The most commonly reported comment was that parents said they did not know that such young babies could join the library.

All members of the health center team considered the project successful and were pleased to support it. They saw their roles in delivering the project as important and also saw the project as complementary to their roles in supporting children's health and overall development. The health visitors commented,

> I think it has been successful. It has clearly, in my mind, brought parents' attention to the fact that this can be an issue at this stage—that it's nice to have books around. The fact that health workers are bringing it up as an issue—we're saying that this is a good idea. It's positive, and we're not expecting them to do anything other than look at a simple book with their baby and point at pictures.

> I do consider the project to have been very successful. It reiterates advice that we give anyway. It's concrete—"Here's the book"—and we say to them that children who do read books early have an excellent start.

The delivery of the packs at the end of the hearing test enables health professionals to reinforce and develop their good practice in encouraging children's general development and literacy. A slightly different message is also clear—that reading and books are additional forms of stimulation (or possibly even a behavior-management strategy) for parents and caregivers to use with babies. As one health visitor said,

> I think it's made me more aware of it as an issue, to be honest, and more likely, I suppose to, say, sit down and talk to a young baby about books. I can think of maybe a couple of occasions in the past when we've talked to parents about reading a book. I will now confidently say to a parent of a 1-year-old to sit down with their child and look at a book, instead of, for example, put them on the changing mat and show them a mobile. It adds to the repertoire of what you can do with your baby.

Some evidence exists that the packs serve as a reminder and ensure that health visitors and their supporting staff more consistently promote literacy. One health visitor commented that it was simply nice to be giving such a positive message:

> It's very nice to be doing something that isn't just browbeating parents—don't smoke, don't do this or that—something positive.

All those interviewed emphatically recommended that the project be continued, with one health visitor expressing concern over whether subsequent children in families who had received a pack would also get one. Other recommendations follow:

> There could be some guidance notes on what to do, even though your baby can't read or speak. Possibly the designs of the "tips" could be improved. —Health visitor

> There could be more dual language books—Panjabi and Urdu—and more in translation.... Perhaps it could be expanded to include the 18-month or 3-year child health surveillance review, when other age-specific books could be introduced. —Health visitor

The Boots Company is only mentioned once as a promoter by those interviewed about the project, but this was in an entirely positive way:

> It's nice that Boots is a local firm. It reinforces partnership. Boots has always been good to the people of Sneinton. —Health visitor

LIBRARIES AND LIBRARY STAFF

I conducted interviews with four key members of library services staff in the target community: the community librarian, the children's librarian for the area including the target area, the library assistant in the launch library, and a library assistant in a smaller, local library that had not hosted a launch party.

The role of library service staff in delivery of the Boots Books for Babies project is in processing library registration forms that are passed on from the health center via the project coordinator who decides which library is the closest one for each baby's family. (This contrasts with several other books for babies projects in which library staff are expected to make up the packs.) The library assistant in the library in which the launch party was held does not see this ongoing administrative task as burdensome; however, in the smaller, local library, the library assistant commented negatively about the time spent on this task, "I must have done 30 or 40 forms. It's an awful lot of effort if we're not seeing people come in."

The main project activity was a launch party in the central library in the target area. This launch played an important role in attracting parents to that particular library. The children's librarian noted,

> I just think that the launch is very different—the hot drinks, cakes, rusks. It's tied in with a big push for literacy. The freebies, of course, are a huge draw, but it's mostly because of community involvement.... At the launch, we had people coming from the housing queue. [The housing office shares the same entrance.]

Some evidence exists that there is a greater sense of ownership in launch libraries than in other, smaller libraries, and that additional events in the latter would be beneficial.

The interviews with library services staff also provide evidence of the success of Boots Books for Babies in attracting more parents and caregivers and babies to libraries. In the library in which the launch took place, there were reports of more babies being brought to the library and higher levels of borrowing of baby books. The Boots Books for Babies project also provides displays and toys for the libraries, which prompts further interest from parents and caregivers visiting the library.

> Absolutely [the project has had an effect]. Generally in the area there has been a rise in under twos joining: about 6% in Sneinton and about 65% in Bulwell [another area of the city]. Membership and issues are going up…. Kinder boxes and displays are almost empty here. We have had to spend a greater proportion of money on board books.... We are seeing so many more mums and babies coming through the doors and borrowing books, and our observations are supported by the figures. People have been saying, "I didn't think you could join at such a young age."
> —Children's librarian

The children's librarian and community librarian, both of whom work over a wider area than just the target area, have been able to report that similar effects can be seen in other areas where Boots Books for Babies has been launched. Library staff are also very aware of other local factors (such as summer vacation events for children run in the case study launch library) and national publicity for literacy initiatives being introduced in schools that may have led to the increased library use. They are, therefore, cautious in interpreting the changes they have observed. The community librarian observed, "But I do think that the link with the health visitor is important—someone mothers are seeing early who is saying, 'library.'"

All those interviewed regarded the project as highly successful, despite their caution in interpreting their impressions. Comments on the success of the project were generally integrated with discussion of the evidence of increased library use or of the positive impact on supporting good practice. Again, the librarians saw the link between health visitors and the library as a particularly important success of the project:

> The health visitors have been absolutely brilliant and have grasped it straight away—just what we've wanted—giving parents access to books. The example of the lady living in a women's refuge coming shows the benefits of talking between the library service and health visitors.

As with health visitors, library services staff see the Boots Books for Babies project as reinforcing and developing good practices. It supports strategies already being used or planned, such as reminding staff to put out toy collections, and it also provides a basis or catalyst for further development, such as, the reinstatement of storytime for children under 5 years of age. Library colleagues are aware that Boots Books for Babies introduces to the library some parents, caregivers, and babies who might not have come otherwise, but it is up to library staff both to meet this demand and to encourage participants to stay and visit again:

> We are getting more Asian [Indian and Pakistani British] women into the library. A lady from the Asian Ladies Group was at the launch and was interested in a special event for Asian mums—it's yet to happen, though. —Children's librarian

> We have moved the parenting books into the children's library, which was [the community librarian's] idea.... The room is very attractive.... It's getting to the stage now that we might be starting up storytimes again for under-fives.... My role is making sure that people stay—making it a good place to be is really important, getting attitudes right. —Library assistant at the launch library

Library services staff all strongly recommended that the project be continued and hoped that further funding would be forthcoming for the project. The community librarian said,

> I hate the idea of this cohort getting books and it coming to an end. Just getting this particular group of parents valuing the library isn't enough.

Ending it will almost be counterproductive if people have already heard about it. I really would like to see it continue. We'll just about be getting a buzz going, and it will stop.

There were also specific recommendations for following up on the project's launch:

Trying to follow up on ones that we haven't snared, if you like. People who have registered but who haven't used us—check the figures after three, six, nine months. Send personal invitations to events?... But maybe a free book if you keep coming.... But you don't want them to think through their teenage years that you come to the library and get something. —Library assistant at the launch library

Library staff were very positive about the Boots Company's sponsorship of the project:

Because we've got Boots backing now, it's made us. . .because people might not have approached us before...we've suddenly become more attractive. I think it's to do with their image—quality and child care. —Children's librarian

I like the idea of giving books. I like the idea of it being as important as milk powder—like it is being seen as part of health. I like the link with Boots. Boots is seen as the provider of everything for babies. Boots implies [reading] is seen as important as physical nourishment. —Community librarian

PARENTS

I conducted nine interviews with parents—four in person and five over the telephone—and this proved to be the most difficult part of the evaluation to conduct. (All those who were interviewed were parents, rather than other caregivers, so this term is used when discussing specific individuals.) After preliminary discussion with the community health representative on the advisory group and the health visitor team coordinator at the target area health clinic, the evaluation team initially decided that I should invite parents and caregivers to visit the health center for interviews.

I drew a random sample of 30 babies from the Boots Books for Babies database, which contained 126 records for the target area at the time of sampling in November 1999. This sample was then checked by the health visitor team, and six families were eliminated from the sample because of sensitivities around their current circumstances. I then had a list of 24 babies whose families the three health visitors in the target area considered it appropriate for us to contact for evaluation. I offered a suggested appointment time, as well as the option of a different time or a home visit, to the parents of these babies. Parents could, of course, opt not to be involved in the evaluation. I received a total of six responses. Four parents agreed to be interviewed, with two of these requesting home visits, a third parent requesting a workplace visit, and a fourth parent agreeing to be interviewed at the health center. Four face-to-face interviews took place, each lasting between 30 and 45 minutes; three interviews were with mothers and a fourth was with the mother and father together at their home, after work.

Fortunately, from the small number of parents who had provided telephone numbers as part of the Boots Books for Babies registration process, I was able to conduct telephone interviews with five other parents—four mothers and one father—in order to provide additional evidence. The telephone interviews did have the advantage of making contact with two of the parents from the original sample of 24 and 3 other parents from outside this group, all of whom had not responded to letters and at least 2 mothers who, from their circumstances, would have been unlikely to have attended a face-to-face interview.

Thus, a total of nine interviews were conducted with parents (see Table 10.1), which we consider a satisfactory sample from the total of 126 records of babies receiving packs in this area. In the following discussion of the interviews, quotations are identified by the names (pseudonyms) of the babies concerned.

The parents interviewed saw delivery of packs at the hearing test as very positive, and evidence exists that the pack was appreciated all the more for being given at the end of a test about which parents are slightly anxious.

> It's good to have the pack after the test, because there's a bit of anxiety about going. She was so good, and it was like a prize. And because it was the health visitor, it was more significant, better than the receptionist giving it to you or getting it through the post, because it's someone associated with their welfare. (Emma)

TABLE 10.1
Details of Parent Interviews

Baby's "name"	Age Year, Month	Interview Parent Telephone/ Face	Mother's Age/ Occupation (Current / Previous)	Father's Age/ Occupation	Siblings, Age (Year)	Library Previous to BBfB	Library Prompted by BBfB	Bought Books Prompted by BBfB
Katie	0,10	mother + father face	31/classroom asst	42/primary teacher	brother, 16	No	No	No
Megan	1,1	mother face	23/not working	33/technician	sister, 3	No	Yes	Yes
Georgia	1,1	mother telephone	29/former nursery nurse	32/civil engineer	brother, 4	No	Yes	No
Jack	1,2	mother telephone	34/nurse	45/police sergeant	none	Yes	No	Yes
Emma	1,3	mother face	39/part-time administrator	42/ware-houseman	brother, 7	No	No	No
Miriam	1,3	mother face	39/former administrator	?/physicist	brother, 11 sister, 6	Yes	No	No
Jessica	1,3	father telephone	26/not working	35/shop manager	none	No	Yes	No
Eleanor	1,4	mother telephone	29/primary teacher	?/engineer	sister, 2	Yes	No	No
Ricky	1,5	mother telephone	28/disabled	29/disabled	brother, 5 sisters, 8, 9	No	No	Yes

All nine parents appreciated the bag and its contents, particularly the two books. Several parents mentioned the quality of the books and, particularly, the appropriateness of flap books and "feely" books for their babies. The nursery rhyme cards, which also included advice on reading with babies and using the library, were generally appreciated, particularly for their chewable quality. Some parents commented that it was useful to have the information on library opening times and that the bag itself was also appreciated.

Only one of the parents I interviewed had attended the Boots Books for Babies launch party at the library, with both her children and her husband. She told me,

> We were a bit late, but they were really nice and made you all feel welcome. There was tea and biscuits and cake. It was like being at a mother and toddler group. I went with my husband. We got a pack for each of the girls and an extra book. (Megan)

All the other eight parents claimed that they were not aware that there had been a launch party, and in one case, the baby was born after the launch party. However, for the mother who did attend the launch party, the event was significant and much appreciated. It seems to have encouraged her to use the library, which she now does on a regular basis.

> It's prompted me to make the effort now and take the kids every month. They both take books out.... I kept meaning to join her sister before, but I didn't get round to it. The room is good, with a Wendy house [a play house] and things to do. I go to the library every month now. It's really encouraged me. (Megan)

One parent had met the Boots Books for Babies project coordinator through her local baby group and was very positive indeed about this aspect of the project:

> Jack used to go to a baby group, and the Boots Books for Babies lady came round and went through some nursery rhymes and tunes that go with them. It was brilliant for people like me who can't remember the rhymes. She gave Jack a plastic book that I can put in his nappy bag for going out. She was ever so good. Another time she came and brought a big book of Bear Hunt [*We're Going on a Bear Hunt* by Michael Rosen and Helen Oxenbury] and read that with us.... I do think [the program] should

be continued. I found it really useful having the pack, and the contact with the Boots representative was really great. (Jack)

The registration of babies as members of the library is built into the Boots Books for Babies project, so the aim of increased library registration is clearly met as a built-in success. However, the importance of meeting this goal should not be underestimated. The parent interviews provide strong evidence about how important automatic registration is in overcoming this perceived barrier to library use. Six of the nine parents reported that they used the library regularly with their babies, and three of these said that they definitely did this earlier than they would have if they had not received the Boots Books for Babies pack and the library registration card. It would be fair to reiterate at this point, however, that the sample of face-to-face interviewees at least, is probably biased toward parents who are more likely to use the library anyway: Three of the nine parents had registered their babies at the library before they received the packs.

Of the six parents who used the library with their babies, four said that other members of the family also used the library. Evidence exists that in two of the cases in which library use had been prompted by Boots Books for Babies, the project had encouraged parents to use the library for older siblings as well, although for one parent a combination of factors other than the project had influenced library usage. All three parents who did not use the library with their babies noted that other family members had used the local library at some time, although this was clearly not a regular pattern.

No evidence exists from the interviews that Boots Books for Babies had encouraged parents to join the library themselves. One parent, who had been prompted to use the library for her two daughters, made the following comment, which reveals that she was using the library for reference while she was there: "I haven't joined myself, or my husband. You need ID, and I always forget to put it in my bag. When I go with the kids, I browse through the parenting books while I'm there" (Megan). Some parents had received reassurance that they should not worry about babies damaging library books, whereas others worried about this and one specifically said she would not take her son, Ricky, until he grows out of ripping up books. Two parents who did not use the library with their babies mention the deterrent effect of the children's sections in their local libraries being located upstairs. One mentioned that the part-time opening hours at a small library were confusing. However, there are also positive comments about the welcoming features of children's sections, which they noticed once they had visited a library.

All the parents interviewed already had books for their babies in the home, including books bought for the baby concerned. Seven of the nine babies had older brothers and/or sisters and had books passed on to them, but in two of these cases, the parents noted that the Boots Books for Babies pack had prompted them to organize these books and make them more accessible to the babies.

> We went through all of [her older brother's] old books that were suitable for Emma and put them in the basket. She loves it. We get them out and look at the pictures and touch the feely bits. She goes and gets magazines and looks at the pictures.... I think the pack reminded me to start before I would have started, so it was a prompt. I certainly hadn't started to get her brother's books out yet, so it was a timely reminder. (Emma)

The books included in the packs had significance for the parents. The parents said that their babies liked *Twinkle, Twinkle, Little Star* (Taylor & Harker, 1999) and *Stroke Henry* (Campbell, 1995) in particular, as well as bath books (flexible, waterproof books). For two parents, the packs raised awareness of the types of books available and liked by babies, which affected their subsequent book buying. As one parent made clear,

> Until we got the pack with Dear Zoo [by Rod Campbell] in [it], I didn't realize [Jack would] like lift-the-flap books so early. He really liked them, so we went and bought him a load more. We daren't get him them from the library in case he damaged them. I think he reads the one he got in the pack virtually every day. We bought all the other Rod Campbell books we could find. The other book in the pack was *Mr. Bear Says Peekaboo* [by Debi Gliori]. It's just a flat board book. I think he'll like it when he's a bit older. (Jack)

Other comments about where parents buy books are interesting:

> Boots Books for Babies is really good because it encourages [parents] to buy books for their babies. I go to car-boots [similar to flea markets] and to charity shops and the discount bookstore in the shopping center. You can get all sorts of books, and they're fine. (Ricky)

We also have some evidence that the Boots Book for Babies pack encouraged parents to look at books with their babies. As Megan's mother explained,

> Her sister didn't start wanting books until she was about a year old. It's encouraged me to read earlier and to let Megan have them from an earlier age. It's made me realize how important it is and how it can improve their development. I read to her sister a story every night, and Megan joins in. It's encouraged me to get baby books for Megan. (Megan)

Sibling position is an interesting factor that may interact with the effect of the project, which would be worthy of further investigation (Taylor, 1983). Quite possibly, both firstborn and subsequent babies benefited from the project for different reasons.

All the parents interviewed support the Boots Books for Babies project and clearly think it is valuable for their babies, despite feeling, in several cases, that babies from other families might be more in need of the packs than theirs. They implied that, as much as they appreciated the project, it would be even more important for other parents. However, only one parent gave a specific example of another family that did not seem to encourage reading:

> I think Boots Books for Babies is really good. I know from going to mother and baby groups that people think it's good. I know one little girl, and they're the only two books she's got. All she gets is Barbies and other toys for presents. (Eleanor)

It appears, from the profile of those who did agree to the interviews, that those who feel confident discussing literacy matters are more likely to be motivated to participate. Four of the babies in the interview sample had at least one parent working in either the health or education field, which indicates that this group is not representative of the general local population (see Table 10.1 on page 216). However, as the evidence already presented indicates, the Boots Books for Babies project seems to have had a worthwhile impact, even if just in confirming parental practices and providing two more books for each baby concerned. In several cases, the effects were greater than this, in serving as a prompt or reminder to engage children in literacy-related activities, ranging from organizing books in the home to borrowing and buying more books. These findings are consistent with Millard, Taylor, and

Watson's (2000) results from the evaluation of the early stages of a similar books for babies initiative that was "clearly shown to influence parents' views on when it is appropriate to introduce babies to libraries and to increase their willingness to provide earlier book experiences both for existing and future children" (p. 133).

All the parents interviewed strongly recommended the continuation of the project. Two parents proposed that both books in the packs should be brighter ones for younger children, and one parent suggested including a list of recommended books titles, but it is very clear that these suggestions are not intended as criticisms.

As with the comments made by the one health visitor and the children's librarian already quoted, the parents' comments demonstrate that they see the Boots Company as a particularly good sponsor for local reasons and for the product associations, suggesting that Boots Books for Babies meets this aspect of the company's promotional objectives. Two parents are quoted in this evaluation, quite fully, and others of the parents interviewed expressed similar views.

> Boots is good because they're related to babies in every way because they do clothes, toys, and baby products. Boots is part of your life as soon as you have a baby. Boots do[es] a lot of toys for learning through play, so it's encouraging all that. I think it's a good idea. I was pleased to hear that they're helping out babies. Books are expensive, and it's nice to be given something. (Megan)

> They're not trying to push you to shop at Boots. It doesn't feel like a marketing ploy. I just think it's great that they do it, and it's good to see children's companies doing something for the community. (Emma)

Conclusion

In the view of the evaluators, the Boots Books for Babies project is very successful. The interview evidence indicates that health center staff, library service staff, and parents in the target area have very positive views of the project. Healthcare workers do not see the extra work involved as burdensome. They viewed the delivery of packs as complementary to their own aims in promoting child development and as a useful reminder to talk to parents and other caregivers about literacy. Library services staff all strongly recommended that the project be continued and hoped that further funding would be forthcoming for it.

Staff in a number of libraries noted a rise in infant book borrowing and had to buy additional books, particularly picture books and board books. Library staff claimed that the project was encouraging minority groups to use the library. Parents responded very positively to the packs, and they strongly supported the continuation of the project. Many of those interviewed also made constructive suggestions about ways in which the project could be improved further, and several of these, such as the introduction of more dual-language books and further follow-up events, have been implemented during the pilot project and in a continuation project. The evaluation team considers the flexibility of the project management to be a key factor in its ongoing success.

Project participants saw Boots as a particularly good sponsor for the project partly for local reasons. Although it is a major national company in the United Kingdom, Boots originated in Nottingham and the story of this has almost become part of local folklore. The company also has a good record for employment and community involvement in Nottingham. Boots additionally provides corporate image (quality) and product associations (healthcare, baby care, baby foods, and educational toys) that are viewed positively by many interviewees (see Bailey et al., 2000). This local sponsorship, albeit by a high-profile national company, is an important part of the wider partnership behind the project. Along with the local launch parties and other support events, which enhanced the effectiveness of the project for those families who did attend them, Boots sponsorship contributed to the feeling that the project was adapted to the special needs of the local community.

The links between health and library staff were perceived as very important by both of these professional groups and are clearly a significant factor in the project's success. As Millard and colleagues (2000) also found, these partnerships allow health and library professionals to develop their own awareness of literacy and the ways in which it can be supported in the community, prompting or reinforcing more explicit promotion of literacy in their professional practice. Although this development is beneficial, it is not neutral, and it is interesting to consider how the concept of literacy becomes associated with that of health because of the Boots sponsorship and the health visitors' involvement.

Furthermore, the health visitors' delivery of the packs gives the literacy message authority, with associations in the minds of some parents interviewed of test-passing and prizes, because of its incorporation into the script of advice to parents. However, this advice can also be offered with sensitivity to the increasingly evident acceptance that parents are the "senior partners" in family literacy, whereas professionals have relatively junior roles (Harrison, 1995).

The role of professionals in literacy initiatives presents an area of possible tension, given the extra work entailed for both health center teams and library staff, as well as the potential for implied criticism of existing practice. It is just as important not to have a deficit model of the professional participants in books for babies programs as it is not to have a deficit model of parental literacy practices. The interviews with health visitors and library staff made it clear that some individuals were keen to stress what they had been doing to support literacy prior to the project and to construct the project as prompting or reinforcing what they were doing anyway, rather than radically changing their behavior (in similar ways to that in which some parents described the impact of the project). However, there was no sense during the interviews that any of the professionals felt that they had been criticized in any way, which is testament to the sensitive management of partnerships by the project advisory group and coordinator. In fact, many respondents stressed the particularly important part that the project coordinator plays in the project's success, which the evaluation team also identifies as another significant factor.

Although this chapter has not reported the quantitative strand of the evaluation, the results of this strand support the case study conclusions. The statistical data also show that the goals of significantly increasing new baby registrations and loans to babies have been met (Bailey et al., 2002). In 21 libraries in which launch parties took place during the period of the project up to December 1999, baby library registrations increased 5%, and in some libraries there was a 400% increase in new baby registrations. In an unseen control group of seven other libraries that were matched on socioeconomic and demographic variables, baby registrations increased by only 6% over the same period, and in some of the seven nonproject libraries, baby registrations fell by 20 to 30% over the same period.

Clearly, this evaluation is very positive in its overall findings. Nevertheless, the evaluation team must admit that the scope of the evaluation has been constrained in a number of respects. The case-study data are limited, because they are based primarily on a single area, albeit a carefully chosen one, and the parents interviewed are not representative of the population in this area. In particular, it would be useful to have been able to make case-study comparisons between different areas and to look for possible differential effects of enthusiasm of health visitors or library staff for the project.

Finally, there is the issue of sustainability and long-term impact of the project. Do babies who begin to read early as a result of this project go on to become readers, and if they do, what can be said about the long-term gains? To answer these questions, a longitudinal study would be necessary, and these types of studies, as we observe in the review of the literature in our full report (Bailey et al., 2000), remain rare.

Following the success of the pilot program, Boots agreed to continue its £53,000 (approximately US$85,000) annual sponsorship for at least another four years, with Nottinghamshire County Council contributing £89,000 (approximately US$142,000) a year and the Nottingham City Council £40,000 (approximately US$64,000). This means that more than 12,000 babies a year across Nottinghamshire will continue to receive free books and nursery and action rhyme cards, and their parents will continue to receive advice on reading with children under age 5.

ACKNOWLEDGMENTS

The author wishes to thank the project coordinator, the parents who gave up time to be interviewed, the health and library staff who gave time to assist the evaluation team, and colleagues from the Boots Company who supported our efforts.

REFERENCES

Auerbach, E.R. (1989). Toward a socio-contextual approach to family literacy. *Harvard Educational Review, 59,* 165–181.

Auerbach, E.R. (1995). Which way for family literacy: Intervention or empowerment? In L.M. Morrow (Ed.), *Family literacy connections in schools and communities* (pp. 11–28). Newark, DE: International Reading Association.

Bailey, M., Harrison, C., & Brooks, G. (2000). *The Boots Books for Babies project evaluation.* Nottingham, UK: University of Nottingham School of Education.

Bailey, M., Harrison, C., & Brooks, G. (2002). The Boots Books for Babies project: Impact on library registrations and book loans. *Journal of Early Childhood Literacy, 2*(1), 45–63.

Bentley, A., Cook, M., & Harrison, C. (1995). Family literacy: Ownership, evaluation and accountability. In B. Raban-Bisby, G. Brooks, & S. Wolfendale (Eds.), *Developing language and literacy* (pp. 179–187). London: Trentham Books in collaboration with the United Kingdom Reading Association.

Cairney, T.H., & Munsie, L. (1992). *Beyond tokenism: Parents as partners in literacy.* Carlton, Victoria, Australia: Australian Reading Association.

Hannon, P. (1995). *Literacy, home and school: Research and practice in teaching literacy with parents.* London: Falmer.

Harrison, C. (1995). Family literacy practice in the United Kingdom—An international perspective. In L.M. Morrow (Ed.), *Family literacy connections in schools and communities* (pp. 223–235). Newark, DE: International Reading Association.

Harrison, C., Bailey, M., & Dewar, A. (1998). Responsive reading assessment. In C. Harrison & T. Salinger (Eds.), *Assessing reading: Theory and practice* (pp. 1–20). London: Routledge.

Heath, S.B. (1983) *Ways with words: Language, life and work in communities and classrooms.* Cambridge, UK: Cambridge University Press.

Millard, E., Taylor, C., & Watson, S. (2000). Books for babies means books for parents, too: The benefits of situating the earliest stages of literacy in the framework of the wider community. *Reading, 34*(3), 130–133.

Morrow, L.M. (1995). Family literacy: New perspectives, new practices. In L.M. Morrow (Ed.), *Family literacy connections in schools and communities* (pp. 5–10). Newark, DE: International Reading Association.

Morrow, L.M., Tracey, D.H., & Maxwell, C.M. (1995). *A survey of family literacy in the United States.* Newark, DE: International Reading Association.

National Centre for Research in Children's Literature at the University of Surrey–Roehampton. (2001). *Evaluation of the Bookstart programme.* London: Booktrust.

National Literacy Trust. (1999). National Literacy Trust Database and Information Service. Retrieved June 27, 1999 from http://www.literacytrust.org.uk

Neuman, S.B., & Celano, D. (2001). Access to print in low-income and middle-income communities. *Reading Research Quarterly, 36*, 8–26.

Nottingham City Council. (2001). *Poverty in Nottingham 2001.* Retrieved August 28, 2002 from http://www.nottinghamcity.gov.uk/coun/department/chief_execs/policy/povertypro file/foreword.htm

Stake, R. (1979). Program evaluation, particularly responsive evaluation. In W.B. Dockrell & D. Hamilton (Eds.), *Rethinking educational research* (pp. 72–87). London: Hodder & Stoughton.

Taylor, D. (Ed.). (1983). *Family literacy: Young children learning to read and write.* Portsmouth, NH: Heinemann.

Taylor, D., & Dorsey-Gaines, C. (1988). *Growing up literate: Learning from inner-city families.* Portsmouth, NH: Heinemann.

Wade, B., & Moore, M. (1993). *Bookstart.* London: Booktrust.

Wade, B., & Moore, M. (1996a). Home activities: The advent of literacy. *European Early Childhood Education Research Journal, 4*(2), 63–76.

Wade, B., & Moore, M. (1996b). Children's early book behaviour. *Educational Review, 48*, 283–288.

Wade, B., & Moore, M. (1998a). *Bookstart: The first five years. A description and evaluation of an exploratory British project to encourage sharing books with babies* (Bookstart report 2). London: Booktrust.

Wade, B., & Moore, M. (1998b). An early start with books: Literacy and mathematical evidence from a longitudinal study. *Educational Review, 50*(2), 135–145.

LITERATURE CITED

Campbell, R. (1995). *Stroke Henry*. London: Campbell.

Taylor, G., & Harker, J. (1999). *Twinkle, twinkle, little star*. London: Ladybird.

CHAPTER 11

Learning From Soweto: The Story of Two Family Learning Programs in South Africa and the United Kingdom

Letta Mashishi and Margaret Cook

This chapter tells the stories of two family literacy programs operating in very different contexts with distinct initial objectives and very disparate levels of funding, staffing, and resources. One program, the Parents and Schools Learning Clubs (PASLC), is situated in Soweto, South Africa, a city famous internationally for the role it played in the struggle for the country's freedom from apartheid. (The name of this program changed in 2001 to the Families Learning Together Trust [FLT], which reflects the widening of the program's clientele and strategies it employs. Throughout the chapter, the acronym PASLC/FLT is used to denote the whole program from its 1990 inception to the present and the individual acronyms are used to distinguish between particular stages of the program.) The other program, Families and Schools Together (FAST), is located in Merseyside, United Kingdom, one of the European Union's poorest regions, which was the temporary home in the 19th century to thousands of emigrants en route to the United States. What has brought these two programs together is a friendship that developed between Letta and Margaret during the visits we paid to each other's programs. Yet, as we shall see, our stories have much more in common than their contexts of urban deprivation and the friendship that has developed between us.

Historical Context

The occasion for our first meeting was a conference in South Africa at which Margaret spoke about family literacy—specifically the dangers of its reduction to a deficit model if families were seen as recipients of knowledge rather than equal participants in education—and its potential for success for African countries if it were based in an alternative "wealth" model of language and learning, giving due place to oral texts in the development of literacy (Cook 1999; see below for a brief discussion of these issues). Margaret had already read some of Letta's work, realized we had much in common, and briefly exchanged e-mail messages with her. Letta generously invited Margaret to stay with her while she was in South Africa. We talked for three days, and Margaret visited some of Letta's programs, immediately noticing the significance of what was being done and its likeness to the FAST program of which Margaret was then the project officer. This meeting was at a time when Letta's award-winning program, PASLC, was in danger of reduction—or possible closure—because, although parental enthusiasm was still high, the program's funding was unlikely to be renewed for a variety of unconnected reasons.

Margaret could do little about the funding situation (except to comment wryly to herself that lack of funding seems a worldwide phenomenon), but, fortunately, was able to bring Letta to the United Kingdom for a study visit with financial support from the Southern Africa British Council and the United Kingdom Reading Association (UKRA), of which Margaret was the incoming president. With this joint funding, Letta attended and spoke at the UKRA Annual International Conference in 2000. She was heard by a lecturer from Sheffield University, where much has been done over the years to further insightful approaches to family literacy, and the lecturer arranged a further conference, the proceeds from which were donated to Letta's program. Thanks to Sheffield University's initiative, Letta's program was not only saved but reestablished as a trust with a management board that now includes a number of eminent people, such as the wife of South Africa's chief judge. Meanwhile, through her several sponsored visits to the United Kingdom, Letta visited a range of family learning educators and several major family literacy initiatives, and she acquired a number of practical ideas (some of which she describes in this chapter) together with confirmation that her own program is soundly based in good family learning principles, sometimes more so than many Western programs.

Principles, Aims, and Objectives of the PASLC/FLT and FAST Programs

These principles, as we see them, are those of the wealth models of family literacy that Taylor (1997) and Auerbach (1997), among others, describe and that resonate strongly with Paolo Freire's work (1996). These models view literacy as empowering; they value and build on the literacies and literacy learning opportunities of home and neighborhood and acknowledge families as having the resources, skills, and opportunities necessary for teaching literacy. School literacy is seen as different from many home literacies and additional to them, and families and schools are recognized as equal partners in teaching shared curricula (Barton, 1994; Hannon, 1995; Mashishi, 1997). Typical of such programs' activities are the recognition and praising of literacy achievements in nonschool as well as school environments, interaction between children and adults in home literacy events, and parents' modeling of literacy activities typical of home and community settings (Hannon, 1995; Weinberger, 1996). Some programs, FAST among them, also are characterized by pedagogies appropriate to home learning and to some aspects of early childhood learning in school (Cook, 2002).

Conversely, deficit models, including some now current in the United Kingdom and the United States, are based on the perception that economically and educationally disadvantaged families need support in providing the early educational experiences schools believe to be necessary for children's success. In this scenario, families are recognized as having an essential role in relation to their children's school education that only some of them have the knowledge and resources to perform effectively. Typical of these programs is that, although families (or at least parents), achieve visibility in the educational enterprise, their contributions to it comprise implementing the school's intentions and promoting its culture within the home. The school, its language of instruction, and its curricula are seen as preeminent, with parents being taught the pedagogies and syllabuses that the schools think their children need for later achievement. Taylor (1997), Auerbach (1997), and others have rightly criticized these kinds of family literacy programs. Those programs (and they often seem to be the majority) principally targeted at families with young children also have been criticized more recently on the following grounds: (1) the way in which this early intervention can be construed as remediation for a culturally produced construct of early failure to thrive and (2) for providing a single focus solution to school failure that excludes, for example, the adolescent years, which may have potential equal to or greater than the younger ages for educational and cultural change (Luke & Luke, 2001). Operationally, early intervention programs also tend to involve only mothers as caregivers of young children, rather than all family members. (See chapter 5 for discussion of the role of fathers in family literacy.)

Both PASLC/FLT and FAST have mission statements and operational objectives that reflect their bases in a wealth model of family literacy and the distinct ways in which they seek to enact this model in their separate contexts. For example, PASLC/FLT aims "to promote literacy and learning in communities by involving family members in literacy development activities that utilise skills, values, knowledge(s) and attitudes that reside in families" (Families Learning Together, 2000, p. 2). (See chapter 6 for discussion of a program with the same goals.) The term *family members* refers not only to parents and their children residing in the same home but also other members of the extended family, such as grandparents, aunts, and uncles who may or may not be residing together with the participating family. Therefore, the ages of the participants at PASLC/FLT workshops range between 5 and 75 years. By involving this wide age range, the program ultimately aims "to develop learning communities that are able to contribute to the social, economic and political development of society" (p. 2). Program objectives include involving families in the effort to entrench reading, writing and learning as part and parcel of the culture in African homes; using resources that reside in the family in order to teach reading and writing to family members (including cultural knowledge); bridging the gap between the home and the school by working closely with teachers; and identifying parents who could be trained as volunteer parent educators.

A more detailed description of the program's activities that implement these objectives is provided later in the chapter.

FAST's policy includes an explicit commitment to the wealth model of family literacy, with clear statements that all homes already provide resources appropriate to literacy learning, that all education should be inclusive, that both children's and adults' new learning should start with their existing experiences, and that all participants—including program staff—should make opportunities for learning together. The program aims to develop a clearly identified family learning curriculum and pedagogy that is shared with all participants and underpins all the program's activities; to celebrate and support lifelong learning, especially in and through families; to involve all families as significant partners with schools in their children's education; to maximize educational opportunities and access to accredited learning for all family members through multigenerational learning; and to support underachieving communities, families, and schools. (See chapter 6 for another example of this type of program.)

The FAST program has three main operational strands with the implementation coordinated from a well-equipped resource center that also houses the program manager, four outreach workers, and administrative staff. The first strand supports the development of children's literacy at home and at school for children from birth to age 11 (with a concentration on those up to about age 7) through home visiting, the establishment of literacy-based play groups, loans of books and toys for home use from the resource center, the development of assessment and recording procedures appropriate to the program, and the provision of inservice training for teachers. The second strand involves the establishment of appropriate management structures for the center, the parents' rooms, and the service as a whole. These structures include parents and provide opportunities for parents' groups to plan activities for schools' parent rooms. The third strand consists of the development of parents' own education, often through activities shared with their children, such as bookmaking, but also through the completion of observations and analyses of their children's home literacy behaviors, workshops, and accredited courses. With help from an outreach worker from the center, the program also offers support to schools and other agencies wishing to set up short-term literacy- and numeracy-focused preschool play groups.

Orientations

Both PASLC/FLT and FAST were conceived in relation to local school provisions but in quite different ways. Letta's response to the problems of access and underachievement in black education in South Africa was to set up PASLC/FLT. Originating and remaining as a volunteer program with business and charitable funding, PASLC/FLT started as an individual initiative in the context of an overburdened and underfunded school system, which for a variety of reasons often was failing students. The program originally aimed to help families provide their children with essential study support in one-on-one situations and often in a home language different from the medium of instruction of the school, and this goal remains a main focus. Although the educational opportunities PASLC/FLT offers are often ones that schools do not or cannot provide, the main intention is not to alter school provision but to provide additional ways of accessing it. The program complements the local school system, rather than aiming to change or develop it. The support provided is informed from the start by substantial understanding of patterns of home and community learning, including multiliteracies, and how these patterns can be used as powerful resources in making meaning from a largely alien school curriculum. (See chapters 6 and 7 for discussion of working with families of students who may diverge from the mainstream.)

This valuing of local cultures and ways of knowing has the potential to be a powerful force in the reestablishment of local communities, disrupted and humiliated during the apartheid years, and can be an effective way of improving access to the school curriculum. In the PASLC/FLT example, the process of making aspects of the school curriculum accessible to children means that the whole family often works in a collaborative meaning-making exercise in which discussion and transliteration between and across languages is as important as the learning of the English-language study skills that are the ostensible object of the program. In this process, siblings, parents, and grandparents become the experts, and the culture of the home and its language is celebrated, while the school and its teachers remain, in this respect, undeveloped. In fact, the program's valuing of the languages of home, which are rarely the medium of instruction in the South African school system and have been impoverished as a result of the South African education system under the apartheid regime, offers the opportunity of a radical reconceptualization both of the relationship between communities and schools and of the traditional role of the teacher.

In contrast to the voluntary nature of PASLC/FLT, Margaret and a team of paid professionals designed the FAST program as part of a government-funded program of urban regeneration to "deliver" higher standards of literacy via parental partnerships with local schools in which positive outcomes (i.e., a large increase in levels of parental accreditation) were needed in order to receive funding over a five-year period. Although the FAST program itself is based on a positive view of families and their cultures, this viewpoint was not held initially by the government funders or their political culture. This group saw the development of home-school partnerships in terms of the designated outputs and as a means of raising standards of school literacy in the area by redressing inequalities of performance on school entry and the early years of schooling. This viewpoint clearly followed a deficit model of family literacy that took some ingenuity on the part of the FAST program managers to turn around. (See Bentley, Cook, & Harrison [1995] for a description of how this turnaround was accomplished.)

Because of their different originating contexts, purposes, and patterns of funding, PASLC/FLT and FAST have faced different challenges, as well as different patterns of external pressures and levels of resources. Knowledge of both school and home curricula and pedagogies, and of the means by which the latter can be foregrounded, has been highly significant for FAST in order to establish an equal relation between home and school. This method contrasts with the Soweto approach in which knowledge of the home culture has always been the dominant feature and which accepts that the school's culture will necessarily remain in its current condition. Concern about school failure had been identified by parents, not government, and parents took the first steps in setting up the initiative, rather than being the subjects of its activities. Likewise, peers, fathers, and grandparents are commonly involved. Parental motivation—often the reason why U.K. schools want to develop good parental partnerships—has not been at issue: most South African parents still see education as highly desirable and the reasons why they may not send their children to school usually involve a lack of resources, rather than a lack of motivation. In contrast, the FAST parents are often the products of several generations of families with histories of school failure, and they have become alienated from education at least in its most institutionalised forms. For them, successful motivation is a key factor in developing more positive attitudes toward learning.

FAST, therefore, although set up with official support and generously funded by South African standards, has faced challenges quite different from and potentially more difficult than PASLC/FLT's, and must overcome these challenges to achieve its aim of giving equal power to all program participants in the construction of a shared curriculum. Ensuring good relations between schools and parents will not be enough if schools have to change their culture as much as families are being asked to change theirs. Positive measures will need to be taken to ensure that the school's role stays secure but not dominant. These measures include strategies specifically designed to change the school's culture and knowledge base, make parents and teachers aware of the value of existing home cultures and resources, encourage schools to use home-based pedagogies and contexts, train teachers—often together with parents—in the use of home contexts and pedagogies, ensure that parental training is of the same quality and depth as that expected by school staff, and ensure that everyone's achievements are revealed and celebrated, including providing routes to accreditation for all adults.

A further, and perhaps even more insidious, danger (and one into which the FAST program partly fell, like so many others) is that of presuming that the development of literacy must have as a prime focus the sharing of someone else's written texts, thus flying in the face of many language educators' understandings—including the understandings of the FAST and PASLC/FLT program managers—about the dominance of oracy (i.e., speaking and listening) in homes and in early childhood learning (see Crystal, 1987, p. 248, for a description of oracy) and about the need to ensure that readers and writers have ownership of the texts with which they engage. However, FAST suc-

cessfully changed schools' cultures so they recognized parents as playing an essential part in their children's educations, and the program also
established an appropriate pedagogy based on play. The play texts produced by parents and children together signal an important shift away
from the written focus of most U.K. family literacy programs and, using the Opportunities, Recognition, Interaction, and Modeling (ORIM)
paradigm (Hannon, 1995), form the basis for engaging parents in close
observation and assessment of their children's self-initiated engagement
in activities with literacy potential. Nevertheless, the program's explicit
aims remain, as demanded by their funders, largely related to the development of conventional literacy. Great care also is taken that all incoming workers understand the service's philosophy and have the
personal skills to communicate it in everything they do.

In separately subscribing to a wealth view of literacy and how it
should be taught, PASLC/FLT and FAST, in different ways, have both
overturned the stereotypical role each might have had in relation to
schools by seeing families as powerful meaning makers and educators
with access to community resources from which a rich curriculum
capable of being shared between home and school might be formed
(Bentley, Cook, & Harrison, 1995).

The History of PASLC/FLT

The original PASLC program, established in 1990, followed a request by
parents of children who attended Nkholi primary school in Pimville,
Soweto, that Letta should assist them with strategies that they could use
to support and promote their children's learning at home. The gradual
erosion of the culture of teaching and learning in South African schools
since the early 1970s precipitated this request. The erosion occurred because the system of apartheid in education had been deliberately designed to train African children to become "hewers of wood and
drawers of water" (Christie & Collins, 1984, p. 161). By the 1990s, the
cultural erosion had assumed crisis proportions. In a lead article in
Johannesburg's *City Press* on September 3, 1995, the paper describes the
situation as a "national tragedy" exhorting readers to "(g)o to Soweto,
for instance, and witness this national tragedy playing itself out everyday [sic] in every classroom" (p. 16).

At the time of the parents' request, Letta was employed as a teacher-in-service trainer at the University of the Witwatersrand, Johannesburg. Because she had been responsible for training the teachers at Nkholi in language-across-the-curriculum methodologies and was also a parent at the school, both the teachers and the parents asked Letta to think of ways of responding to the parents' needs. She got involved in the area of parental involvement in education in this manner. The PASLC/FLT staff organized parents' workshops and, after a few months, received requests from other schools for similar parents' workshops. At the height of its operation, PASLC employed a full-time staff of two people, engaged six volunteer parent educators, worked in 30 schools, and, between 1994 and 1996, ran workshops once every two weeks for over 1,000 parents at 10 schools. In 1996, PASLC received the Presidential Award from Nelson Mandela in the category of Early Childhood Development in recognition of its contribution to reviving the culture of learning in South African schools. After 1996, the program had to be reduced somewhat through a decrease in funding but, with new funding, it has now been reestablished as the Families Learning Together (FLT) program. Staffing is not yet at pre–1996 levels, but the program's scope has nevertheless been extended, including work with crèche managers (day-care providers who are usually unqualified in early years day care or education) based mainly in garages, in people's backyards, and in informal settlements, promoting story-telling and story reading, extended work with libraries, and work with some school districts. Some new ways of working have been included, especially since Letta's visits to the United Kingdom, but the program's character, aims, and main priorities have not changed.

Developing PASLC/FLT's Theoretical Framework

When Letta attended the 42nd Annual Convention of the International Reading Association in 1994, she came into contact with Elsa Auerbach, Denny Taylor, and others who follow a family literacy approach to parental involvement in education, and she acquired their books and articles. In her discussions with colleagues and after reading some of their writings, Letta saw clear parallels between what they suggest and what she had been doing in Soweto. Letta also realized that their family literacy approaches to parental involvement would provide her with the theoretical framework on which to ground the PASLC/FLT work. These family literacy proponents refer to the necessity for educators to be sensitive to the needs and cultures of the communities in which they work (Auerbach, 1989; Taylor, 1993, Taylor & Dorsey-Gaines, 1988). Taylor further states that "parents and children, teachers and administrators can work together to reduce their failure-producing ways" (1993, p. 26).

THE PASLC/FLT CURRICULUM APPROACH

The PASLC/FLT curriculum has evolved over a period of more than 10 years, and because the curriculum design is based on collaborative action research in which the knowledge, experiences, and concerns of the parents are allowed to interface with the knowledge of PASLC/FLT parent educators, the curriculum has tended to integrate knowledge, skills, attitudes, and values that are reflective of the families, schools, and communities in which the original PASLC program operated.

PASLC/FLT PARENT WORKSHOPS

Parent workshops have always formed a major part of PASLC/FLT activities. Issues and activities covered in the workshops include

- story reading and writing
- monitoring school work and working collaboratively with volunteer teachers
- learning strategies such as time management, note-taking, and summary writing
- using family histories, family trees, and family praise poems to teach writing and research skills
- researching and writing down folk tales and having parents read these with children in the home
- researching the kinds of services provided at various community service points such as clinics, police stations, and fire stations
- using available resources such as junk mail, scraps of material, and cereal boxes to produce teaching and learning aids

- involving families in projects that will help them to develop do-it-yourself skills such as sewing, knitting, cooking, creative writing, creating art, and elementary bookmaking
- creating parents' awareness of possible career paths that can be pursued by family members and their children
- encouraging parents and children to use community libraries where these are available
- linking school knowledge and home activities

Program staff have discovered that parents generally have mistaken perceptions about the role of the library in the community. (See chapter 10 for a discussion of how another program uses the library in its community.) Letta surveyed 480 parents to find out what they thought the function of a library was. The majority of the parents said that only school-going high school students are allowed in libraries, that libraries are places where high school students go if they want places to study, and that children learn to read in school and nowhere else. Because of these findings, PASLC/FLT entered into a partnership with the Carletonville Library to help familiarize parents and their children with the workings of a library. The first activity was to take parents and children on a tour of the library, during which the children were given tasks that required them to do extra reading there. The activity resulted in a dramatic increase in the use of the Khutsong Library (a Carletonville Library branch that is closer to where the families live) by children and parents, an increase commented on by the chief librarian, Riëtte Myburgh:

> We had 427 [library] members in total for a community of 120,000. We joined 175 members (since PASLC/FLT began running workshops for parents), which brings us to 602 members in total. Daily use of library picked up by 60 kids per day. Issue of books improved by 750 books per month.

Besides increasing library usage, PASLC/FLT has made a conscious attempt to help parents and their children connect school knowledge with activities that take place at home. For example, parents and children discuss recipes and (a) guess measurements (What quantity do you need for your family?), (b) make estimations (About how many cups of maize meal do you think will be needed to cook porridge in the pot we use for cooking porridge at home?), (c) choose units of measurement (What instrument can we use to measure water, green leaves, or meat?), (d) learn to do conversions (reading in the library or in recipe books about conversions of temperatures from Fahrenheit to Celsius or weights from pounds to kilograms, (e) practice reading time, and (f) use the conventions of recording time. Also, once a year, parents and children go on an educational tour organized by PASLC/FLT. A trip to the National Zoological Gardens, for instance, entails the preparation of worksheets and activities based on animals in the zoo and the study of the map of the zoo so parents and children can preview its layout. Parents teach their children in the African languages they use at home (such as Sesotho, Setswana, Sepedi, IsiZulu, and IsiXhosa) the names of the animals that they know, particularly those that connect with their totems (an animal or natural object that symbolizes an important trait in which the family prides itself, such as bravery for those whose totem is a lion or beauty and elegance for those whose totem is a bird). Each child is encouraged by their parent to read more information on their favorite animal, make his or her own animal alphabet book, and read more extensively about his or her totem.

THE PASLC/FLT LANGUAGE FOR LEARNING

When the PASLC program started, the staff produced materials written in English This language choice resulted in minimal parent participation because most parents were not fluent in English. During the review sessions, parents complained that they were not able to use the program worksheets when they tried to work with their children at home. Program staff then decided that materials should be produced in English and in African languages such as those mentioned previously. This decision completely transformed the tone of the workshops. The parents who tended to be more knowledgeable about their own languages helped the program staff with the translations. Conversely, the program staff and volunteer parent educators, who mainly had urban backgrounds, discovered that they had to rely heavily on the parents when it came to understanding the cultural ways of the different African communities in South Africa. Some parents complained that they identified similar gaps in the cultural knowledge of their own children and requested that the program address this issue. In addition, parents requested that issues of immediate concern to them should also be addressed in the workshops. For example, some parents living in informal settlements expressed concern about poisons in the home because the children sometimes drank kerosene that was stored in drink bottles. Mainly through such activities, PASLC/FLT has been able to develop its mission statement, aims, and curriculum.

THE USE OF LOCAL GENRES AND TEXT FORMS: PRAISE POEMS, FAMILY TOTEMS, AND FAMILY TREES

The use of genres and text forms characteristic of participants' home languages and cultures form an important aspect of the program. The genres include family praise poems, family totems, and family trees, all of which develop the writing skills of family members. The projects on which these writing activities are based involve extensive collaboration and research that has involved not only members of the immediate family but also members of the extended family who were not residing in the same household.

Praise poetry is a form of African oral literature that is found in many communities on the African continent. Okpewho (1992) states that oral literature serves

> members of the society, whether individually or in relation to one another, making it possible for them to come to terms with the world in which they live. A much wider service provided by oral literature is to give the society—whether isolated groups within it or the citizenry as a whole—a collective sense of who they are and to help them define or comprehend the world at large in terms both familiar and positive to them. The justification for this kind of service is essentially that as society develops and becomes increasingly complex, a variety of interest groups invariably emerge, each united either by similar professional concerns or by the knowledge that its members derive from a common stock. To protect these interests, they often tend to develop and circulate pieces of oral information (whether in songs or in stories) that will help them feel a certain sense of security in the face of other contending groups within society. (p. 110)

Families usually perform praise poems at very important stages of a member's life, such as at a child's birth, a child's graduation from initiation school, during a marriage ceremony, at a burial, or when the family or relatives feel that someone has achieved something exceptional.

Family totems (usually animals or birds) and clan names are often built into the fabric of the praise poem. The power, ability, agility, and determination of the crocodile as it swims against the flow of the current are shown in the following lines of the praise poem of the Bakwena ba Makgwakgwa (a people for whom this creature is a totem).

Kwena ha e hlape e thulame	The crocodile never swims with the flow of the current
E hlapa e nyolosa madiba	It swims up against the drift of the current

The qualities manifested in individual praise poems are discussed at workshops, and after an example has been used, program staff encourage parents to read with their children and see which of these qualities they can find in their praise poems. See Figure 11.1 for another example of a praise poem that incorporates a totem.

The workshops also focus on the teaching points suggested by the praise poem of Vadau. The following examples show other possible teaching points to cover:

• map reading to locate the geographical area of the Balobedu in the Limpopo Province

---

Figure 11.1
Praise Poem of Vadau

Tau	Lion (A person whose totem is a lion)
Agee Molobedu moana	Greetings Molobedu (a Bapedi clan found in the
Tatja, Tatja, Laga mogale	Limpopo Province) whose totem is a lion. A
wa ga Mmalea	lion of the brave one of Mmalea.
Subela ga bo kgoši ya mosadi	Go yonder to the place ruled by a female, queen
Modjadji.	Modjadji.
Ke le molobedu ke ana tau	Being a molobedu, my totem is a lion
Ke setlogolo sa Khuvhe	I'm the grandchild of the old man Khuvhe
Mokgalabje wa bo Mushathama	a descendent of Mushathama.
Mushathama wa bo Ravele	Mushathama, a descendent of Ravele who
la peu o tswetsweng Venda	originates from Venda, a place known
la ga sekga morogo	for the harvesting of morogo (any green edible leaves)

- reading up further on the habitat of a lion, and its diet, for example, or conducting a debate on the caging of animals in zoos
  versus leaving them in the wild
- reading up on Queen Modjadji, who was reputed to have rain-
  making power
- discussing the value of eating green leaves versus eating meat
- drawing the animal that represents the family totem
- writing to a friend and telling him or her about the issues contained
  in the praise poem

Parents are also encouraged by program staff to research their lineage
and document it in any way they liked. For instance, parents can begin
their family tree with one of their children in relation to his or her other
siblings, followed by the parents themselves in relation to their siblings,
and ending with the parents' grandparents and great-grandparents, or
they can arrange their family trees in reverse order, beginning with their
great-grandparents and working their way down to their children. This
activity is used to teach hierarchical ordering and family relationships
and also can be used to teach the concept of a timeline.

THE USE OF LOCAL GENRES AND TEXT FORMS: ORAL STORY SACKS

Another workshop activity involves the making of story sacks, an idea
Letta had been introduced to by the FAST staff in the United Kingdom.
A story sack normally contains a children's storybook, a nonfiction book
thematically linked to the story, an audiotape, activities, and puppets
and other props that go with the story. However, the FAST and
PASLC/FLT's contexts are different in that PASLC/FLT does not have a
ready supply of children's reading books for use by parents because
these families come from homes that do not have books and because the
program operates in a multilingual context. These contextual differences
have resulted in a new dimension being added to story sacks. The
PASLC/FLT staff ask the parents to narrate folk tales that they know to
their children and get the children to write them down. If the parents
do not know any folk tales (some young urban parents born and bred
in Soweto do not know any), they are asked to do research and ask
older members of the family to narrate to them stories that they know.

One child, asked what this meant for her family, commented that her grandmother had been a very quiet person when she came to live in Soweto but that, by contributing to the story project, she had at last started to talk to her family and this "had bonded [them] together." Other parents created their own stories that were not necessarily folk tales. The stories were group edited and added to the reading material that parents read with their children, and the stories also formed the central written texts in completed story sacks for use with other families.

The parents and children next use the stories to make their own books. So far, PASLC/FLT has a collection of about 50 stories written and group edited by parents and their children. Figure 11.2 shows an

Figure 11.2
An Example of a Group-Edited Story

The Lady and the Bird

Once upon a time, there was a lady and a bird. One day, the lady went to the river to draw water. When she came back, she found bird droppings on her baby's head. She then ran out of her hut to find the bird. She saw the bird sitting on a tree. Under the tree, there were goats. When she tried to catch the bird, the goats bleated, "*Meeee! Meee!*"

The lady said, "You go '*Meeee! Meee!*' when I want to catch the bird that sprayed its droppings on my child's head!" The lady chased the goats.

The herdboys shouted, "Hey! Careful of those goats of ours!

The lady said to the herdboys, "You say, 'Those goats of ours, those goats of ours.' They bleated, '*Meeee! Meee!*' when I tried to catch the bird that had sprayed its droppings on my baby's head." The lady chased the herdboys.

Women shouted out, "Hey! Careful of those children of ours!"

The lady said to the women, "You say, 'Those children of ours, those children of ours.' The herdboys said, 'Those goats of ours, those goats of ours.' The goats bleated '*Meee!*' when I tried to catch the bird that sprayed its droppings on my baby's head." The lady gave chase to the women.

Men shouted, "Hey! Careful of those wives of ours!"

The lady said to the men, "You say, 'Those wives of ours, those wives of ours.' They said, 'Those children of ours, those children of ours.' The children said, 'Those goats of ours, those goats of ours.' The goats bleated '*Meee!*' when I tried to catch the bird that sprayed its droppings on my baby's head." The lady chased the men.

The king shouted, "Hey! Careful of those people of mine!"

The lady said, "You say, 'Those people of mine, those people of mine.' They said, 'Those wives of ours, those wives of ours.' They said, 'Those children of ours, those children of ours.' They said, 'Those goats of ours, those goats of ours.' They said '*Meee!*' when I tried to catch the bird that sprayed its droppings on my baby's head." The lady tried to chase the king.

When the king's men caught the lady, they all said, "She is not well."

example of such a story first written in Sesotho, one of the African languages used in Matatiele in the Eastern Cape, Soweto, and Lesotho.

While working on story sacks, the staff discovered that a few parents had been trained to make puppets and dolls. The parents volunteered to train other parents in these skills, often using scraps of material and trash that they previously would have ignored. In the process, the parents became fiercely proud of their own ingenuity and dismissive of those U.K. version of story sacks they had seen in which items and materials had been bought. This pride was in itself a celebration of their own creativity and resourcefulness in the face of often demoralizing life conditions. It also came to the staff's attention that some parents had not taught their children how to sew (particularly true with parents of boys). Sewing then became part of the skills that parents taught their children during the story–sacks–making process. Because story writing and sewing cannot (and should not) always be part of all workshops and because the program staff do not want the children to be limited to local reading materials only, program staff also make story sacks in the usual way with a published book providing a theme. A number of parents who have completed their story sacks use the sacks to promote their children's literacy. Program staff hope that when there are a sufficient number of story sacks, old and new parents will exchange story sacks.

In writing the stories, discussions in the PASLC/FLT workshops center around the South African orthography, grammaticality of sentences, punctuation, logical ordering, the ways the stories begin and end, the use of repetition in stories, and elements that make stories interesting. In a different session, the focus might shift to a discussion of the characters, their actions, and the values and attitudes that they reflect. Program staff encourage the children to consider how these values would play out in their own lives.

As well as learning about and adapting the idea of story sacks from FAST, the PASLC/FLT staff have been impressed by the way FAST values young children's early attempts at writing and encourages parents to engage their children in this kind of writing. Early writing activities have the same status in PASLC/FLT as storytelling and story reading.

Now program staff also have realized the importance of play and of providing toys for young children, so they have begun to use the FAST program's idea of creating a library of toys for parents to share with their preschool children. The toys include puppets, dolls, and kitchen utensils. Easily available materials, such as empty toilet paper rolls, are used to make the toys for children who are not yet able to read on their own. From the wide-ranging Read On, Write Away program in Derbyshire, U.K., which includes multiple strategies for involving parents and children in learning focused activities, the PASLC/FLT staff also learned the value of communal play activities, such as the use of parachutes to develop cooperative thinking and action. This activity has given rise to a joint research project between the two programs on the use of parachute games in the development of literacy.

Yet another idea that PASLC/FLT gained from Letta's visit to the FAST program is that of training a practicing teacher to be responsible for promoting family literacy to the parents of the children at the teacher's school. This effort has the benefit of ensuring that someone at the school both trains parents on what to do to help their children learn to read and write and helps make the school a friendly environment for parents. Other useful ideas have been the idea of accrediting parents who have had training in promoting family literacy at home—something PASLC/FLT also hopes to do in the near future—and recognizing the importance of networking with other family practitioners.

Major Recent Outcomes

A number of parents at the PASLC/FLT workshops have shared the view that they now communicate with others more and have a lot to talk about. For example, many parents have reported that whenever they attend family weddings, parties, or funerals, they ask their relatives to explain how they are related in order to extend their knowledge of their family trees. Working on family histories and family trees has promoted intergenerational communication, and writing folk tales has encouraged family storytelling.

Using stories families contribute themselves has reduced the pressure on families living in depressed conditions who do not have the money to purchase published books to read with their children. Parents and children have learned about the process of book production from the group editing, revising of first drafts, and simple bookmaking activities. A commissioning editor from one of South Africa's national book publishers was present when Letta presented a paper at a literacy conference hosted by the department of adult education at the University of Cape Town. The editor informed one of her colleagues about the parents' and children's stories Letta had discussed in her presentation. Her colleague then contacted Letta and asked that she send some of the stories for publishing consideration. Five of the stories will be published, and the proceeds from the sale of these stories will be shared between the program and the parents and children who contributed the stories. The editor also advised Letta to submit the rest of the stories to a small printer whose charges would not be excessive. Families Learning Together has arranged to have one trial run of such stories in African languages because there is a dearth of children's storybooks written in African languages in South Africa. Perhaps this publishing project could be a way to begin solving this problem.

Children in FLT also have developed their letter-writing skills by writing to children in the United Kingdom. This activity has not only helped them to develop a sense of audience when writing but also has broadened their minds about the experiences of children in other parts of the world.

Conclusion

When we (Margaret and Letta) visited each other's programs, we were both struck by the similarity of our approaches, particularly in our underlying assumptions that parents know a lot and can contribute to their children's educational development, that parents should be invited to engage in activities that use the skills that they already have, and that all participants should learn from one another, including the program leaders. Both programs are successful in achieving their aims, with exceptionally high parental participation and retention in both cases in spite of adverse circumstances. Both programs inspire a great deal of enthusiasm, and face-to-face sessions in both Merseyside and Soweto are characterized by much talk and laughter and a general sense of having fun. The FAST and PASLC/FLT programs both have incorporated the learning opportunities and resources of homes into their activities and have recognized the particular needs of young children. The programs also have responded to the special features of their own contexts—PASLC/FLT in its emphasis on local languages, use of a predominantly oral culture, and involvement of whole families, and FAST in its impact on schools' relationships with parents, its creation of a learning culture involving school staff and parents as equal participants, its moves toward the development of a pedagogy and curriculum transferable between home and school, and its widespread success in getting accreditation for parents and teachers.

Some significant differences between the programs remain, however. Although FAST has been successful in causing an impact on parents and schools, its involvement with libraries has not been successful, and it has not involved children's siblings, peers, or grandparents to any substantial degree. FAST may be unusual in the United Kingdom in having successfully rolled out the program to the so-called leafy suburbs, but it has done so in the context of what it knows most about— early childhood pedagogies, including play; the development of early reading and writing; and how to make parents enthusiastic about teaching their children, all of which are major concerns of United Kingdom early years educators. It also has moved both families and schools some way toward recognition of children's play as an important feature of home culture. However, the example of Soweto, with its whole-family involvement; its prime focus on the cultures, texts, and languages of home and community; its celebration of improvisation and resourcefulness; its persistence; and above all, its avoidance of the domination of the already written text, must make us all pause for thought. If we are committed to a positive model of family learning, are most of us starting in the right place? If family learning is going to draw from the richness of all its participants' cultures, we should surely be first recognizing that home literacies, unlike those of schools, have their roots in oral interchanges, family histories, and the traditional and improvised texts—including playful ones—that arise from families' use and exploration of these literacies. These issues are not matters solely for South African townships but for all of us committed to a wealth model of family literacy.

REFERENCES

Auerbach, E.T. (1989). Toward a social-contextual approach to family literacy. *Harvard Educational Review, 59,* 165–181.

Auerbach, E.T. (1997). Reading between the lines. In D. Taylor (Ed.), *Many families, many literacies* (pp. 71–81). Portsmouth, NH: Heinemann.

Barton, D. (1994). *Literacy: An introduction to the ecology of written language.* Oxford, UK: Blackwell.

Bentley, A., Cook, M., & Harrison, C. (1995). Family literacy: Ownership, evaluation and accountability. In G. Brooks & B. Raban-Bisby (Eds.), *Developing language and literacy* (pp. 179–188). Stoke-on-Trent, UK: Trentham for the United Kingdom Reading Association.

Christie, P., & Collins, C. (1984). Apartheid ideology and labour reproduction. In P. Kallaway (Ed.), *Apartheid and education: The education of black South Africans* (pp. 160–183). Johannesburg, South Africa: Ravan.

Our "education" is a national tragedy. (1995, September 3). *City Press,* p. 16.

Cook, M.A. (1999, August). *Family literacy: Issues in designing successful programmes.* Paper presented at the First Pan-African Reading for All Conference, Pretoria, South Africa.

Cook, M.A. (2002). Bringing the outside in: Using playful contexts to maximise young writers' capabilities. In S. Ellis & C. Mills (Eds.), *Connecting, creating: New ideas in teaching writing* (pp. 8–20). Royston, UK: United Kingdom Reading Association.

Crystal, D. (1987). *The Cambridge encyclopedia of language.* Cambridge, UK: Cambridge University Press.

Families Learning Together. (2000). *FLT Policy Document.* Unpublished manuscript.

Freire, P. (1996). *Pedagogy of the oppressed* (Rev. ed.). London: Penguin. (Original work published 1970)

Hannon, P. (1995). *Literacy, home and school: Research and practice in teaching literacy with parents.* London: Falmer.

Luke, A., & Luke, C. (2001). Adolescence lost/childhood regained: On early intervention and the emergence of the techno-subject. *Journal of Early Childhood Literacy, 1*(1), 91–120.

Mashishi, L.M. (1997). Soweto, South Africa: A parent involvement model. In D. Taylor (Ed.), *Many families, many literacies. An international declaration of principles* (pp. 109–111). Portsmouth, NH: Heinemann.

Okpewho, I. (1992). *African oral literature: Backgrounds, character and continuity.* Bloomington, IN: Indiana University Press.

Taylor, D. (1993). *From the child's point of view.* Portsmouth, NH: Heinemann.

Taylor, D. (Ed.). (1997). *Many families, many literacies: An international declaration of principles.* Portsmouth, NH: Heinemann.

Taylor, D., & Dorsey-Gaines, C. (1988). *Growing up literate: Learning from inner city families.* Portsmouth, NH: Heinemann.

Weinberger, J. (1996). *Literacy goes to school. The parents' role in young children's literacy learning.* London: Paul Chapman.

Evaluating Family Literacy Programs and Their Participants

CHAPTER 12

Assessment and Evaluation of (and for) Family Literacy Programs

Nancy D. Padak and Dianna Baycich

The Ravenna, Ohio, Even Start Family Literacy Program is in its eighth year of operation. Consequently, its coordinator, Odessa Pinkard, has a great deal of experience thinking about the evaluation of family literacy programs. Recently, we asked her what evaluation advice she would give a new family literacy program. She laughed, and then said,

> That's a big question! I remember being overwhelmed at the beginning, so I think I'd advise an initial focus on the "big picture." Beyond that, programs need to be clear about their goals and objectives so that they can be clear about what needs to be evaluated. Finding tools for evaluation can be challenging, and then there's the issue of developing a system for keeping track of what you have. We have found that working with an outside evaluator helps us understand what all our information means. This person needs to be someone who will work with the program, someone with whom we can communicate informally, effectively, and often. (personal communication, June 20, 2002)

Pinkard's comments serve to remind us about the complexity of assessment and evaluation of (and for) family literacy programs. This chapter focuses on this important and often problematic aspect of family literacy programming. First, we offer some general guidelines for evaluation and identify key issues related to evaluation design. The second section of the chapter centers on finding and using assessment and evaluation tools for the people involved in family literacy programs (parents and children), as well as for aspects of the program itself (e.g., collaboration). The third section of the chapter presents a model for using evaluation results for program improvement. To conclude the chapter, we identify and comment on several persistent concerns or issues related to family literacy program evaluation.

General Guidelines for Evaluation

Why evaluate? From a programmatic perspective, evaluation serves to identify successes or goals met and areas that might benefit from alteration—either fine tuning or complete overhaul. This type of evaluation, often called formative, is particularly useful early in a program's life. Except when external funding is received for implementing a complete family literacy program, such as Even Start in the United States, programs typically begin by offering one component, such as adult education or early childhood education, and then expand to address other components. (See chapter 8 for more about Even Start programs.) Inclusion of external family support services is often the last stage in program refinement (Knell & Geissler, 1992), and program expansion often necessitates collaboration with other agencies. Formative evaluation can identify changes in participants, programs, and collaborative relationships over time and can provide valuable information for program improvement in any or all these areas.

Many family literacy programs receive financial support from public or private entities, so another practical reason for evaluation is to ensure continued funding, which often depends on evidence of participants' progress. This sort of evaluation, often called summative, aims to inform funders about the effects of the program on participating families, and it thereby serves as a form of accountability.

A third reason to evaluate family literacy programs centers on the education profession. Other family literacy professionals have an interest in evaluation data so they can learn what works, under what circumstances, and with what types of families. Whether evaluation data are used to demonstrate the effectiveness among alternative approaches or to delineate models for replication, sharing evaluation information can advance knowledge in the field of family literacy and enable new programs to learn from others' experiences.

Finally, as a stance, evaluation or assessment *for* learning involves students in the process; its goal is to advance student learning, not just to check on it. Practitioners who assess for learning have clear instructional goals that program participants understand, know how to assess these goals in ways that accurately reflect achievement, use the assessment process to build participants' confidence in themselves as learners and to enhance their sense of responsibility for their own learning, translate assessment results into specific, descriptive (not evaluative or judgmental) feedback that participants can use to foster their own achievement, and adjust instruction based on assessment results. (See chapter 14 for an example of this type of assessment.) Stiggins (2002) says of this model, "In short the effect of assessment for learning, as it plays out in the classroom, is that students keep learning and remain confident that they can continue to learn at productive levels if they keep trying to learn" (p. 762).

Part of the challenge of evaluating family literacy programs should be apparent from the preceding discussion of possible goals for the evaluation. In addition, family literacy programs are complex enterprises that typically attempt to provide (a) educational opportunities for parents, from basic skills instruction to high school equivalency studies; (b) early literacy learning opportunities for children, from birth onward in the case of Even Start; and (c) opportunities for parents to learn why and how to support their children's language development and literacy learning. Some programs also feature a focus on employment or other social issues as well. Moreover, because family literacy programs should be designed to meet the needs of participating families within the contexts of their communities, their particular emphases may differ, even if at a broad level they attempt to achieve similar goals (e.g., goals established by Even Start legislation). To say the least, given these layers of complexity, the evaluation design requires careful thought and planning.

Assessment and evaluation approaches, therefore, may need to be tailored specifically to reflect the unique aspects of programs (Holt, as cited in Sapin & Padak, 1998). Although no single plan for evaluation is likely to meet the needs of all programs, several guidelines may assist in evaluation planning:

- Evaluation should be an ongoing, collaborative effort. Evaluation can be viewed as part of the comprehensive cycle of planning, implementing, and improving family literacy programs, rather than a single event that occurs annually or at a project's conclusion.
- Evaluation should focus on a program's goals and objectives. In essence, evaluation should attempt to determine the extent to

which goals are being met. In most cases, then, the evaluation will be more than a description of program activities. The evaluation will offer judgments about the impact of the activities. The perspectives of participating families are critical in this regard, and input from other agencies or groups may be beneficial as well.

- The evaluation model should be multidimensional, and evaluation results should be based on multiple indices. Unless restricted by funders' requirements, assessment data should probably include qualitative information (observations, interviews, analysis of performance samples) as well as quantitative information. Key differences between quantitative and qualitative approaches to evaluation research are summarized in Table 12.1. Those persons responsible for evaluation design might use this table to discuss and decide on a basic framework to guide evaluation.

TABLE 12.1
Quantitative and Qualitative Approaches to Evaluation Research

	Quantitative Research	Qualitative Research
Basis/Purpose	Probability and mathematical perspectives. To determine possibility that some measured change occurred by chance; to compare individuals to norm groups.	Anthropology and naturalistic perspectives. To understand something from the perspectives of those who participate in it.
Sources of Information	Standardized tests, scales	Informal tests, observations, interviews, documents
Quality Concerns	Validity (truthfulness) and reliability (consistency); adequacy of norming procedures; similarity of norm group	Skill of observer/ interviewer; length of observation; analysis procedures; use of multiple data sources
Results	Standard scores (percentiles, stanines); probability (odds of a chance occurrence)	Categories; frequencies and percentages
Usefulness	Summative evaluation; Reports to present or future funders	Formative evaluation; Summative evaluation; Reports to present or potential funders

Adapted from Sapin, C., & Padak, N. (1998). *Family Literacy Resource Notebook*. Kent, OH: Ohio Literacy Resource Center. Reprinted with permission.

The evaluation design itself should proceed logically from program goals, whether they are related to changes in participants or aspects of program delivery. The first step in designing an evaluation is to articulate the goals, and the next step involves making the goals concrete in terms of particular participants in particular programs. To make the goals concrete, evaluation planners might work with program personnel to describe people or program aspects that reflect goal attainment. For example, if improving parents' basic skills in reading were a goal, it would be necessary to decide what adults who had increased their reading abilities satisfactorily would know and be able to do. Likewise, programs aimed at helping parents support their preschool children's literacy learning would need to describe the attributes of families who had achieved this goal. In other words, the second stage of planning the evaluation design focuses on what behaviors, attitudes, and skills will count as evidence of goal attainment.

Having determined the program's goals—which are usually abstract statements of what the program hopes to accomplish—and its attributes—which are more concrete descriptions of people or programs that have achieved the goals—the next step in planning an evaluation is to determine the evidence that can be gathered to allow judgments about goal attainment. Will test results be enough to decide the amount of progress toward achievement of a particular goal, or might other indices be necessary? What kinds of information are already available within a program? What sorts of additional information might be needed? Program designers should ask these questions to match evidence available from assessment information to the goal being evaluated. Finally, evaluation planners must decide on logistics, such as who will be responsible for gathering evaluation and assessment information, when evaluations will occur, how to record results, and who the audience for the evaluation information will be.

Why evaluate? A carefully conceptualized evaluation can yield significant findings about family literacy programs. Evaluations can document the development of the program and the resulting changes in program participants. Some attention to the general issues described above can help family literacy professionals craft evaluation designs that will address both the formative and the summative needs of their programs.

Finding and Using Assessment and Evaluation Tools

A strong evaluation design facilitates the selection of assessment tools, which may be used to evaluate changes in program participants (adults, children, families), as well as to explore aspects of the program itself such as recruitment, retention, or collaboration. As mentioned above, program evaluators first should consider information already available within the program that may have use in the evaluation. For example, parents may keep lists of books they read to their children, or they may write about their children's literacy progress in journals. Evaluators can use this information to draw conclusions about parents' support of their children's literacy learning and understanding and appreciation of developmental progress. Taking advantage of this already-existing information is efficient; it also may yield a more natural and, therefore, valid (or truthful) look at programs than is possible with assessment tools such as tests.

In most cases, however, existing information will not provide enough data to evaluate the program thoroughly. Moreover, single assessments, whether standardized or informal, do not offer enough information to evaluate a family literacy program or even a single aspect of the program, such as adult reading achievement, effectively. Those responsible for family literacy program evaluation, then, will most likely need to select additional assessment tools. In this section, we offer some guidance for this process.

Family literacy programs frequently use standardized assessments to measure participants' progress. In fact, external funders may mandate the use of these standardized assessment methods. If these types of assessments are used at program entry and then periodically thereafter, results can document participant gains over time. Standardized assessments also can compare the achievements of participants in family literacy programs with participants in single focus programs, for example, by comparing adults in family literacy programs with adults in adult education programs or by comparing children in family literacy programs with children in early childhood education programs. A recent review of the research (Padak, Sapin, & Baycich, 2002) concludes that among the many standardized assessments available, the most often-used assessments for adults were the Test of Adult Basic

Education (TABE), the Comprehensive Adult Student Assessment System (CASAS), the Basic English Skills Test, and the General Educational Development (GED) Practice Test. The Arlington (Virginia) Education and Employment Program's (REEP) writing assessment for second language learners is a standardized performance-based assessment. Standardized tests most often used for children in large-scale studies of family literacy programs have included the Preschool Inventory and the Peabody Picture Vocabulary Test (PPVT). Publishers for all these tests are listed in Figure 12.1.

Alternative assessments abound as well. Samples of nearly 30 different assessment tools are provided in Chapter 11 of the *Family Literacy Resource Notebook (FLRN)* (Sapin & Padak, 1998). Samples collected from Ohio family literacy programs in 1997–1998 include (a) general program assessment tools, such as observation guides, checklists, written surveys, and interview questions; (b) suggestions for evaluating parents' reading, writing, and math achievements; (c) a variety of checklists and written surveys related to home-school communication and collaboration, use of community resources, such as museums and public libraries, and parents' perceptions of their children's literacy learning; and (d) a variety of assessments appropriate for gauging young children's developmental growth as literacy learners. These assessment tools can be downloaded and printed from the website (http://literacy.kent.edu/), used as is, or modified to meet particular program needs.

Figures 12.2 and 12.3 (see pages 258 and 259) provide samples of assessments available in *FLRN*. Figure 12.2 is a log, developed by evaluators for the Northwest (Ohio) Even Start program to document home visit activities. The home visitor and parent(s) complete this log together. Figure 12.3 is a survey used in Pinkard's Even Start program to document perceptions about the extent to which the Even Start program is achieving its mission. Adult participants, staff members, and members of Pinkard's advisory council all complete the survey so evaluators can examine the perceptions of a single group and compare perceptions among the groups.

Using alternative assessments in addition to standardized measures can give a better overall picture of participants' progress. Staff and adult family members can work together to tailor alternative assessments to outcomes that both groups consider important. Examples of alternative

Figure 12.1
Publisher Information for Standardized Tests

Basic English Skills Test
Center for Applied Linguistics
4646 40th Street NW
Washington, DC 20016-1859
Phone: 202-362-0700
Website: www.cal.org/BEST

Comprehensive Adult Student
    Assessment System (CASAS)
8910 Clairemont Mesa Boulevard.
San Diego, CA 92123
Phone: 800-255-1036
Website: www.casas.org

GED Practice Test
American Council on Education
1 DuPont Circle
Washington, DC 20036
Phone: 202-939-9300
Website: www.acenet.edu

Peabody Picture Vocabulary Test (PPVT)
American Guidance Service
4201 Woodland Road
Circle Pines, MN 55014-1796
Phone: 800-328-2560
Website: www.agsnet.com

Preschool Inventory
McGraw Hill
1221 Avenue of the Americas
New York, NY 10020
Phone: 212-512-2000
Website: www.mcgraw-hill.com

REEP Writing Assessment
Arlington Education and Employment
    Program (REEP)
2801 Clarendon Boulevard #218
Arlington, VA 22201
Phone: 703-228-4200
Website:
    www.arlington.k12.va.us/departments
    /adulted/REEP

Test of Adult Basic Education (TABE)
McGraw Hill
1221 Avenue of the Americas
New York, NY 10020
Phone: 212-512-2000
Website: www.mcgraw-hill.com

assessments are interviews to gather detailed information from participants, observations used to collect information about group interactions or literacy performance, and performance samples–examples of learners' work that are collected and saved (Holt & Van Duzer, 2000). Assessments can be kept in portfolios for adults, children, families, or both. In most cases, portfolio contents reflect program goals (i.e., parents' personal goals, parents' goals for children, and family goals). Evaluation of portfolio contents involves looking for evidence of progress toward meeting the goals. (See chapter 13 for additional information about portfolios.)

No limits exist as to how "alternative" an assessment can be. For example, participants and staff at a family literacy program in Chicago,

Figure 12.2
Home Visit Log

Family Visited _____ Parent's Signature _____

Date of Visit _____ Staff Member _____

Goal: _____

Materials: _____

Who was present in the home during the visit? (List names.)

Briefly recap what you did while at the home.

How was the interaction between parent and child(ren)?

Do you feel the visit went well? Please explain.

If this is a second visit (or more), did you observe any improved learning or parenting behaviors?

Home Visit Chart

1. How much time have you and [child] spent reading or looking at books in the past week?

   None   less than 1 hr.   1–2 hrs.   3–4 hrs.   more than 5 hrs.

2. What books have you read or looked at? [list]

3. What have you helped [child] learn?

   colors   reading   speaking   numbers   writing letters
   spelling   math   name, address, phone number   other (list)

4. Why?

   to learn   parent wants   child wants   needs for school   other (list)

5. How did it go?

   positive   neutral   negative

From Sapin, C., & Padak, N. (1998). *Family Literacy Resource Notebook*. Kent, OH: Ohio Literacy Resource Center. Reprinted with permission.

Figure 12.3
Achievement of Mission

1. I am [check one]
   [ ] an Even Start parent
   [ ] an Even Start staff member
   [ ] an Even Start advisory board member

2. I know what Even Start is supposed to do.
   [ ] yes
   [ ] no

3. I learned about Even Start by _____

   _____

   _____

4. I think Even Start is helping

	yes	somewhat	no	not sure
a. parents	[ ]	[ ]	[ ]	[ ]
b. preschoolers	[ ]	[ ]	[ ]	[ ]
c. school-age children	[ ]	[ ]	[ ]	[ ]
d. families	[ ]	[ ]	[ ]	[ ]

5. The three best things about Even Start are
   a. _____
   b. _____
   c. _____

6. The Even Start program could be even better if
   a. _____
   b. _____
   c. _____

From Sapin, C., & Padak, N. (1998). *Family Literacy Resource Notebook*. Kent, OH: Ohio Literacy Resource Center. Reprinted with permission.

Illinois, used photographs and videos of their program to document progress (Landerholm, Karr, & Mushi, 1999). The Appendix (see page 265) contains websites and books that offer additional ideas about alternative assessments and other aspects of family literacy evaluation.

The success of any family literacy program depends on its ability to attract families to the program (recruitment) and to keep them coming back (retention). Measuring the effectiveness of recruitment and retention strategies is an important part of family literacy program evaluation. A needs assessment can be done before the program starts to find out what the intended participants expect from a family literacy program. During the course of the program, staff can use questionnaires or interviews to find out how participants heard about the program, why they decided to attend, how the program has helped them, and what they would change about the program. Staff can maintain and evaluate lists of recruitment strategies and events. Follow-up conversations with those families who indicate interest in the program but do not enroll and exit interviews with those who leave the program before their individual goals are met also reveal recruitment and retention issues.

Community collaboration is a prominent feature of many family literacy programs and may, therefore, be an important aspect of programs to evaluate. Evaluation might focus on such issues as (a) which agencies are (and should be) partners in the family literacy program, (b) how partners learn about the program and what they do with this information (e.g., advertise the program to possible participants and encourage attendance among clients), and (c) how partners provide support for the program. Additionally, partners' perceptions of program impact on the community can be valuable. Surveys or interviews with representatives of partnering agencies can be used to gather this information, and the minutes of advisory board or partners' meetings can be good sources of information as well.

A final issue related to the nuts and bolts of evaluation is whether to work with an external evaluator. In some cases, external evaluation is a condition of financial support for the program; funding agencies may require an outsider's look at the operation and impact of the family literacy program. In other cases, details of the evaluation are left to program discretion. In the latter case, the decision about who will evaluate the program should be made early in the program's life. Before identifying possible evaluators, program staff should agree about the extent of the evaluator's involvement with the program. The evaluator's level of involvement may depend on his or her time, the financial resources available for his or her compensation, and the evaluation expertise that exists among staff members.

Ideally, an external evaluator will understand both the program and how to conduct evaluation research. Expertise in only one area—family literacy or evaluation—may lead to evaluation reports that are unhelpful and incomplete. In addition, a good evaluator needs to be familiar with program requirements, including any conditions imposed by external funders. The evaluator must have strong communication skills for both the effective collection of evaluation information and the sharing of results through writing and speaking with stakeholders—both funders and all others with interest in the program. Cultural sensitivity is another critical evaluator attribute (Sapin & Padak, 1998). Informal conversations with those involved with established family literacy programs can help new programs identify possible evaluators, including college and university faculty who do this type of work.

By using a combination of available information, standardized tests, and alternative assessments, program staff can gather a wealth of information about the program and the participants. If the program has an outside evaluator, he or she will make good use of these data for the evaluation report, but the program staff may be wondering, What else can we do with all this information?

Using Evaluation Results Formatively

Information about changes in the people involved in family literacy programs and in the operation of the programs themselves can be used to identify particular strengths and needs in programs, especially relatively new ones. Padak and Rasinski (1994) present and explain a six-step model for using evaluation data to improve program delivery:

1. Convene a team. This five- to eight-person team should represent various aspects of the program: parents, teachers, community partners, and literacy experts from schools or universities.

2. Understand the results. The team should examine and discuss evaluation results related to a particular need or weakness. The goal is to determine if the results are true, and the process may involve such issues as determining the validity of assessment measures and considering definitions used to frame the evaluation. Evaluation always relies on the definitions used for particular program elements. "Successful retention," for example, might mean participation for a month, a year, or an accumulated number of hours, so the extent to which a program is judged successful depends on the definition used.

3. Explore reasons for the results. Most problems associated with complex delivery systems such as family literacy programs are themselves complex, and the team's efforts at understanding these reasons may point toward solutions for problems. Efforts at understanding the reasons for problems should be as objective as possible, and blame-the-victim thinking should be avoided. As possible reasons for program difficulties are uncovered, additional information might be sought. For example, if retention is identified as a problem, to gain additional perspectives on reasons for the problem each member of the evaluation team might interview three people who left the program.

4. Generate and evaluate possible solutions. This is essentially a brainstorming step in which the team identifies as many solutions to the problem as possible, evaluates them, and identifies one or more solutions for implementation. Factors such as economic feasibility, availability of program resources, and funders' restraints, if applicable, may influence the selection of a solution. Unanimous support for a solution is the goal at this stage.

5. Develop and implement a plan to solve the problem. This may involve strategic planning and attention to issues such as activities that need to be accomplished (and, perhaps, the order in which they should occur), financial and human resources that are needed, the time line to be followed, and person(s) to be responsible for oversight.

6. Evaluate the plan's success. After an appropriate amount of time has passed—perhaps six months or a year—the team should reconvene to ascertain the success of its plan. Further refinements may be necessary.

No matter how effective a family literacy program, refinements are always possible. This model offers a framework that family literacy professionals can use to evaluate program-related problems, understand their causes, and develop effective plans for solving them.

Conclusion

The National Institute for Literacy (NIFL) sponsors several electronic lists to foster communication and sharing among adult education professionals. We examined the archives of the NIFL-Family discussion list (http://www.nifl.gov/lincs/discussions/nifl-family/family_literacy.html)

to identify evaluation- or assessment-related issues of concern to list subscribers, which we describe below. Where pertinent, we add some of Pinkard's observations

One group of evaluation concerns focuses on alternative assessments. Practitioners see the value of alternative assessments, but they have questions about their validity (truthfulness) and reliability (consistency). Pinkard comments, "The best evaluation data might be subjective, but it's very hard to get teachers to think alike across one program, let alone the state or nation." A related issue involves developing valid ways to assess parents while remaining sensitive to differences in cultures and parenting styles.

Many comments from the NIFL-Family archive address the time-consuming nature of alternative assessments, especially portfolio developments and analyses, a point that Pinkard underscores:

> Portfolios are very time-consuming, but we think they're worth it. Analysis of our families' portfolios shows us things about their growth and our program that standardized tests cannot. Still, time is always an issue. It takes so much time to pull all the evaluation information together.

Additionally, some respondents on the NIFL-Family list expressed the belief that self-reports from parents just beginning programs tend to be inflated. Lack of commonly accepted alternative assessments for evaluating program components such as Parents and Children Together (PACT) time and parenting education also was viewed as a problem Pinkard believes that "sometimes the most natural or authentic way to do something is very hard to evaluate." Writers on the NIFL-Family list also decried the lack of ways to measure changes in the family as a whole.

The people who communicate on the NIFL-Family list also raised questions about the type of assessment and evaluation information that is reported to funders and legislators. Practitioners see value in information from alternative assessments, especially measures of improvements in "soft skills," but reports of these aspects of programs are not requested, and the field lacks a consistent way to share this type of information. Consequently, practitioners believe that reported assessment results often do not fully represent the benefits of the complex interactions in family literacy programs.

For the most part, family literacy evaluation is in its infancy. Whether because of lack of staff, lack of funding, or lack of priority placed on evaluation, many programs have only minimal evaluation methods in place. Yet ongoing assessments of participants and evaluations of programs are necessary to ensure that programs meet families' needs and to ensure continued funding. This issue, then, is among the most pressing concerns facing family literacy practitioners and policymakers (Padak et al., 2002). In this respect, family literacy professionals face many of the same assessment and evaluation questions as others in public education: "Are our current approaches to assessment improving student learning? Might other approaches to assessment have a greater impact? Can we design...assessment systems that have the effect of helping our students want to learn and feel able to learn?" (Stiggins, 2002, p. 759). None of these questions has an easy answer. Making evaluation a program priority, developing systematic and comprehensive plans for evaluation, and attending to evaluation for (as well as *of*) programs, however, offer three effective beginning points.

REFERENCES

Holt, D., & Van Duzer, C. (Eds.). (2000). *Assessing success in family literacy and adult ESL.* Washington, DC: Center for Applied Linguistics and Delta Systems.

Knell, S., & Geissler, B. (1992). *Fine tuning the mechanics of success for families* (Report No. 3). Rantoul, IL: Illinois Literacy Resource Development Center. (ERIC Document Reproduction Service No. ED357156)

Landerholm, E., Karr, J., & Mushi, S. (1999). *A collaborative approach to family literacy evaluation strategies.* Springfield, IL: Illinois State Board of Education. (ERIC Document Reproduction Service No. ED435465)

Padak, N., & Rasinski, T. (1994). *Using evaluation results to refine family literacy programs.* Kent, OH: Ohio Literacy Resource Center. (ERIC Document Reproduction Service No. ED374230)

Padak, N., Sapin, C., & Baycich, D. (2002). *A decade of family literacy: Programs, outcomes, and future prospects.* Columbus, OH: ERIC Clearinghouse on Adult, Career, and Vocational Education. (ERIC Document Reproduction Service No. ED465074)

Sapin, C., & Padak, N. (1998). *Family literacy resource notebook.* Kent, OH: Ohio Literacy Resource Center. Available: http://literacy.kent.edu/Oasis/famlitnotebook/

Stiggins, R. (2002). Assessment crisis: The absence of assessment FOR learning. *Phi Delta Kappan, 83,* 758–765.

Appendix
Resources for Further Learning

Websites

Assessment and Evaluation Strategies in Family Literacy Program Development
www.nald.ca/clr/aestrat/cover.htm

Evaluation, Measurement Issues in Family Literacy
www.literacyvolunteers.org/ppe/ppe.html

NIFL Family Literacy Special Collections
literacy.kent.edu/Midwest/FamilyLit/

One Family Literacy Program's Assessment Story
www.sabes.org/resources/adventures/vol10/10greene.htm

A Practical Guide to Family Literacy
www.nald.ca/clr/pgtfl/cover.htm

Synthesis of Local and State Even Start Evaluations
www.ed.gov/pubs/evenstart_final/synthesis/synthesisa_h.html

Books

Epstein, A. (1995). *A guide to developing community-based family support programs.* Ypsilanti, MI: High/Scope Press.

> This book has five sections: "An Overview of Family Support Programs," "Getting Started," "Designing the Program," "Implementing the Program," and "Evaluating the Program." The evaluation section addresses designing, conducting, and using the evaluation.

Holt, D., & VanDuzer, C. (Eds.). (2000). *Assessing success in family literacy and adult ESL.* Washington, DC: Center for Applied Linguistics and Delta Systems.

> Helpful chapters in this book are "Alternative Approaches to Assessment and Evaluation," "Initial Assessment," "First Step to Success," "Next Steps: Using the Results to Refine the Project," and "Assessing Progress: Are We Progressing?"

Lyons, P., Robbins, A., & Smith, A. (1984). *Involving parents: A handbook for participation in schools.* Ypsilanti, MI: High/Scope Press.

> The second part of this book provides a self-assessment model that will enable a school to evaluate parental involvement.

Morrow, L.M., Neuman, S.B., Paratore, J.R., & Harrison, C. (Eds.). (1995). *Parents and literacy.* Newark, DE: International Reading Association.

> The first part of this book discusses family literacy and younger children; the second part covers family literacy with teenagers and adults. The chapter titled "The Family Portfolio: Using Authentic Assessment in Family Literacy Programs" shows that the family portfolio is a useful alternative for evaluation in family literacy programs.

National Center for Family Literacy. (1996). *Outcomes and measures in family literacy.* Louisville, KY: Author.

> The first several chapters discuss the terms, concepts, and issues associated with family literacy program assessment. The bulk of the book covers assessment tests; inventories; and checklists for adults, families, and children. Each test entry contains a description, administration, scoring, reliability, validity, price, and ordering information.

Popp, R. (1992). *Family portfolios: Documenting change in parent-child relationships.* Louisville, KY: National Center for Family Literacy.

> This publication discusses the concept of authentic assessment and focuses on the use of portfolios as assessment tools in family literacy programs. The report defines the types of information and artifacts that can be included in portfolios and provides ways to analyze portfolio data.

CHAPTER 13

Using Family Literacy Portfolios as a Context for Parent-Teacher Communication

Barbara Krol-Sinclair, Alisa Hindin, Julia M. Emig, and Kelly A. McClure

arent–teacher contact is increasingly viewed by both educators and researchers as a critical element in children's school success. Evidence suggests that parents and teachers best serve children when they work as partners in supporting children's learning in compatible ways (Kellaghan, Sloane, Alvarez, & Bloom, 1993; Schneider & Coleman, 1993). Parent–teacher conferences serve as the most consistent, institutionalized forms of communication between parents and teachers. At the same time, the conferences traditionally have been directed by teachers, with parents primarily receiving information about their children's school achievements and behaviors. This imbalance between parents and teachers may be further exacerbated for nonmainstream parents who may not have a frame of reference for the information received at conferences, thus leaving them confused about what they have heard and, consequentially, less certain of their abilities to support their children's academic success (Ada, 1993; Delgado–Gaitan, 1991).

This chapter describes a project in which U.S. immigrant parents and classroom teachers collaborate in the development and use of home-based literacy portfolios to support children's developing literacy.

This chapter presents data collected over a three-year period. Preliminary results based on the first year's data are reported in a paper that was presented at the National Reading Conference's 1998 annual meeting and published in EDUCATION AND URBAN SOCIETY. Parts of this chapter are drawn from that paper and from a paper presented at the 1999 National Reading Conference annual meeting.

We will explain the construction and use of portfolios by families, report on the nature of the conferences in which portfolios were shared, and provide teachers with strategies for using children's home-based literacy portfolios to strengthen home–school relationships.

Parent-Teacher Communication and Conferences

Ample evidence suggests that parents play critical roles in their children's success in school, through both home literacy practices and parent–school collaborations (e.g., Anderson, Hiebert, Scott, & Wilkinson, 1985; Durkin, 1966; Epstein, 2001a, 2001b; Epstein & Becker, 2001; Henderson & Berla, 1994; Hewison & Tizard, 1980; Hoover-Dempsey & Sandler, 1997; Tangri & Moles, 1987; Teale, 1984). Convincing evidence also exists of the negative consequences of discontinuities between home and school literacy practices, particularly for children who are linguistically and culturally different from the mainstream (e.g., Heath, 1983; Purcell-Gates, 1995; Taylor & Dorsey-Gaines, 1988). Despite a number of efforts to instruct parents about schools (e.g., Morrow, 1995) and similar efforts to instruct teachers on ways to build on what researchers Moll and Greenberg (1990) have called "household funds of knowledge" (p. 321), evidence suggests that children's home and school literacy lives remain largely disparate (e.g., McCarthey, 1997).

Because conferences are a mainstay in most school systems and serve as the primary means of parent–teacher communication, we became interested in them as a context for improving collaboration between parents and teachers. In our previous studies (Paratore et al., 1995; Paratore, Hindin, Krol-Sinclair, & Durán, 1999; Paratore et al., 1999), we found that when parents collect evidence of their children's literacy uses at home and share examples with elementary classroom teachers during parent–teacher conferences, the nature of the conferences changes. Parents are able to take more active roles in the conferences and to provide teachers with new information about how their children learn and use literacy at home. Conversations about home literacy activities become more collaborative, and teachers are able to see concrete examples of how parents participate in their children's educations. Finally, parents and teachers report that they have better understandings of home and school literacies. According to both parents and teachers, this collaborative style is different from the patterns of previous, more traditionally structured conferences.

The Community, the Families, and the Schools

We implemented the Home-School Portfolio Project as one element of an intergenerational literacy program located in a geographically small, urban community identified by 1990 census data as the most ethnically diverse in the Commonwealth of Massachusetts. (See chapter 1 for further description of the program.) Seventy-five percent of the school-age children in this community speak a first language other than English. The community is economically impoverished, with over 85% of elementary school children identified as members of low-income families.

Parents participating in the Home-School Portfolio Project attended adult literacy classes in an intergenerational literacy program (ILP), located in the public school system's learning center. The program primarily served immigrant families and focused on (a) strengthening parents' abilities to read and write in English, (b) helping parents support their children's literacy development at home, (c) providing parents with information about school culture and ways they could help their children succeed in school, and (d) supporting the language and literacy development of preschool- and school-age children attending the ILP's children's classes. Parents attended classes three or four days per week for two hours per day. (See chapter 6 for further discussion of a program focused on second language learners.)

The data this chapter presents were gathered from 20 parent-teacher pairs who participated at different times during the three years of the Home-School Portfolio Project. The parents are all Latino, and the group included 19 mothers and 1 father. The participating families had emigrated from Puerto Rico, Mexico, and various countries of South and Central America. The parents had, on average, attended school for 9 years and had lived in the mainland United States for an average of 6 years. The average length of parents' participation in the ILP was 36 weeks.

Thirteen of the children were enrolled in transitional bilingual (Spanish-English) education classrooms, two attended two-way bilingual (Spanish-English) classrooms, and five were enrolled in general education classrooms. Three children were enrolled in prekindergarten classrooms, four in kindergarten, seven in first grade, three in second grade, and three in third grade. The parents who participated in the project received US$50 worth of children's books appropriate to the ages of their children.

Of the 20 teachers, 15 were Spanish–English bilinguals and 5 were monolingual English speakers. Eight of the teachers were raised and schooled outside the mainland United States for at least part of their childhoods, and on average, they had been teaching for 5 years. Each teacher received a US$50 voucher for books from a local bookstore as a stipend for participation.

What We Did: Creating and Using Home-Based Literacy Portfolios

Parents participating in the Home–School Portfolio Project attended ILP classes, in which a component of the overall instruction focused on observing their children's uses of literacy at home and understanding family literacy portfolios. We began the project by giving parents large, colored, accordion-style folders to be used as portfolios in which to save home literacy materials. Parents received a portfolio for each of their children and were encouraged to have their children personalize them by writing their names on them and decorating the folders as they chose. When introducing the concept of portfolios in parents' classes, we discussed the reasons parents might want to keep these portfolios and the types of materials to collect. See Figure 13.1 for a short article the parents read on keeping a portfolio and Figure 13.2 for a list of typical portfolio contents. We emphasized the importance of including both samples of children's written work (e.g., drawings, stories, letters) and parents' own written notes on how they saw their children use reading and writing.

In earlier attempts to encourage parents to use portfolios, we found that merely providing the folder and explaining the rationale for observing their children's literacy uses at home and collecting examples to include in the portfolio did not provide parents with enough support. They often began collecting items, but they did not continue using the portfolios on their own long enough to be able to see evidence of their

Figure 13.1
Article on the Value of Portfolios

Why Keep a Portfolio?

As a parent, you already spend a lot of time watching your children—seeing how they are growing and how they behave with other children—and teaching them things. Sometimes, it helps to write down what you are seeing. This way you will not forget the day your son said his first word or the day your daughter read her first book.

You can collect information about your children on a routine basis, too. For example, you can collect pictures that your child has drawn, words that your child knows, songs that you sing with your child, and many other things. You can put all these things in your child's portfolio. Writing notes about your child and saving things that your child has done helps you to observe your child's growth and learning.

By watching your children, writing notes about what you see them do, and collecting what they draw and write in your home, you can do many things. First, collecting information about your child at home will show your child that you are interested in his or her work and learning. Second, the portfolios make it very easy to collect information about your child. You can put everything in your portfolio. Third, by putting the date on everything in the portfolio, you can see the changes in your child over time. For example, one month you may put in the portfolio a number game that you played with your child. The next month, you can look back and see that your child only knew 10 numbers then, and now your child knows 20 numbers. Fourth, you can share this information with your child's teacher. Teachers love to see what children are doing at home, and taking your child's portfolio to your parent-teacher conference is one way that you can help your child's teacher learn more about your son or daughter.

Figure 13.2
List of Sample Portfolio Contents

- Photocopies of book covers (books read by children alone or with their parents)
- Notes and special-occasion cards written by children to their parents
- Shopping lists
- Drawings
- Coloring book pages
- Parent-generated learning activities (such as parent-created math worksheets)
- Craft projects
- Parent observations of children's literacy use

children's literacy development. In instituting this project, then, we decided to provide parents with ongoing support in developing and sharing their portfolios. On a weekly basis, parents were asked to bring their children's family literacy portfolios to a session and to share examples from them with other members of their ILP class. Figures 13.3 and 13.4 are examples of artifacts included in the portfolio of a kindergartner. Often, particular examples shared by parents served as models, inspiring other parents to adapt these literacy activities for use with their own children. Parents worked collaboratively in these sessions to discuss other types of reading and writing that could be included in their children's portfolios.

We also taught the parents strategies for sharing their children's portfolios with teachers during informal meetings and gave the parents opportunities to rehearse parent-teacher conferences in their adult literacy class. They discussed what they were learning about their children's literacy from the portfolios and how they could use that knowledge in talking with teachers about school-based literacy learning and in asking teachers questions about how to support their children at home.

Figure 13.3
Portfolio Artifact Sample: A Discount Coupon Completed by a Kindergartner While Waiting for Her Mother in the Drugstore and Annotated by Her Mother

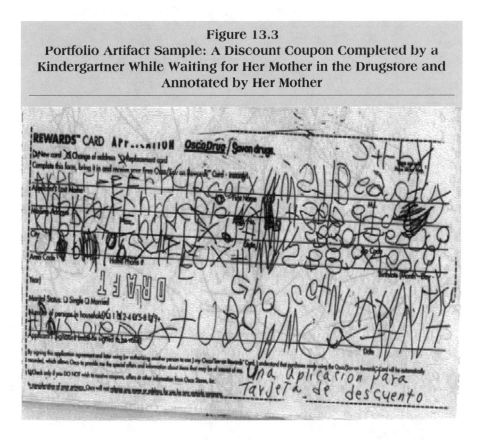

Figure 13.4
Portfolio Artifact Sample: A Letter Written by a Kindergartner to Her Mother's Friend and Annotated by the Mother

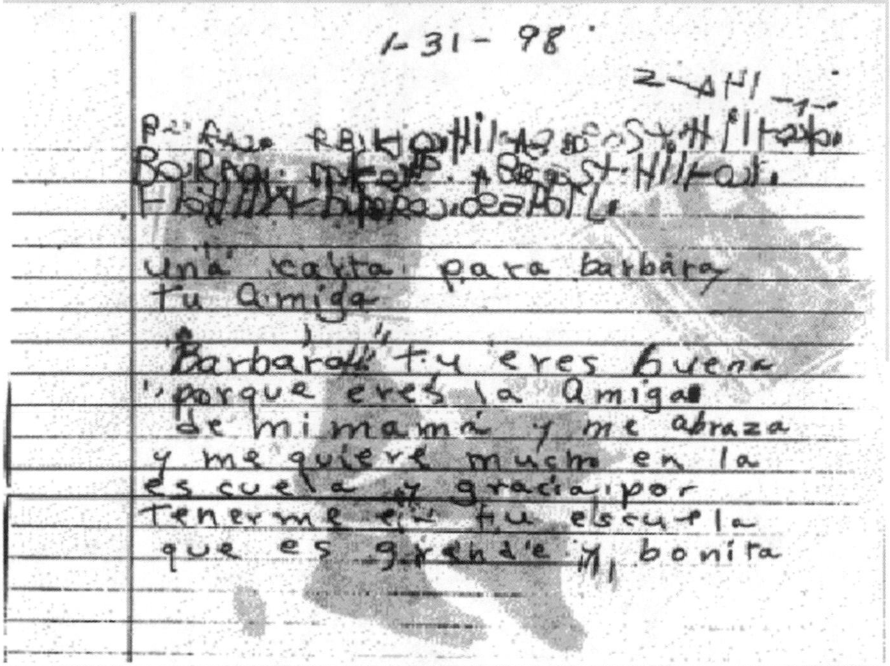

Translation of annotation: Barbara, you are good because you are my mother's friend and you hug me and you like me a lot in school, and thank you for having me in your school, which is big and beautiful.

Likewise, classroom teachers attended a series of three after-school seminars per year, led by ILP staff. Teachers attending the seminars read and discussed key texts and articles about family literacy and about establishing and supporting home–school partnerships. (See Figure 13.5 for a list of articles reviewed in the seminars.) The meetings provided a forum to identify and discuss opportunities for collaborating with parents in the development of family and school literacy. During these seminars, teachers learned about the home literacy portfolios being assembled by families participating in the ILP. A key topic of discussion was how to use routine parent-teacher conferences as opportunities for these groups to pool their knowledge of children's developing

Figure 13.5
Articles Read and Discussed by Teachers in Professional Development Seminars

Ada, A.F. (1988). The Pajaro Valley experience: Working with Spanish-speaking parents to develop children's reading and writing skills through the use of children's literature. In T. Skutnabb-Kangas & J. Cummins (Eds.), *Minority education: From shame to struggle* (pp. 223–238). Clevedon, UK: Multilingual Matters.

Auerbach, E.R. (1989). Toward a socio-contextual approach to family literacy. *Harvard Educational Review, 59,* 165–81.

Chavez, L. (1996, September 5). Hispanic parents want English education. *Wall Street Journal,* p. A16.

Corno, L. (1989). What it means to be literate about classrooms. In D. Bloome (Ed.), *Classrooms and literacy* (pp. 29–52). Westport, CT: Ablex.

Delgado-Gaitan, C. (1992). School matters in the Mexican-American home: Socializing children to education. *American Educational Research Journal, 29,* 495–513.

Delpit, L.D. (1988). The silenced dialogue: Power and pedagogy in educating other people's children. *Harvard Educational Review, 58,* 280–98.

Goldenberg, C. (1990). Research directions: Beginning literacy instruction for Spanish-speaking children. *Language Arts, 67,* 590–598.

Goldenberg, C. (1996). The education of language-minority students: Where are we, and where do we need to go? *The Elementary School Journal, 96,* 353–362.

Goldenberg, C., Reese, L., & Gallimore, R. (1992). Effects of literacy materials from school on Latino children's home experiences and early reading achievement. *American Journal of Education, 100,* 497–536.

Hoover-Dempsey, K.V., & Sandler, H.M. (1995). Parental involvement in children's education. Why does it make a difference? *Teachers College Record, 97,* 310–331.

Krol-Sinclair, B. (1996). Connecting home and school literacies: Immigrant parents with limited formal education as classroom storybook readers. In D.J. Leu, C.K. Kinzer, & K.A. Hinchman (Eds.), *Literacies for the 21st century: Research and practice* (45th Yearbook of the National Reading Conference, pp. 270–283). Chicago: National Reading Conference.

Lareau, A. (1996). Assessing parent involvement in schooling: A critical analysis. In A. Booth & J.F. Dunn (Eds.), *Family-school links: How do they affect educational outcomes* (pp. 57–64). Hillsdale, NJ: Erlbaum.

Moles, O.C. (1993). Collaboration between schools and disadvantaged parents: Obstacles and openings. In N.V. Chavkin (Ed.), *Families and schools in a pluralistic society* (pp. 21–49). Albany, NY: State University of New York Press.

Moll, L.C., & González, N. (1994). Lessons from research with language-minority children. *Journal of Reading Behavior, 26,* 439–456.

Paratore, J.R. (1994). Parents and children sharing literacy. In D. Lancy (Ed.), *Children's emergent literacy: From research to practice* (pp. 193–216). Westport, CT: Praegar.

Paratore, J.R. (1995). Implementing an intergenerational literacy project: Lessons learned. In L.M. Morrow (Ed.), *Family literacy: Connections in schools and communities* (pp. 37–53). Newark, DE: International Reading Association.

Paratore, J.R., Homza, A., Krol-Sinclair, B., Lewis-Barrow, T., Melzi, G., Stergis, R., et al. (1995). Shifting boundaries in home and school responsibilities: Involving immigrant parents in the construction of home-based literacy portfolios by immigrant parents and their children. *Research in the Teaching of English, 29,* 367–389.

Paratore, J.R., & Krol-Sinclair, B. (1996). A classroom storybook-reading program with immigrant parents. *The School Community Journal, 6,* 39–51.

Parra, E., & Henderson, R.W. (1982). Mexican-American perceptions of parent and teacher roles in child development. In J.A. Fishman & G.D. Keller (Eds.), *Bilingual education for Hispanic students in the United States* (pp. 289–299). New York: Teachers College Press.

Peel, B.B. (1991). Making the right connection: Conferencing with parents of different cultures. *Education, 9,* 575–579.

Rosenthal, D., & Sawyers, J.Y. (1996). Building successful home/school partnerships: Strategies for parent support and involvement. *Childhood Education, 72,* 194–200.

Taylor, D. (1993). Family literacy: Resisting deficit models. *TESOL Quarterly, 27,* 550–553.

literacy and talk about how to use their shared knowledge to continue support of family literacy and children's academic learning.

In the school system involved with the program, teachers were required to hold at least one parent-teacher conference each year. Parents were asked to bring their children's family literacy portfolios to share with the teachers during the regularly scheduled parent-teacher conference. Teachers had a tape recorder and an audiotape and recorded the full conference at our request. No observer was present during the conference. In addition, we interviewed the participating parents and teachers at the beginning of the school year and after their parent-teacher conferences, and we audiotaped all the interviews. In all, we recorded and analyzed a total of 34 parent-teacher conferences and 108 interviews.

What We Learned: Potential for the Portfolio-Based Conference to Influence Children's Learning Opportunities

In order to examine the extent to which the conversation during the portfolio-based conferences might lead to new insights into children's literacy learning or otherwise influence their opportunities to learn at home or at school, we reviewed conference and interview transcripts, focusing on excerpts in which the speaker made specific recommendations about how to support a child's literacy development or in which the speaker affirmed or provided feedback on a reported action or interaction. We also searched for instances in which the parent or teacher reported extending or revising a previous practice in response to feedback during the conference.

In each of the 20 pairs of parents and teachers, we found at least one incident, and usually two or three, in which we believed that the exchange offered evidence that the home portfolio itself provided a foundation for improved or increased literacy learning opportunities at home or at school. We also found evidence that sharing the portfolio led to increased or improved learning opportunities at home or at school. In the following case, the first example comes from the first of three conferences between the mother and her child's teacher. The parent, Ms. Salazar, described to the teacher, Ms. Thomas, how she read with her child, Gabriela, and the teacher affirmed her actions:

Ms. Salazar: When I read a book to her, right, she retains in her head what I have read to her. Later, I have turned the pages like this slowly, and she tells me what I have told her.

Ms. Thomas: That is good. That is how she learns to read.

However, the teacher's feedback did not stop at merely affirming the parent's actions. As the parent continued, the teacher helped her acquire new strategies for guiding the child's response to literature:

Ms. Salazar: I would always tell her, "Gabriela, what do you like most about the story?" And she told me "here," and I told her, "Why do you like that page here?" She told me because of the girl's scream. She liked it completely; she says that she is not afraid of monsters.

Ms. Thomas: When you ask a question, things like "Why?" you should ask more...she has to think or recall things about the story.

We concluded that such exchanges have the potential to lead to ongoing parent–child learning interactions, a finding that is supported by interview data. In her third interview, Ms. Salazar, commented,

> I am going to continue...that is something that motivates me more...to continue providing my product, contributing with my ideas. And contributing here in the school. To continue working, right, with the school with the portfolio...because...I see that they value the work that one does, right? They value the work that one does.

The teacher, Ms. Thomas, also commented on the influence she thought the interactions during the conference had on Ms. Salazar's interactions with Gabriela at home:

> During the first conference, we had talked about [the fact that] Gabriela's basic literacy skills were really good and her numeracy skills weren't so great, or they weren't at the same level as her literacy. So, I had mentioned that and I said maybe that's something you [Ms. Salazar] could work on because you obviously work on the literacy stuff. And, that was one of the areas where we saw a big change, and I said that I'm sure it was from the work that she was doing with her at home.

Keeping and sharing a portfolio also seems to encourage the parent to seek ways to collaborate with the teacher. During the first interview, Ms. Thomas reported that when Ms. Salazar drops her daughter off at school each day, "At least once a week, she'll ask me, 'So, what are we doing this week?' So I'll point things out that are going on around the room." Ms. Salazar also commented on these interactions and provided explicit evidence of her follow-through, "This week, now, they are going to study the fish and the ocean in Gabriela's classroom. Well, I have looked for books in the library that talk about fish and the ocean, right?"

Finally, during the last conference, the home portfolio itself became the object of continued collaboration. When Ms. Thomas told Ms. Salazar that she found the project so useful that she hoped to continue it the following year with more parents, Ms. Salazar offered to give her a copy of the portfolio:

Ms. Thomas: That's what I want to do, as a personal goal next year. I want to do that with more parents. I am going to ask them if they want to and I know that they [the portfolios] are not going to be as beautiful as yours and as...

Ms. Salazar: But you can take these things as an example for them. You can show them the work that is done, so they can have an idea about how they are going to work, because I didn't know and one acquires knowledge through the ideas of other people.

Ms. Thomas: So it can be that I'll call you next year to come to show [the portfolio] because I can see the progress in Gabriela. And I think it is because we are talking and doing the same things at school and at home.

Later, during her final interview, Ms. Thomas reiterated this plan:

In fact, for my goal, we have to do a professional development kind of goal each year, because I saw such a change in Gabriela, what I want to do, actually I want to expand it a little bit and ask three or four parents to do a portfolio.... And Gabriela's mom said..."I'll come in and show them mine and tell them how to do it."

Across our sample, we found that the home portfolio influenced parents and teachers in three ways: (1) parents effectively and enthusiastically shared what they were doing, (2) teachers affirmed the interactions and used them to inform parents about ways to continue to support their children's literacy learning, and as a result, (3) children were provided opportunities for increased or improved literacy learning.

Transforming Classroom Practice: Using Portfolios as a Means of Strengthening Parent-Teacher Understanding and Communication

In elementary classrooms, home literacy portfolios can provide teachers with common ground for conversations with parents. By involving parents in collecting portfolio artifacts and writing down their observations, teachers enlist parents as coresearchers into children's literacy development. Parents increase their understanding about their children's literate lives at home and at school, and teachers learn about children's home literacy practices and strategies that can be adapted for classroom use. In the Home-School Portfolio Project, however, the instruction in portfolios and ongoing portfolio sharing time offered in parents' own literacy classes served to validate portfolios for our parents in a way that is unavailable to most classroom teachers. Nonetheless, evidence exists that portfolios can be implemented as part of routine parent-teacher communication, even without the consistent support that the ILP provided parents. In an earlier study, Paratore, DiBiasio, Turpie, and Sullivan (1993) recruited parents of first graders in two classrooms to contribute home-based literacy artifacts to their children's classroom portfolios. The communities of the two classrooms differed greatly: One of the classrooms was in a largely white, upper middle-class, suburban community, and the other was in a large, ethnically diverse, urban community. Paratore and colleagues found that the types of home literacy samples varied across communities, demonstrating differing purposes for literacy use at home. The parents reported learning about classroom practices, and both teachers noted increased understanding of their students' home lives. Across sites, both teachers had successfully engaged parents in the project, although substantially more portfolio submissions were obtained by the urban classroom teacher who consistently and actively encouraged parents to bring samples. The findings from this study suggest that, even without the intervention of an outside agency such as the ILP, parents and teachers can collaborate in collecting artifacts of children's literacy practices at home and at school and, in so doing, can strengthen their own abilities to communicate with one another.

School-based portfolios form a part of routine assessment activities in classrooms. Teachers can encourage parents in several ways to build connections with their children's learning at school through the use of these already existing portfolios. Parents can contribute both home-based literacy artifacts and their own observations of how they see their children using reading and writing in their daily lives to their children's classroom portfolios. The following suggestions can help classroom teachers strengthen communication with parents through the use of portfolios:

Ask parents how their children use reading and writing at home in their daily lives. They are, after all, the experts in their children's home lives. Asking for parents' insight serves the dual purposes of demonstrating that teachers recognize the importance of the parents' role in their children's learning and of providing teachers with information about children's literacy backgrounds.

Share samples from children's school-based portfolios with parents. A routine component of the ILP class instruction helps immigrant parents learn about school culture in the United States: how elementary classrooms are organized, how reading and writing are taught, how children learn at school, and how parents can support their children's learning. Sharing samples of children's work at school with parents provides an opportunity for parents to learn about instructional routines and the language of the classroom.

Invite parents to bring in examples of children's home literacy activities. Home-based work can be sent in with the children on a weekly basis, or, when possible, encourage parents to bring artifacts to the teachers themselves.

Provide parents with examples of the types of home-based literacy interactions that could be included in their daily lives, such as those listed in Figure 13.2 (see page 270). The types of activities children engage in at home do not have to be and should not be duplications of school-based literacy activities. Artifacts should reflect the ways children are actually using reading and writing in their daily lives.

Prompt parents by asking them for specific examples of home literacy activities at different times. For example, one week, ask for a copy of a shopping list and, another week, send home a simple form (see Figure 13.6 for an example) that focuses parents on observing their children's literacy uses at home. Although, initially, parents should simply note their children's reading and writing, over time the parent and teacher can use what they have learned from parents' observations to make suggestions about additional ways that children can read and write at home, both alone and with their parents.

Review children's home literacy artifacts with parents and consider their comments. What do parents believe these samples reveal about their children's learning? How do teachers see classroom instruction being carried into home activities?

Figure 13.6
Sample Parent Form for Reporting Observations of Home-Based Writing

Student's name _____ Date _____

Over the next week, please watch your child to learn about how he or she uses writing at home. Please record your observations on this page and return it to school with your child next Monday. The first line is filled in as an example.

What did your child write during the past week?	How often did he or she write this?	What did you notice about the writing?
List of gifts she wants for her birthday	Every day	She kept showing us the list. Then she'd think of something more and add to it or cross something out. She spent a lot of time reading it over, and she made sure to let us know whenever she made a change.

Include samples of children's reading and writing—both at school and at home—in discussions with parents during parent-teacher conferences. Finding and nurturing connections between home and school literacy enables both the teacher and the parent to use common strategies in supporting children's literacy development.

Connect parents with other parents in workshops, open houses, and meetings in order to give them opportunities to learn from one another, to build greater understanding of school policies and practices, and to allow them to share their knowledge of their children's learning in ways that can influence instruction at school.

Use increased knowledge of children's home literacy practices in developing classroom activities and in assigning homework that will lessen the gap between home and school.

Conclusion

The use of home literacy portfolios in parent-teacher conferences and other home-school interactions may provide a means for building bridges between parents whose understanding of the culture of U.S. schools and their children's teachers may be limited. When parents assemble portfolios, they not only gain understanding of their children's home literacy activities but they also build a means to demonstrate their awareness of their children's literacy learning and, as a result, they participate in school conferences on more equal footing with teachers. Further, when teachers express interest in the portfolios, they are opening doors to learning about home literacy activities and to strengthening classroom instruction by building on children's literacy bases. We hope that these activities may be steps toward improving the opportunities to support children's school success that parent-teacher conferences can provide.

REFERENCES

Ada, A.F. (1993). *A critical pedagogy approach to fostering the home-school connection.* (ERIC Document Reproduction Service No. ED358716).

Anderson, R.C., Hiebert, E.H., Scott, J., & Wilkinson, I. (1985). *Becoming a nation of readers: The report of the Commission on Reading.* Washington, DC: National Institute of Education.

Delgado-Gaitan, C. (1991). Involving parents in schools: A process of empowerment. *American Journal of Education, 100,* 20–46.

Durkin, D. (1966). *Children who read early*. New York: Teachers College Press.

Epstein, J.L. (2001a). Homework practices, achievements, and behaviors of elementary school students. In J.L. Epstein (Ed.), *School, family, and community partnerships: Preparing educators and improving schools* (pp. 236–252). Boulder, CO: Westview Press.

Epstein, J.L. (2001b). Parents' reactions to teacher practices of parent involvement. In J.L. Epstein (Ed.), *School, family, and community partnerships: Preparing educators and improving schools* (pp. 155–175). Boulder, CO: Westview Press.

Epstein, J.L., & Becker, H.J. (2001). Teachers' reported practices of parent involvement: Problems and possibilities. In J.L. Epstein (Ed.), *School, family, and community partnerships: Preparing educators and improving schools* (pp. 120–133). Boulder, CO: Westview.

Heath, S.B. (1983). *Ways with words: Language, life and work in communities and classrooms*. Cambridge, UK: Cambridge University Press.

Henderson, A.I., & Berla, N. (1994). *A new generation of evidence: The family is critical to student achievement*. St. Louis, MO: Danforth Foundation; Flint, MI: Mott (C.S.) Foundation.

Hewison, J., & Tizard, J. (1980). Parental involvement and reading attainment. *British Journal of Educational Psychology, 50*, 209–215.

Hoover-Dempsey, K.V., & Sandler, H.M. (1997). Why do parents become involved in their children's education? *Review of Educational Research, 67*, 3–42.

Kellaghan, T., Sloane, K., Alvarez, B., & Bloom, B.S. (1993). *The home environment and school learning: Promoting parental involvement in the education of children*. San Francisco: Jossey-Bass.

McCarthey, S.J. (1997). Connecting home and school literacy practices in classrooms with diverse populations. *Journal of Literacy Research, 29*, 145–182.

Moll, L.C., & Greenberg, J.B. (1990). Creating zones of possibilities: Combining social contexts for instruction. In L.C. Moll (Ed.), *Vygotsky and education: Instructional implications and applications of sociohistorical psychology* (pp. 319–348). Cambridge, UK: Cambridge University Press.

Morrow, L.M. (Ed.). (1995). *Family literacy connections in schools and communities*. Newark, DE: International Reading Association.

Paratore, J.R., DiBiasio, M., Turpie, J., & Sullivan, K. (1993, December). *Learning from home literacies: Inviting parents to contribute to literacy portfolios*. Paper presented at the 43rd annual meeting of the National Reading Conference, Charleston, SC.

Paratore, J.R., Hindin, A., Krol-Sinclair, B., & Durán, P. (1999). Discourse between teachers and Latino parents during conferences based on home literacy portfolios. *Education and Urban Society, 32*, 58–82.

Paratore, J.R., Hindin, A., Krol-Sinclair, B., Durán, P., Emig, J., & McClure, K. (1999, December). *Deepening the conversation: Using family literacy portfolios as a context for parent-teacher conferences*. Paper presented at the 49th annual meeting of the National Reading Conference, Orlando, FL.

Paratore, J.R., Homza, A., Krol-Sinclair, B., Lewis-Barrow, T., Melzi, G., Stergis, R., et al. (1995). Shifting boundaries in home and school responsibilities: Involving immigrant parents in the construction of literacy portfolios. *Research in the Teaching of English, 29*, 367–389.

Purcell-Gates, V. (1995). *Other people's words: The cycle of illiteracy*. Cambridge, MA: Harvard University Press.

Schneider, B., & Coleman, J.S. (Eds.). (1993). *Parents, their children, and schools*. Boulder, CO: Westview.

Tangri, S., & Moles, O. (1987). Parents and the community. In V. Richardson-Koehler (Ed.), *Educators' handbook: A research perspective* (pp. 519–550). White Plains, NY: Longman.

Taylor, D., & Dorsey-Gaines, C. (1988). *Growing up literate: Learning from inner-city families*. Portsmouth, NH: Heinemann.

Teale, W.H. (1984). Reading to young children: Its significance for literacy development. In H. Goelman, A. Oberg, & F. Smith (Eds.), *Awakening to literacy* (pp. 110–121). Portsmouth, NH: Heinemann.

CHAPTER 14

Evaluating Adult/Child Interactive Reading Skills

Andrea DeBruin-Parecki

The phrase "the parent is the child's first teacher" is well established as the credo of family literacy programs (Barbara Bush Foundation for Family Literacy, 1989; McKee & Rhett, 1995; Taylor, 1983; see also chapter 1 for an overview of theoretical frameworks of family literacy). Along with this notion comes responsibility. To assist their child in establishing good literacy habits that lead to clearer understandings, improved critical thinking, consistent use of strategies, and motivation to learn, parents must establish good habits themselves. Instruction in these areas can take place within the context of interactive sessions. Research has shown that the incorporation and practice of specific behaviors during joint book reading can promote future academic success for children as they enter school (Cochran-Smith, 1984; Flood, 1977; Jordan, Snow, & Porche, 2000; Morrow, 1983; Senechel, Cornell, & Broda, 1995). Although improving interactive reading skills is certainly not the only goal of family literacy programs, it is a major goal. The desire to help their children learn to read so they will become academically successful is one of the primary reasons parents choose to enter family literacy programs (Brizius & Foster, 1993; Cairney, 2000; Edwards, 1995).

If one were to walk into most family literacy programs in communities and/or schools almost anywhere in the United States today and ask to see evidence of improved adult-child joint book-reading practices, it is unlikely that staff members would be able to provide this information in a systematic manner (DeBruin-Parecki, Paris, & Siedenburg, 1997). Standardized tests, which are most commonly used to provide information on the progress of program participants, are not useful for this evaluative purpose because they measure only adults' development of reading skills and cannot indicate any form of interactive growth. The tests do not demonstrate how the adult has learned to provide more positive and interesting reading experiences for his or her children, nor do the tests measure how young children initiate or respond to conversation during joint book-reading—clear goals of the majority of family literacy programs and their participating families (Brooks, 1998; Morrow, 1990; Purcell-Gates, 2000). The U.S. government, in its definition of the components of family literacy programs, also identifies these goals as appropriate ones for programs and participating families. Required program components comprise provision of interactive literacy activities between parents and their children and training for parents regarding how to be the primary teachers for their children as well as full partners in their children's education (U.S. Government, 2001).

In order to provide a means of evaluating interactive reading practices and to assist programs and families in measuring the progress being made as adults and children learn to read together, I designed a tool called the Adult/Child Interactive Reading Inventory (ACIRI) (see Appendix on page 300). This instrument offers teachers and participants information about interactive literacy behaviors that promote positive outcomes. The reasons why specific interactive reading behaviors, particularly those included on the ACIRI, are important during adult-child joint book-reading behaviors will be detailed in the next section.

Background: Why Is Joint Storybook Reading Important?

Children are not born knowing how to connect their knowledge and experience in "literate" ways to printed and pictorial texts. Rather, they must learn strategies for understanding texts just as they must learn the ways of eating and talking that are appropriate to their cultures or social groups. (Cochran-Smith, 1986, p. 36)

Over the past decade, both popular media and academic research have drawn attention to the benefits of reading to young children. Most recently, the International Reading Association (IRA) and the National

Association for the Education of Young Children (NAEYC) have supported this idea by issuing a joint position statement on learning to read and write (IRA/NAEYC, 1998). The release of the National Research Council report *Preventing Reading Difficulties in Young Children* also confirms the widespread support of this notion (Snow, Burns, & Griffin, 1998).

Politicians, volunteer organizations, government programs, librarians, and teachers all implore adults to make reading with their children a part of their everyday lives. A desire to further children's chances for achieving success as they progress through school is the underlying reason for promoting this activity. Encouraging family members and friends to read with children answers not only a social and emotional need but also an important instructional one.

For years, researchers have stated that interactive book reading can enhance language development (Crain-Thoreson, Dahlin, & Powell, 2001; Durkin, 1966, 1972; Storch & Whitehurst, 2001; Teale, 1978, 1981) and help children learn that printed words, although different from oral language, represent sounds and carry meaning (Clay, 1979). Numerous studies have shown that early readers come from homes in which adults read to them regularly and books and reading materials are readily available (Bus, van IJzendoorn, & Pellegrini, 1995; Clark, 1976, 1984; Lancy, Draper, & Boyce, 1989; Morrow, 1983; Purcell-Gates, 2000; Teale, 1978; see also chapter 3 for discussion of shared literacy and chapter 2 for information on early literacy development). Questions remain, however, about the specific characteristics of these interactive sessions that lead to children's success in reading. It is not only the frequency with which a parent reads to a child that affects the child's success but also what that parent does during shared reading and how he or she mediates the shared text.

There appear to be specific joint storybook reading behaviors and practices that enhance children's reading skills and comprehension. Children gain comprehension skills, increase their understandings of literacy conventions, and are encouraged to enjoy reading primarily because of interactive dialogue. Book-reading episodes provide an opportunity for adults and children to co-construct knowledge in social settings and negotiate meanings together. Adults can collaborate with children and adjust the amount of scaffolding they provide as children gain understanding and complete tasks. This process requires that the adults be able to judge children's current levels of knowledge and know how to push their children a bit beyond that comfort zone. Vygotsky (1934/1978) calls this *working within the child's zone of proximal development*. His theory claims that intellectual skills arise from social interactions that occur during practical activities. In the context of literacy learning, Teale (1981) interprets this to mean that, over time, children can internalize co-constructed parent-supported behaviors and strategies used during joint book-reading sessions. This process, Teale argues, can eventually lead children to independent functioning and self-regulated reading behaviors.

Morrow (1990) identifies nine interactive reading behaviors that researchers have investigated. These behaviors are questioning, scaffolding dialogue and responses, offering praise or positive reinforcement, giving or extending information, clarifying information, restating information, directing discussion, sharing personal reactions, and relating concepts to life experiences. In addition to these behaviors, adults must promote positive attitudes toward reading through enthusiasm, animation, and modeling (Bergin, 2001; Hiebert, 1981; Holdaway, 1979). Reading sessions also provide natural contexts for adults to assist children in forming concepts about books, print, and reading, such as directionality and book handling (Clay, 1979).

When conversation takes place around joint storybook reading, adults and young children have the opportunity to construct meaning together and positively affect the development of the children's literacy skills. Cochran Smith (1986) states, "The task of becoming literate and learning to make sense of printed and pictorial texts requires more than simply breaking the sound-symbol code" (p. 39). Equally important is the negotiation of meaning and understanding of literacy conventions that can occur through interactive reading sessions.

A number of studies have indicated that behaviors such as mutual questioning and responding, making stories relevant to children's lives, giving praise and feedback, explaining, physically sharing the book, monitoring children's understanding, and adjusting dialogue to acknowledge mutual understanding are all behaviors that enhance children's literacy skills and comprehension (Cochran-Smith, 1984, 1986; Flood, 1977, Jordan et al., 2000; Ninio & Bruner, 1978; Roser & Martinez, 1985; Whitehurst et al., 1988). The studies support the notion that when these behaviors are practiced during joint storybook reading time, children become more engaged in reading and are better able to comprehend the story and understand the conventions of books.

The Impact of Cultural, Economic, and Environmental Differences

Teale (1978, 1981, 1984) has extensively reviewed the literature on early reading and states that, although storybook reading may not be necessary for becoming literate, it does have an extremely facilitative effect on children's acquisition of emergent literacy skills. He acknowledges that students who come from disadvantaged environments with few books in their homes and few opportunities to read with adults may do fine in school. However, he also emphasizes that "the more conducive to learning to read we can make that environment, the more responsible it will be in the long run for enabling children to read and for fostering within children the desire to read" (Teale, 1978, p. 931). (See chapter 6 for an example of a program that supports this philosophy.)

Within her larger ethnographic study of language use and communication in the white working–class community of Roadville, the black working–class farm community of Trackton, and the mainstream community of Maintown (all town names are pseudonyms), Heath (1983, 1986) looked specifically at storybook reading. She discovered that Trackton parents did not read to their children, although Roadville and Maintown parents did. Maintown parents mediated the text for their children, taught them to label things and pay attention to specific aspects of the text, demonstrated how to link old and new knowledge, and gave "what" explanations (i.e., known–answer questions). Also in Maintown, children learned to answer decontextualized knowledge questions and became cooperative partners with adults in negotiating meaning from books. Conversely, Roadville children were taught letters, words, and labeling but little generalization to other contexts. The children were expected to listen and not interrupt their parents and focus on the truth in stories. The use of imagination was not considered desirable by these children's parents, who practiced direct instruction as they read books to children. Rarely did Roadville parents ask their children to relate a book's content to other areas. When Maintown children entered school, they usually did quite well, and this success continued throughout elementary school. Roadville children appeared to do well when they first entered school because they understood adherence to rules and norms of participation. When they entered the third or fourth grade and were expected to think more creatively and conceptually, they began to fail. Trackton children came to school without understanding the need for "what" explanations, and, therefore, they rarely participated. Collectively, they had a hard time adjusting to the social interaction patterns of school learning and, frequently, did not meet with academic success. Heath's work demonstrates that it is not joint book reading itself but what goes on during the parent-child reading time that may make a strong difference in children's literacy development.

Swift (1970) designed a project to assess the effectiveness of a training program meant to enhance the storytelling and communication skills of low-income mothers with limited educational backgrounds. Swift's design focuses on aspects of maternal language and communication that are shown to be related to a child's future success in school. Mothers of 3- to 5-year-old children in a Get Set preschool program were taught to use children's books to increase interactive communication with their children. The program emphasized the elaboration of thought, the sharing of the books themselves, the mothers' abilities to relate the books to their children's lives and experiences, and the retelling of stories. The mothers also were shown techniques for observing and responding to their children's reactions. As a result of the intervention, mothers developed the ability to tell stories and interact with their children around books and began to better understand their roles as their children's teachers. Their children also became more attentive and responsive. Swift concluded that if mothers who are known to lack these skills could be taught to use preschool books as vehicles for communicating with their children, then their own language and literacy development would be positively affected, as would the literacy development of their children.

After examining a number of studies focusing on families and literacy, Rogers (2001) documented three important things to remember about the status of literacy in families and communities. She acknowledges that (1) a wide range of literary practices exist; (2) literacy is a social practice that shapes and is shaped by social institutions; and (3) social debates concerning family literacy are often connected to discussions of the mismatch between home, community, and school discourses. With these issues in mind, educators must continue to be aware that being literate means different things in different cultures. Parents encourage literacy in a variety of ways within the home and community. It does appear, however, that certain literacy practices that occur within joint book-reading episodes can help to promote the type of skills children need to master in order to ensure success in school, and evidence exists that nonmainstream groups agree with this viewpoint (Heath, 1983; McCarthey, 2000). The types of interactive behaviors discussed earlier in this chapter can be taught to parents within different cultural contexts, in different languages, using culturally relevant texts. Furthermore, parents can be encouraged to practice them during storybook reading with their children.

Paradigms for Measuring Adult-Child Behaviors During Joint Reading Sessions

Guinagh and Jester (1972) developed the Parent As Reader Scale (PARS) in order to assess the quality of mother-child interaction during reading and to determine the quality of the mothers' teaching abilities. The measure focuses on the mothers' behavior. The items on the scale reflect those dimensions of the mother-child interaction that are assumed to be related to positive growth in children. There are 10 different rating scales assessed by scores ranging from 1 to 5. The highest score possible is a 50. The PARS items cover introduction to the book, language use, encouragement of child participation, elaboration, feedback, identification, and affect. The authors of this instrument have used it with low socioeconomic status populations to determine which important reading and teaching behaviors parents may not use when reading with their children. Guinagh and Jester promote this tool as a springboard for training parents to read more effectively during storybook time.

Resnick and colleagues (1987) developed an evaluation tool for observing behaviors during maternal reading to infants. This instrument comprises four categories: mother's body management, management of book, language proficiency, and attention to affect. There are a total of

56 separate behaviors listed under these categories. Although the authors are familiar with theory on early reading, they chose to arrive at these behaviors by observing what occurs during mother-infant reading sessions that they videotaped. Resnick and colleagues feel that they want to be open to all aspects of sharing behavior and do not want to narrow their instrument based on others' findings. The instrument does ultimately include many of the well-researched behaviors, such as labeling, praising, describing, observing affect, identifying, making text relevant to life, and inviting participation. However, it also has a stronger emphasis on physical behaviors, such as holding the child close, removing distractions, and sharing the book. When scoring mothers, the instrument considers both positive and negative behaviors.

In their initial study, Resnick and colleagues found that mothers became more involved as their children grew older and were able both to express their understanding of reading materials and participate frequently. Martin (1998) supports this viewpoint and found that as children get older, their mothers can provide them with more factual information about book concepts, and more demands are placed on the children to label and participate in dialogue. Resnick and colleagues believe that use of their instrument helps to identify those parents who may benefit most from some type of training in positive reading behaviors. Helping parents practice reading behaviors that have been shown to enhance the reading readiness of children when they enter school boosts the academic success of children who might have previously met with frustration toward success. Most notable, Edwards (1991, 1995) has used Resnick and colleagues' evaluation tool to assist her in determining the types of behaviors parents are taught in her training program, Parents as Partners in Reading, which is a nationally known family literacy program that empowers parents to help one another promote literacy in the home.

Few attempts have been made to construct instruments that assess the interactive reading behaviors of parents and their preschool children, particularly in their home environment. Some studies have examined interactive behaviors between teachers and students in schools using devised rating scales (Klesius & Griffith, 1996; Morrow, 1990), but these scales have not been promoted as evaluation tools for parents and children. The two instruments developed by Guinagh and Jester and

Resnick and colleagues focus exclusively on rating the adult's behavior, not the corresponding behaviors of the child. If the quality of interaction between adult and child promotes literacy development, then it is important to evaluate the behaviors of both participants in order to determine instructional strategies that may assist them both. Understanding parents' beliefs about reading practices and the effect of these practices on their children's literacy development also may prove helpful when designing future instruction based on observations of reading dyads.

The Adult/Child Interactive Reading Inventory (ACIRI)

I designed the ACIRI as an observational interactive reading instrument that would not be patronizing, insulting, or threatening to participants and that would help family literacy teachers assess joint storybook reading, while teaching parents effective techniques for making reading more interesting and useful to their children. The reading instrument also has been translated into Spanish for use with Spanish-speaking populations. Furthermore, the ACIRI has been used as a major evaluation component in a number of programs composed of diverse populations, including Even Start, Head Start, and other family literacy programs over the past five years. Teachers use the ACIRI to observe parent–child dyads under natural conditions during joint storybook reading time either at program centers or in participants' homes. The instrument consists of categories and behaviors selected for inclusion based on the research previously discussed. I created the inventory primarily to provide teachers working with parent–child dyads with a means of evaluating the dyads, thereby helping them decide how to focus their future teaching to best help these families. I also intended the ACIRI to introduce parents and guardians to a greater range of strategies that they could use to help their children develop the kinds of literacy skills that appear to be most helpful when entering school. Another purpose of the ACIRI is to provide data for program evaluation purposes.

ACIRI COMPONENTS

Areas for both quantitative scoring and qualitative comments are contained in the ACIRI. For both the adult and the child portions, the observed interactive reading behaviors are defined within three categories: (a) enhancing attention to text, (b) promoting interactive reading and supporting comprehension, and (c) using literacy strategies. Each component assesses four interactive behaviors for a total evaluation of 12 specific literacy behaviors. These 12 behaviors are directly linked to the literature on promoting good reading practice (Cochran-Smith, 1984; Flood, 1977; Jordan et al., 2000; Morrow, 1983; Senechel, Cornell, & Broda, 1995). A copy of the ACIRI is attached in the Appendix (page 300). The actual inventory is on a legal-size form.

ACIRI ADMINISTRATION

The administration of the ACIRI takes 15–30 minutes. The length of time spent on the inventory depends on the complexity of the book being read and the number of observed behaviors the teacher wishes to discuss with the adult after the observation. The step-by-step procedure for using the ACIRI is as follows:

1. The adult, child, and teacher select an age-appropriate book. Wordless picture books are available, permitting adults with low conventional literacy skills to participate.

2. The adult and child read together while being observed by their home-visiting or center-based teacher. The teacher notes adult and child behaviors on the inventory and writes comments as the reading progresses.

3. When the reading is complete, the teacher studies his or her comments, then discusses with the adult the areas of strength and those that need improvement in a nonthreatening, helpful manner. The teacher uses the inventory as a teaching tool, thus linking teaching directly to assessment.

4. After the session, the teacher reads over his or her comments and numerically scores the behaviors, entering the scores in the appropriate columns. The numerical scores are used for program evaluation purposes only and are not meant to be shared with participants. The goal in using the ACIRI with families is to be encouraging, friendly, and nonthreatening. Numerical scores can only serve to associate the ACIRI with a testing rather than a teaching situation, and this creates discomfort in the majority of participants

ACIRI Scoring

For program evaluation purposes, the ACIRI can be quantitatively scored. Qualitative data in the form of written comments are also available to support numerical scores and provide teachers with detailed pictures of what has occurred during the reading interactions. The numerical scoring is based on a 0–3 scale as follows: *0* indicates "no evidence of the behavior, *1* indicates that the behavior occurs infrequently, *2* indicates that the behavior occurs some of the time, and *3* indicates that the behavior occurs most of the time. As the adult and child read together, the teacher makes observational notes near each listed behavior as he or she sees it occur. Some teachers choose to use a combination of written comments and check marks that indicate the number of times a behavior occurs, such as the number of times a parent asks the child a question. The combination of these data assists the teacher in quantitatively scoring the inventory when the reading ends. The parent's and child's reading behaviors are separately indicated by scores on each individual item, mean scores on the three broad categories, and by the total mean score of the inventory.

ACIRI Reliability

Without reliability, an instrument cannot be used for any type of uniform evaluation. Reliability indicates score consistency over time or across multiple evaluators. Reliable assessment assures that the same answers receive the same score regardless of who performs the scoring or how or where the scoring takes place. (See chapter 12 for further discussion of the importance of reliability.)

When I originally piloted the ACIRI, inter-rater reliability was calculated among eight raters from a group consisting of family literacy teachers, administrators, and community service workers, all of whom had become familiar with the instrument through workshops. The raters watched three sets of dyads on videotape, each set reading two books matched for difficulty and vocabulary level. Frequency counts of raters' scores across individual items were done for each dyad and each book to find how many raters scored each item the same. This process provided the means of showing inter-rater agreement on each book for each dyad. A percentage of agreement was then calculated for each dyad. The percentage of agreement for all dyads and all books was then averaged, giving the total agreement figure. Having the same dyad read two different books also allowed for examination of the effect of varied materials on the scoring procedure. The "materials" reliability (two books by the same author read by the same dyad) was calculated with frequency counts of raters' scores on individual ACIRI items of the same dyad over two episodes reading matched books. The percentage of agreement across each matched pair was then calculated. These three total percentages were then averaged, resulting in the total agreement figure. The examination of the ACIRI for inter-rater reliability resulted in 97% agreement among eight raters across six observed reading dyads. When materials reliability was calculated for dyads who read two different books matched for author, vocabulary, and difficulty, raters agreed 99% of the time on scores for the pairs. This high degree of reliability has been achieved in multiple settings over a number of years. It is extremely important that teachers in all programs understand the category and behavior definitions (see DeBruin-Parecki, in press) in order for reliability to be established among those who administer the ACIRI.

ACIRI VALIDITY

For an instrument to be useful to literacy programs, it must measure what it was designed to assess, or it is not valid. Because of the ACIRI's uniqueness, it was difficult to assess concurrent validity—that is, to compare it to other instruments that measure the same interactive behaviors across both adults and children. Therefore, I decided to examine construct and consequential validity. Construct validity of an instrument is determined by examining the items on that instrument and deciding if they are fair and representative samples of the general domain that the instrument was designed to measure (American Educational Research Association, American Psychological Association, and National Council on Measurement in Education, 1985). This type of validity is most often ascertained through reference to related research and theories. The ACIRI behaviors (items) are based on research and theory in the field of joint storybook reading, as reviewed in the beginning of this chapter. Those interactive reading behaviors that seem important to the development of literacy skills in children and the transfer of those skills to positive school outcomes are contained in and measured by the ACIRI.

Consequential validity occurs when a designed instrument has positive consequences for those who use it. In the case of the ACIRI, this type of validity would mean that the implementation, concepts, and content of the ACIRI promote future improved interactive reading and learning experiences over time. Consequential validity has tremendous implications for newly developed authentic assessments such as the ACIRI:

> High priority needs to be given to the collection of evidence about the intended and unintended effects of assessments on the ways teachers and students spend their time and think about the goals of education. It cannot just be assumed that a more "authentic" assessment will result in classroom activities that are more conducive to learning. (Linn, Baker, & Dunbar, 1991, p. 17)

To provide evidence of consequential validity, I offer the following excerpts about the administration, purpose, and usefulness of the ACIRI from interviews done with two teachers who piloted and continue to use this instrument. Their comments address the positive implications of the ACIRI for both teaching and learning.

Teacher 1: After it's been done, I'll talk about some of the things like, "You did really well on this. One thing that I noticed you weren't doing that you might want to think about doing is…. And this is why this is important when you read to your children." It really helps them stay focused on the story, and it makes them really think about more than just the words. They have to think about things they are doing while they read, and that's a good way to develop skills.

Teacher 2: I think the Interactive Reading Inventory is helpful for initial diagnosis of joint reading behaviors. It's really helpful because I can say to a mom, "Do you notice that when you do this that this happens? Maybe if you try something else…. Try this, and I don't think that will happen anymore." It really is good to have both of them there together. It's valuable as a teaching tool because I can always say to the mom, "You did really well. There are only one or two places where I think..." It gives me a jumping-off place. This definitely provides valuable information to me, and I think to the family members and administrators.

It appears from these comments and others offered in formal and informal interviews that teachers have found the ACIRI useful and feel it accomplishes its purposes of being a teaching, learning, and evaluation instrument that has positive consequences for adults, children, and teachers. Adults are able to discover the joint storybook reading skills they need to improve or learn and get focused skill instruction from teachers. Children benefit by participating in interactive reading sessions, and they ultimately profit when their parents or guardians learn how to encourage the development of important literacy skills. The teachers gain information that allows them to design lessons concentrated more closely on the skills parents and guardians need to improve. This information allows them to note participants' strengths and provide individual recognition, as opposed to teaching the same curriculum to everyone and risking participant boredom and lack of motivation.

Linking Assessment and Curriculum

If program teachers are going to measure behaviors or skills, they must be sure the skills being tested are being taught. This link between curriculum and assessment is crucial if the objective is to measure authentic progress over time (Wiggins, 1992). In other words, it is imperative that a teacher using the ACIRI to evaluate joint storybook reading skills also teach these skills.

In the summer of 2002, a family literacy program was created in Waterloo, Iowa, at the YWCA as a community service project. The basis for this program was the ACIRI and the skills emphasized by it. Each week, the teacher emphasized a particular skill or set of skills and built the week's lesson around this focus. Teachers gave families books to read and activities that focused on the skill(s) taught in each specific lesson to take home each week. Using the ACIRI, staff assessed each family before and after program instruction. Because of the small number of families, each one was treated as its own case study. Across all families, positive differences on the ACIRI were evident (DeBruin-Parecki & Severson, 2002).

Conclusion

According to data that researchers have collected and analyzed (see DeBruin-Parecki, 1999), the ACIRI has achieved its original purposes of being sensitive to growth and change over time and being useful to teachers as a measurement of adult and child reading behavior and progress. This tool provides a means to promote joint storybook reading and to observe the interactive behaviors of adults and children at home as they engage in this collaborative process. The scoring of the ACIRI provides quantitative information to satisfy those persons who require a numerical means of judging progress and qualitative data in order to enrich the numerical data and expand on the reasons for assigning certain scores. While family literacy programs can compile useful data for their funders to help ensure continued financial support, teachers can focus on the *teaching and learning* aspects of the instrument. Using time and adult and child development as natural interventions, the ACIRI is meant to encourage good instruction, as well as authentic and friendly assessment. The inventory also helps teachers determine how to focus their efforts when it comes to promoting good reading behaviors.

Two key goals of family literacy programs are improving the literacy skills of both adults and children and encouraging adults to practice reading behaviors in family settings with their youngsters to enhance these children's abilities to do well in school. The behaviors listed in the inventory are supported by research demonstrating that learning and practicing these skills gives children a head start when they begin school, assists adults in improving their own literacy skills, and further provides positive opportunities for families to interact around literacy together. These positive opportunities may help dispel any negative feelings adults may retain from their own school experiences. The inventory enables teachers to ascertain which skills adults and children already practice, permitting the teachers to design individualized instruction that will improve these skills and introduce others. Teachers also can use the ACIRI as a teaching tool by reviewing it with the adult and child after the reading of the initial story, explaining why they received certain scores and the reasons for learning and practicing the behaviors listed. The design of the ACIRI provides a unique means of authenticating the progress adults and children are making as they learn to read together. By documenting the positive outcomes, the ACIRI also appears to satisfy the criteria for having consequential validity.

In the future, it might be helpful for programs to have lessons, interactive reading tips, and lists of storybooks that match each of the interactive reading skills on the ACIRI so teachers can easily move forward in teaching those skills that specific adults and children need to improve. Teachers could then consult and modify sample lessons and activities and find books that promote needed skills for individual families. Later, they can spend time with individual families, revisiting the behaviors that require improvement in order to determine the progress made over the school year in these areas. A book to meet this need is currently in progress (DeBruin-Parecki, in press).

REFERENCES

American Educational Research Association, American Psychological Association, and National Council on Measurement in Education. (1985). *Standards for educational and psychological testing.* Washington, DC: Authors.

Barbara Bush Foundation for Family Literacy. (1989). *First teachers: A family literacy handbook for parents, policy makers, and literacy providers.* Washington, DC: Author.

Bergin, C. (2001). The parent-child relationship during beginning reading. *Journal of Literacy Research, 22*(4), 681–706.

Brizius, J.A., & Foster, S.A. (1993). *Generation to generation: Realizing the promise of family literacy.* Ypsilanti, MI: High/Scope Press.

Brooks, G. (1998). The effectiveness of family literacy programmes in England and Wales for parents. *Journal of Adolescent & Adult Literacy, 42,* 130–132.

Bus, A.G., van IJzendoorn, M.H., & Pellegrini, A.D. (1995). Joint book reading makes for success in learning to read: A meta-analysis on intergenerational transmission of literacy. *Review of Educational Research, 65*(1), 1–21.

Cairney, T.H. (2000). The construction of literacy and literacy learners. *Language Arts, 77*(6), 496–505.

Clark, M.M. (1976). *Young fluent readers: What can they teach us?* London: Heinemann.

Clark, M.M. (1984). Literacy at home and at school: Insights from a study of young fluent readers. In H. Goelman, A.A. Oberg, & F. Smith (Eds.), *Awakening to literacy* (pp. 122–130). London: Heinemann.

Clay, M.M. (1979). *The early detection of reading difficulties: A diagnostic survey* (2nd ed.). London: Heinemann.

Cochran-Smith, M. (1984). *The making of a reader.* Westport, CT: Ablex.

Cochran-Smith, M. (1986). Reading to children: A model for understanding texts. In B.B. Shiefflin & P. Gilmore (Eds.), *The acquisition of literacy: Ethnographic perspectives* (pp. 35–54). Westport, CT: Ablex.

Crain-Thoreson, C., Dahlin, M.P., & Powell, T.A. (2001). Parent–child interaction in three con-versational contexts: Variations in style and strategy. *New Directions for Child and Adolescent Development, 92,* 23–37.

DeBruin-Parecki, A. (1997). *The identification of effective practices and the development of authentic as-sessments for family literacy programs.* Unpublished doctoral dissertation, University of Michigan, Ann Arbor.

DeBruin-Parecki, A. (1999, August). *The Adult/Child Interactive Reading Inventory: An assessment of joint storybook reading skills* (Tech Rep. No. 2-004). Ann Arbor, MI: The National Center for Improvement of Early Reading Achievement.

DeBruin-Parecki, A. (in press). *Assessing Adult/Child Interactive Reading: The Adult/Child Interactive Reading Inventory.* Baltimore: Brookes.

DeBruin-Parecki, A., Paris, S.G., & Seidenberg, J. (1997). Family literacy: Examining practice and issues of effectiveness. *Journal of Adolescent & Adult Literacy, 40,* 596–605.

DeBruin-Parecki, A., & Severson, A. (2002, October). *Promoting interactive storybook reading in fam-ily literacy programs.* Paper presented at the 29th Plains International Reading Association Regional Conference, Topeka, KS.

Durkin, D. (1966). *Children who read early: Two longitudinal studies.* New York: Teachers College Press.

Durkin, D. (1972). *Teaching young children to read.* Boston: Allyn & Bacon.

Edwards, P.A. (1991). Fostering early literacy through parent coaching. In E.H. Hiebert (Ed.), *Literacy for a diverse society: Perspectives, practices and policies* (pp. 199–213). New York: Teachers College Press.

Edwards, P.A. (1995). Combining parents' and teachers' thoughts about storybook reading at home and school. In L.M. Morrow (Ed.), *Family literacy connections in schools and commu-nities* (pp. 54–69). Newark, DE: International Reading Association.

Flood, J.E. (1977). Parental styles in reading episodes with young children. *The Reading Teacher, 30,* 864–867.

Guinagh, B.J., & Jester, R.E. (1972). How parents read to children. *Theory Into Practice, 11*(5), 171–177.

Heath, S.B. (1983). *Ways with words: Language, life and work in communities and classrooms.* Cambridge, UK: Cambridge University Press.

Heath, S.B. (1986). What no bedtime story means: Narrative skills at home and at school. In B.B. Schieffelin & E. Ochs (Eds.), *Language socialization across cultures* (pp. 97–124). Cambridge, UK: Cambridge University Press.

Hiebert, E.H. (1981). Developmental patterns and interrelationships of preschool children's print awareness. *Reading Research Quarterly, 16,* 236–260.

Holdaway, D. (1979). *The foundations of literacy.* Sydney, Australia: Ashton Scholastic.

International Reading Association and the National Association for the Education of Young Children. (1998). *Learning to read and write: Developmentally appropriate practices for young chil-dren.* A joint position statement of the International Reading Association (IRA) and the National Association for the Education of Young Children (NAEYC). Newark, DE: Author; Washington, DC: Author.

Jordan, G.E., Snow, C.E., & Porche, M.V. (2000). Project EASE: The effects of a family literacy project on kindergarten students' early literacy skills. *Reading Research Quarterly, 35,* 524–546.

Klesius, J.P., & Griffith, P.L. (1996). Interactive storybook reading for at-risk learners. *The Reading Teacher, 49,* 552–560.

Lancy, D.F., Draper, K.D., & Boyce, G. (1989). Parental influence on children's acquisition of reading. *Contemporary Issues in Reading,* 83–93.

Linn, R.L., Baker, E.L., & Dunbar, S.B. (1991). Complex performance–based assessment: Expectations and validation criteria. *Educational Researcher, 20*(8), 15–21.

Martin, L.E. (1998). Early book reading: How mothers deviate from printed text for young children. *Reading Research Quarterly, 37*, 137–160.

McCarthey, S.J. (2000). Home-school connections: A review of the literature. *Journal of Educational Research, 93*(3), 145–53.

McKee, P.A., & Rhett, N. (1995). The Even Start family literacy program. In L.M. Morrow (Ed.), *Family literacy connections in schools and communities* (pp. 155–166). Newark, DE: International Reading Association.

Morrow, L.M. (1983). Home and school correlates of early interest in literature. *Journal of Educational Research, 76*, 221–230.

Morrow, L.M. (1990). Assessing children's understanding of story through their construction and reconstruction of narrative. In L.M. Morrow & J.K. Smith (Eds.), *Assessment for instruction in early literacy* (pp. 110–133). Englewood Cliffs, NJ: Prentice Hall.

Ninio, A., & Bruner, J. (1978). The achievement and antecedents of labeling. *Journal of Child Language, 5*(1), 1–15.

Purcell-Gates, V. (2000). Family literacy. In M.L. Kamil, P.B. Mosenthal, P.D. Pearson, & R. Barr (Eds.), *Handbook of reading research* (Vol. 3, pp. 853–870). Mahwah, NJ: Erlbaum.

Resnick, M.B., Roth, J., Aaron, P.M., Scott, J., Wolking, W.D., Larsen, J.J., et al. (1987). Mothers reading to infants: A new observational tool. *The Reading Teacher, 40*, 888–894.

Rogers, R. (2001). Family literacy and the mediation of cultural models. In J. Hoffman, D. Schallert, C. Fairbanks, J. Worthy, & B. Maloch (Eds.), *50th yearbook of the National Reading Conference* (pp. 96–114). Chicago: National Reading Conference.

Roser, N., & Martinez, M. (1985). Roles adults play in preschoolers' response to literature. *Language Arts, 62*(5), 485–490.

Senechel, M., Cornell, E.H., & Broda, L.S. (1995). Age-related differences in the organization of parent-infant interactions during picture-book reading. *Early Childhood Research Quarterly, 10*(3), 317–337.

Snow, C.E., Burns, M.S., & Griffin, P. (Eds.). (1998). *Preventing reading difficulties in young children*. Washington, DC: National Academy Press.

Storch, S.A., & Whitehurst, G.J. (2001). The role of family and home in the literacy development of young children from low-income backgrounds. *New Directions for Child and Adolescent Development, 92*, 53–71.

Swift, M.S. (1970). Training poverty mothers in communication skills. *The Reading Teacher, 23*, 360–367.

Taylor, D. (1983). *Family literacy*. Portsmouth, NH: Heinemann.

Teale, W.H. (1978). Positive environments for learning to read: What studies of early readers tell us. *Language Arts, 55*, 922–932.

Teale, W.H. (1981). Parents reading to their children: What we know and need to know. *Language Arts, 58*, 902–912.

Teale, W.H. (1984). Reading to young children: Its significance for literacy development. In H. Goelman, A. Oberg, & F. Smith (Eds.), *Awakening to literacy* (pp. 110–121). Portsmouth, NH: Heinemann.

United States Government. (2001). *No Child Left Behind Act*. Retrieved November 6, 2002, from http://www.ed.gov/legislation/ESEA02/pg107.html

Vygotsky, L.S. (1978). *Mind in society: The development of higher psychological processes* (M. Cole, V. John-Steiner, S. Scribner, & E. Souberman, Eds. and Trans.). Cambridge, MA: Harvard University Press. (Original work published 1934)

Whitehurst, G.J., Falco, F.L., Lonigan, C.J., Fischel, J.E., DeBaryshe, B.D., Valdez-Menchaca, M.C., et al. (1988). Accelerating language development through picture book reading. *Developmental Psychology, 24*(4), 552–559.

Wiggins, G. (1992). Creating tests worth taking. *Educational Leadership, 49*(8), 26–33.

Appendix
Adult/Child Interactive Reading Inventory

CHILD AGE _____ DOB _____
ADULT AGE _____ DOB _____

Teacher's Name _____   General Comments: _____

SCORE (0–3)
3 = MOST OF THE TIME (4 or more times)
2 = SOME OF THE TIME (2–5 times)
1 = INFREQUENTLY (1 time)
0 = NO EVIDENCE

SCORE

ADULT BEHAVIOR	Adult's Name: _____ Date: _____ Case # _____ OBSERVATION	CHILD BEHAVIOR	Child's Name: _____ Date: _____ Case # _____ OBSERVATION
I. Enhancing Attention to Text 1. Attempts to promote and maintain physical proximity 2. Sustains interest and attention through use of child-adjusted language, positive affect, and reinforcement 3. Gives child opportunity to hold book and turn pages 4. Shares book with child (i.e., displays sense of audience in book handling when reading)		**I. Enhancing Attention to Text** 1. Child seeks and maintains physical proximity 2. Child pays attention and sustains interest 3. Child holds book and turns pages on his or her own or when asked 4. Child initiates or responds to book sharing that takes his or her presence into account	
II. Promoting Interactive Reading and Supporting Comprehension 1. Poses and solicits questions about the book's content		**II. Promoting Interactive Reading and Supporting Comprehension** 1. Child responds to questions about book	

(continued)

Appendix (Continued)
Adult/Child Interactive Reading Inventory

CHILD AGE _____ DOB _____
ADULT AGE _____ DOB _____

SCORE (0–5)
5 = MOST OF THE TIME (4 or more times)
2 = SOME OF THE TIME (2–3 times)
1 = INFREQUENTLY (1 time)
0 = NO EVIDENCE

Teacher's Name _____

General Comments: _____

SCORE

ADULT BEHAVIOR	Adult's Name: _____ Case # _____ Date: _____ OBSERVATION	CHILD BEHAVIOR	Child's Name: _____ Case # _____ Date: _____ OBSERVATION
2 Points to pictures and words to assist child in identification and understanding 3 Relates book content and child's responses to personal experiences 4 Pauses to answer questions child poses		2 Child responds to parent cues or identifies pictures and words on his or her own 3 Child attempts to relate book content to personal experiences 4 Child poses questions about the story and related topics	
III. Using Literacy Strategies 1. Identifies visual cues related to story reading (i.e, pictures, repetitive words) 2. Solicits predictions 3. Asks child to recall information from the story 4. Elaborates on child's ideas		**III. Using Literacy Strategies** 1. Child responds to parent and/or identifies visual cues related to the story himself or herself 2. Child is able to guess what will happen next based on picture cues 3. Child is able to recall information from story 4. Child spontaneously offers ideas about story	

NAME OF BOOK: _____ AUTHOR: _____

Afterword

Barbara Krol-Sinclair and Andrea DeBruin-Parecki

Over the past decade, family literacy has become well established as a construct and as a medium for providing instruction to parents and children. A recent review of the National Center for Family Literacy (NCFL) program directory lists over 2,000 family literacy programs operating in the United States alone, and the National Adult Literacy Database (NALD) comprises more than 300 family literacy initiatives in Canada. It is more difficult to determine the exact number of family literacy programs internationally, but, clearly, those programs are rapidly increasing in number.

The programs and approaches highlighted in this volume represent the diversity of family literacy as a field of research and practice. Family literacy is a range of efforts to strengthen parents' and children's literacy and to foster home–school collaboration (chapter 1). The notion of family literacy involves children developing concepts about language and print (chapter 2); parents and children reading, writing, talking, and listening together at home (chapter 3); and programs building efforts for parents and youth to share in literacy and for families to support their adolescents' success in school (chapter 4). Family literacy includes affirming and supporting the role that fathers play in literacy at home (chapter 5), building literacy instruction on the strengths and cultural values of families (chapter 6), and acknowledging the literate lives of children with significant disabilities and the knowledge families have about their children that can influence instruction at school (chapter 7). Family literacy involves creating opportunities for parents and children to learn together (chapter 8); sharing read–aloud techniques with teen parents (chapter 9); providing books for babies and their families (chapter 10); and tailoring instruction to meet the needs of families, communities, and cultures (chapter 11). Family literacy is stepping back to evaluate our practices as educators so we can support families in developing literacy (chapter 12), building two-way communication between home and school (chapter 13), and assessing and guiding parents in reading with their children (chapter 14). Family literacy programs, their goals, and resulting outcomes are as diverse as the participating families themselves.

Despite the range of approaches that characterize the field of family literacy, this volume does not proportionally represent how various models are implemented in the United States. Of the programs listed in the NCFL directory, more than 83% are designated to use the Kenan Trust four-component model (described in chapter 8). The adoption of the Kenan Trust model by the U.S. government in its extensive funding of family literacy under Even Start has necessarily limited the extent to which other approaches to family literacy are sustained and valued.

In contrast, in Canada, which has avoided promoting a single model of family literacy, the over 300 programs listed in the NALD represent a far greater diversity of programming, including Books for Babies (described in chapter 10), Come Read With Me, and Parent-Child Mother Goose programs. Just over 2% of the Canadian programs follow the Kenan Trust model.

The lack of diversity in U.S. family literacy programs is not surprising, given the increasing emphasis on a one-size-fits-all approach to K–12 education. The No Child Left Behind Act, signed by President Bush in 2002, mandates extensive testing for students at most grade levels that will be used to define students' success in school and that limits the approaches teachers can use in literacy instruction to approved methods grounded in a narrow definition of research-based evidence. Bilingual education, which provides a range of instructional programs to support children who enter school with limited proficiency in English, is also under fire in the United States and has been recently eliminated in three states—Arizona, California, and Massachusetts.

The International Reading Association's position statement *What Is Evidence-Based Reading Instruction?* (2002) notes, "There is no single instructional program or method that is effective in teaching all children to read" (p. 1). Current U.S. educational policy, however, is attempting to reduce classroom instruction to a formulaic process that requires all children to learn the same way, with little regard for their backgrounds, experiences, challenges, or interests.

Just as K–12 education is being driven to what appears to be a one-size-fits-all approach, there are indications that families, and thus programs supporting families, are being targeted to support children's learning in increasingly narrow ways. Superintendent Jerry Weast of Montgomery County, Maryland, recently proposed offering increased English language classes for immigrant parents. Although few would deny that proficiency in English language and literacy are key to families' success in the United States, Dr. Weast's proposal suggests that English should replace families' first languages because, as he says, "These children are not getting the oral English language they need in the quantity that they need it in order to learn to read...they're not exposed to English all day long" ("Weast Plans to Push Language," 2002, p. B1). Such a statement implies that parents should speak to their children only in English and that all parents should strive to emulate the mainstream, suburban, middle-class families who are viewed as offering their children adequate support. This view not only denigrates the funds of knowledge (González et al., 1995) that nonmainstream families add to their children's learning but also flies in the face of an extensive body of research on the positive impact of strong first-language support on children's second language literacy learning (e.g., Cummins, 1981, 2000; Krashen, 1996, 1999; Smith, 1994). Perhaps more important, comments such as Weast's foster the notion that there is one path to academic success, both at school and at home.

The need for continued and expanded family literacy support, both in the United States and throughout the world, is clear. In 2002, the United Nations Educational, Scientific, and Cultural Organization (UNESCO) estimated that 20.3% of adults over the age of 15 worldwide were unable to read or write in the year 2000, a percentage expected to decrease slightly to 18.3% by 2005. One fifth of the world's parents, then, have little or no print literacy, and two thirds of those who cannot read or write are women, the primary caregivers of most of the world's children. No single formula exists for family literacy that can meet the needs of such a diverse global population. Educators must offer a range of programs and approaches that are grounded within the populations and communities being served. Instruction must be based on the strengths, routines, and interests of families and must validate participants' languages, cultures, and values, while offering parents and children opportunities to read and write with greater ease, to engage in activities that are relevant to their lives and their goals, and to expand their knowledge of school practices.

A need exists for programs that support youths—both students and teenage parents. Although existing data on adolescents' school performance clearly indicate that support for learning at home is tied to student achievement, the field of family literacy has primarily focused its efforts on families with preschool- and elementary school–age children. Family literacy programs must expand their focus to more fully include middle and high school students in sharing literacy with their parents, siblings, and children.

A compelling need also exists for a range of assessment tools that will provide families and programs with data that can drive instruction, in addition to evaluating learner gains. Educators must develop a broader range of pre- and postinstruction strategies that offer meaningful information about parents' literacy strengths and needs, families' daily literacy routines, and parent–child reading, all of which can serve as starting points for instruction. Moreover, educators need to be able to document changes in parents' and children's literacy growth throughout their enrollment in family literacy programs both to evaluate their practice and to demonstrate program effects to funders.

A critical need exists for research in several areas of family literacy (Purcell-Gates, 2000). Learning more about the literacy practices of nonmainstream families will provide information necessary to design instruction that builds on families' strengths while addressing their needs. Data comparing the effectiveness of different types of family literacy program models and evidence of the efficacy of specific instructional practices often included in family literacy programs are essential, as are data indicating the intensity or duration of instruction for best assisting families. Few studies (Purcell-Gates, 2000) have compared the literacy gains of parents and children participating in family literacy interventions with changes over time in matched control groups. All these investigations are important starting points if we are to continue to assert that family literacy instruction holds promise for supporting the literacy learning and empowerment of preschool- and school-age children and their parents. Although it is clear that there is a significant need for further research, it is apparent in the reading of the chapters in this book, as well as the broader body of work in family literacy, that there are certain issues common to sustaining and beginning effective programs and improving others.

Family literacy efforts must be focused on literacy. Although comprehensive social services are important and effective, they are not necessarily connected with literacy. A family literacy program is not a panacea and cannot be expected to cure social ills or eliminate poverty, prejudice, or injustice on its own. The focus in family literacy should be on literacy within the family. Connections to other services are useful and important, but they should not be inextricably linked to family literacy instruction—they are not interchangeable. More important is supporting families in advocating for themselves, in gaining access to services on their own, and in taking active roles in their communities, all within the context of instruction in reading and writing rather than as a substitute for actual literacy practice.

Family literacy instruction should be of sufficient duration and intensity to strengthen parents' and children's growth in reading and writing. As the term *family literacy* moves into mainstream vocabulary, increasing numbers of initiatives identify themselves as family literacy programs. Many efforts, however, especially those promoted by celebrities, consist of little more than book giveaways or one-day events stressing the importance of reading at home. While these efforts are laudable, they are not sufficient in and of themselves to be considered family literacy instruction. Research consistently shows that school-age students are best served when literacy instruction is infused throughout the school day year after year. Likewise, programs serving parents and entire families must strive to offer consistent instructional opportunities over a sustained period of time in order to both build and maintain family members' literacy development.

Working with families is a supplement, not a replacement, for effective instruction for school-age students. Abundant data demonstrate that involved and knowledgeable parents and guardians positively influence their children's success in school—a well-publicized rationale for offering family literacy instruction. Providing parents with strategies to support their children's literacy at home and at school can help bridge gaps between the two places of learning and can strengthen the ways that families use literacy in their daily lives. The responsibility for children's school success, however, cannot rest only on parents, and educators should not expect families' home literacy activities to center on school. Educators need to continue building opportunities for children's learning at school, while affirming that the myriad ways that families routinely read and write are as valid to children's literate lives as are homework and other school-generated literacy activities.

No clear evidence links parents' and families' need for literacy support with a parallel need for parents to participate in parenting instruction. Evidence does not show that parents with limited literacy are less effective parents than those who read and write well or that such parenting instruction leads to greater gains in literacy on the part of parents or that it helps them to be better, more supportive parents. Although discussions around issues of interest to parents are logical within the context of a family literacy class and may in fact lead parents to learn new strategies for raising their children and to improve their abilities to support their children, there is no compelling rationale for parenting instruction to be a mandated component of family literacy instruction. The term *comprehensive*, often used in describing four-component programs, can only serve to further disempower parents in need of language and literacy support by equating their lack of formal education or their literacy in English with a need for parenting support.

In conclusion, the future of family literacy is tenuous at best. Although the past decade has seen growth in the numbers and to a lesser extent the types of programs that offer family literacy services, educators are at a crossroad. They can embrace the range of programming that is labeled as family literacy and continue to validate families' home literacy practices, cultures, languages, and values as they support parents' and children's literacy development and the practice of literacy in the home. Educators can use families' experiences, knowledge, and beliefs to build authentic learning experiences for children and for parents that can translate into enhanced use of literacy in their daily lives. Educators can view home–school collaboration as a two-way partnership in which parents and teachers learn from one another in order to provide children with as seamless as possible a transition from learning at home to learning at school. Or, educators can accept a deficit vision of family literacy that employs a unilateral approach, trying to change families so they are moved toward the mainstream, suburban ideal. Educators can insist that families speak only in English and provide them with a range of services under the guise of literacy that will reinforce to them that they do not measure up to what is expected of them as parents and as their children's first teachers. Educators can employ a school-to-home model of parent involvement, viewing schools as the only valid institutions of education and expecting parents to replicate only school learning activities in the home.

As stated in the introduction to this book, Denny Taylor believes, "No single narrow definition of 'family literacy' can do justice to the richness and complexity of families, and the multiple literacies, including often unrecognized local literacies that are part of their everyday lives" (1997, p. 4). This tenet is strongly supported by the programs and approaches described in this book. As educators continue to move forward in the design and implementation of family literacy programs in the United States and internationally, they need to develop their focus on families' strengths, interests, and needs to expand the ways in which programs are developed, rather than reduce family literacy efforts to attempts to transform families and demean the ways they share literacy at home.

REFERENCES

Cummins, J. (1981). The role of primary language development in promoting educational success for language minority students. In California Department of Education (Ed.), *Schooling and language minority students: A theoretical framework* (pp. 3–49). Los Angeles: Dissemination and Assessment Center at California State University.

Cummins, J. (2000). *Language, power, and pedagogy. Bilingual children in the crossfire.* Clevedon, UK: Multilingual Matters.

González, N., Moll, L., Tenery, M.F., Rivera, A., Mendon, P., Gonzales, R., et al. (1995). Funds of knowledge for teaching in Latino households. *Urban Education, 29,* 443–470.

International Reading Association. (2002). *What is evidence-based reading instruction?* A position statement of the International Reading Association. Newark, DE: Author.

Krashen, S.D. (1996). *Under attack: The case against bilingual education.* Culver City, CA: Language Education Associates.

Krashen, S.D. (1999). *Condemned without a trial: Bogus arguments against bilingual education.* Portsmouth, NH: Heinemann.

Purcell-Gates, V. (2000). Family literacy. In M.L. Kamil, P.B. Mosenthal, P.D. Pearson, & R. Barr (Eds.), *Handbook of reading research* (Vol. 3, pp. 853–870). Mahwah, NJ: Erlbaum.

Smith, F. (1994). *Understanding reading: A psycholinguistic analysis of reading and learning to read* (5th ed.). Hillsdale, NJ: Erlbaum.

Taylor, D. (1997). *Many families, many literacies: An international declaration of principles* Portsmouth, NH: Heinemann.

UNESCO Institute for Statistics. (2002). *Estimated illiteracy rate and illiterate population aged 15 years and older, by region 1970–2015*. Paris: Author.

Weast plans to push language: Schools to target non–English–speaking children, parents. (2002, October 2). *The Washington Post*, p. B1.

AUTHOR INDEX

G

GADSDEN, V.L., 2, 12, 86, 87, 90, 98, 99, 105, 106, 112, 114
GALLAGHER, P., 186
GALLIMORE, R., 127, 133, 135, 144
GAMSE, B., 13, 14, 15, 21
GARDNER, H., 163
GARFINKEL, I., 86, 105
GARLAND, J.E., 71
GARY, L., 96
GEE, J.P., 75, 128, 130
GEISSLER, B., 251
GILBRETH, J.G., 86
GOLDENBERG, C., 127, 133
GOMI, T., 193
GONCU, A., 170
GONZALES, R., 74, 305
GONZALEZ, N., 74, 305
GOODALL, J.S., 191, 192
GOODLING, W.F., 172
GOODMAN, Y., 52
GORMAN, T., 15
GREEN, C., 82
GREENBERG, E., 68
GREENBERG, J.B., 12, 267
GREENE, S.M., 174
GREENWOOD, G.E., 69
GRIFFIN, E., 55
GRIFFIN, P., 5, 284
GRIFFITH, P.L., 289
GROLNICK, W.S., 95
GUINAGH, B.J., 288, 289

H

HALPERN, R., 95, 96
HANDEL, R.D., 75, 76
HANLEY, E., 174
HANNON, P., 203, 207, 229, 235
HANS, S.L., 93, 95, 96
HAO, L.X., 98
HARKER, J., 219
HARMAN, J., 15
HARMON, C., 174
HARRIS, K.M., 94, 97
HARRISON, C., 202, 203, 204, 205, 207, 208, 222, 223, 224, 233, 235
HART, B., 50, 51, 55
HASTINGS, L., 104
HAWKINS, A.J., 92
HAYES, A., 10, 11
HEAD, M., 52

HEATH, S.B., 2, 12, 74, 203, 267, 286, 287, 288
HENDERSON, A.T., 69, 70, 267
HENDRIX, S., 68, 119
HENKES, K., 198
HENRY, J., 82
HEWISON, J., 267
HICKMAN, C.W., 69
HIEBERT, E.H., 10, 86, 99, 101, 267, 285
HILL, M.H., 100
HILL, R., 98
HINDIN, A., 267
HOGAN, D.P., 98
HOLDAWAY, D., 285
HOLMES, V.L., 99
HOLT, D., 257
HOMZA, A., 267
HOOVER-DEMPSEY, K.V., 267
HORN, W.F., 174
HUDDELSON, S., 127
HUEY, E.B., vi
HUTCHISON, D., 15

I

IGLESIAS, A., 95
ILLINOIS STATE BOARD OF EDUCATION, 126
INTERNATIONAL READING ASSOCIATION, 5, 28, 31, 33, 35, 37, 39, 43, 46, 80, 171, 283–284, 304

J

JACKSON, J., 106
JACOBS, J.E., 109
JESTER, R.E., 288, 289
JOHNSON, H.L., 68
JOHNSON, M.J., 45
JOHNSON, W.E., 92
JOHNSON-KUBY, S.A., 73
JORDAN, G.E., 19, 20, 21, 24, 282, 285, 291

K

KAMBERELIS, G., 50
KANE, D., 112
KAPLAN, I., 72
KARR, J., 259
KATZ, A., 73
KEITH, T.A., 69
KELLAGHAN, T., 266
KLESIUS, J.P., 289
KLIEWER, C., 150, 151, 152, 153, 156, 162, 164

THE NEW LONDON GROUP, 128, 130
NICHOLSON, P., 34
NINIO, A., 45, 285
NORD, C.W., 86, 95, 96
NOTTINGHAM CITY COUNCIL, 208

O

OKPEWHO, I., 240
OMEROD, J., 197
OOMS, T.J., 97
ORTIZ, R.W., 86, 101

P

PADAK, N., 252, 253, 256, 258, 259, 261, 264
PALKOVITZ, R., 93
PALLAS, A., 169
PARATORE, J.R., 2, 17, 18, 19, 26, 78, 127, 136, 267, 277
PARIS, S.G., 109, 282
PARISH, W.L., 98
PARKE, R.D., 91, 93
PARKER, F.L., 174
PAULL, S., 11
PAYNE, A.C., 55, 56
PEARPOINT, J., 157
PELLEGRINI, A.D., 2, 10, 55, 185, 284
PERKINS, W.E., 93
PERSKE, R., 157
PFLAUM, S., 68
PHARES, V., 90
PINKARD, O., 250, 263
PIOTRKOWSKI, C.S., 174
PITT, F., 90
PLECK, J.H., 91, 92
POLLACK, W.S., 90
POOLE, P., 68
PORCHE, M.V., 19, 20, 21, 24, 282, 285, 291
POTTEBAUM, S., 69
POTTS, M.W., 11
POWELL, T.A., 284
PURCELL-GATES, V., 2, 12, 68, 78, 267, 283, 284, 306

Q–R

QUINTERO, E., 170, 171, 179, 180, 181
RAMIREZ, R.R., 126
RASINSKI, T., 261
RAY, A., 86, 90, 93, 95, 96, 98, 105
REESE, L., 127, 133, 135, 144

REIMERS, T.M., 69
RESNICK, M.B., 288, 289, 290
REYES, M., 127
RHETT, N., 282
RHODES, D., 68
RICH, S.J., 177
RICHGELS, D.J., 28, 29, 30, 31, 32, 33, 37, 39, 42, 43, 45, 46, 58, 60
RIMDZIUS, T., 13, 14, 15, 21
RIOUX, J.W., 71, 72
RISLEY, T., 50, 51, 55
RIVERA, A., 74, 305
RODRÍGUEZ-BROWN, F.V., 16, 17, 78, 128, 129, 131, 134, 145
ROGERS, R., 127, 128, 130, 287
ROSER, N., 285
ROTH, J., 288, 289, 290
RUBIN, S., 158
RUTHERFORD, B., 80

S

SABLE, J., 126
ST. PIERRE, R.G., 8, 13, 14, 15, 21, 172
SANDEFUR, G., 92
SANDLER, H.M., 267
SAPIN, C., 252, 253, 255, 256, 258, 259, 261, 264
SCARBOROUGH, H.S., 10
SCHNEIDER, B., 266
SCHROFF, J.A., 104
SCHWARTZ, A., 197
SCOTT, J., 10, 267, 288, 289
SEAGOE, M.V., 159, 160, 161
SEARFOSS, L.W., 58, 69
SELTZER, J., 93
SENECHEL, M., 282, 291
SERNA, I., 127
SEVERSON, A., 296
SHANAHAN, T., 16, 17, 129, 131
SHANNON, P., 150, 151
SHERMAN, E., 68
SHERRILL, A., 73
SHERWOOD, K., 103
SHOCKLEY, B., 23, 24
SHORE, R., 51, 55
SIEDENBURG, J., 282
SILVERSTEIN, L., 90
SISSEL, P.A., 174
SLOANE, K., 266
SLOWIACZEK, M.L., 95
SMITH, F., 305

SUBJECT INDEX

Note: Page numbers followed by *f* indicate figures; those followed by *t* indicate tables.

A

ACADEMIC ACHIEVEMENT: father's involvement and, 95–96

ACIRI. *See* Adult/Child Interactive Reading Inventory (ACIRI)

ADOLESCENTS: book clubs for, 72, 78–79, 82; booklists for, 79*f*, family effects on home literacy practices of, 73–75; family effects on school performance of, 69–73; family literacy programs for, 75–82

ADULT/CHILD INTERACTIVE READING INVENTORY (ACIRI), 283, 290–301, 300*f*–301*f*; administration of, 291; components of, 290–291; development of, 290; reliability of, 292–293; scoring of, 292; utility of, 294–295, 296–297; validity of, 293–295

ADULT EDUCATION AND FAMILY LITERACY ACT, 172

THE ADVENTURES OF PADDY PORK (GOODALL), 191

AFRICA: family literacy programs in, 227–247. *See also* Parents and Schools Learning Clubs/Families Learning Together Trust (PASLC/FLT)

AFRICAN AMERICAN LOW-INCOME FATHERS, 102–122. *See also* fathers

AFRICAN ORAL LITERATURE, 240–245

ALTERNATIVE ASSESSMENTS, 256–259, 263

ASSESSMENT TOOLS: alternative, 256–259, 263; for family literacy programs, 255–261, 258*f*, 259*f*; for interactive reading skills, 288–301, 300*f*–301*f*; reliability of, 292–293; standardized, 255–256, 257*f*; validity of, 293–295. *See also* evaluation

ATTENTION SPAN, 54; promotion of, 54

AWARENESS AND EXPLORATION PHASE: of literacy development, 30–37, 33*t*

B

BABIES: Boots Books for project, 202–224; exposure of to spoken language, 51–52; reading to, 184–224, 288–289; Read to Me program for, 184–200

BASIC ENGLISH SKILLS TEST, 256, 257*f*

BASIC SKILLS AGENCY'S DEMONSTRATION PROGRAMMES, 15–16

BILINGUAL INSTRUCTION, 126–145, 176, 179–180, 304

BIRMINGHAM BOOKSTART PROJECT, 203, 204

BONDING, 54–55

BOOK(S): access to, 58–60, 202–224; for adolescents, 79*f*; African-language, 246; in awareness and exploration phase, 36; for babies, 184–224; dialogic reading of, 55–56, 185, 285–286; easy reading, 42–45, 43*t*; importance of, 55–56; joint reading of, 56–57, 282–301 (*see also* joint reading); library, 206–208, 217, 218–219, 222–223, 238; reading tips for, 56–57; rereading of, 36; rhyming, 195–196; self-published, 246; wordless, 188*f*, 190–193

BOOK BACKPACK PROGRAM, 177–178

BOOK BAGS, 59–60, 242–245

BOOK CLUBS: for adolescents, 72, 82; mother-daughter, 78–79

BOOKLISTS: for adolescents, 79*f*

BOOK SHARING. *See* shared reading

BOOK TALK PROGRAM, 72

BOOTS BOOKS FOR BABIES PROJECT, 202–224; book packs in, 205–206, 209–210, 216–217; costs of, 224; deficit model and, 223; design and implementation of, 205–206; evaluation of, 206–221; health visitors/health center staff in, 209–211, 222–223; history of, 205; launch parties for, 218–219; libraries in, 206–208, 211–214, 217, 218–219, 222–223; long-term gains from, 224; parents' views of, 214–221, 216*t*; rationale for, 205; results of, 206–221; support activities in, 206; sustainability of, 224

BROWN BEAR, BROWN BEAR, WHAT DO YOU SEE (MARTIN), 41

C

CANADA: family literacy programs in, 304

CEREBRAL PALSY. *See* children with disabilities

CHANGE: ethics of, 143–144

CHICKA CHICKA BOOM BOOM (MARTIN & ARCHAMBAULT), 195–196

CHILD CARE, 136–137, 143

CHILDREN WITH DISABILITIES: creativity of, 153–155, 163; family literacy activities for, 149–152; as literate beings, 147–148, 152; local understanding of, 152–162, 164–165; lowered expectations for, 149–152; mainstreaming of, 148–149, 156–158; school-based literacy instruction for, 147–152; social engagement of, 155–158, 163–165; social generation of competence and, 153–155; symbolic capacities of, 147–148, 152, 155–158; uncertain outcomes for, 162; unique supports for, 161–162; in web of relationships, 164–165

CIRCLE OF FRIENDS, 157

CLASSROOM LENDING LIBRARY, 58–59

COGNITIVE DEVELOPMENT: bonding in, 54–55; communication in, 55; representational thinking in, 52–53; spoken language exposure and, 51–52

COMMUNICATION: multiple modes of, 163; parent-teacher, 278–280

COMMUNITY COLLABORATION: evaluation of, 260

COMMUNITY SERVICES BLOCK GRANT ACT, 170

COMPETENCE: social generation of, 153–155

COMPREHENSIVE ADULT STUDENT ASSESSMENT SYSTEM (CASAS), 256, 257*f*

CONCURRENT VALIDITY, 293

CONFERENCES: family literacy portfolios in, 260–280. *See also* Home-School Portfolio Project

CONSEQUENTIAL VALIDITY, 294

CONSTRUCT VALIDITY, 293–294

CONVERSATION: written language as, 158–161

CULTURAL CONTEXT: for family literacy programs, 22, 127–129, 134–137, 232–235, 239–245; for joint reading, 286–288

CULTURAL LEARNING MODELS, 127–128

CURRICULUM: assessment and, 295–296

D

DEFICIT MODELS: of family literacy, 170, 175–176, 229–230, 233, 309

DEVELOPMENTAL DISABILITIES. *See* children with disabilities

DIALOGIC READING, 55–56, 185, 285–286. *See also* joint reading; shared reading

DISABILITIES. *See* children with disabilities

DIVORCE: father involvement and, 92, 93, 96–98

DOWN ALL THE DAYS (Brown), 153

DOWN SYNDROME. *See* children with disabilities

E

EARLY HEAD START, 104

EARLY READING AND WRITING, 41–47, 43*t*, 67; parental involvement in, 9–10

EASY READING BOOKS, 42–45, 43*t*

EDUCATING: vs. teaching, 133–134

EDUCATIONAL LEVEL: socioeconomic status and, 9, 11

EFFECTIVE PARTNERS IN SECONDARY LITERACY LEARNING (EPISLL), 76–77

ELEMENTARY AND SECONDARY EDUCATION ACT of 1965, 170

EMERGENT LITERACY, 28–47; awareness and exploration phase of, 30–37, 33*t*, 64–66; benchmarks of, 29–30; continuum of, 28; early reading and writing phase of, 41–47, 43*t*, 67; experimental reading and writing phase of, 37–41, 39*t*; joint reading and, 284–285; overview of, 29; spoken language development and, 32–36. *See also* literacy development

ENGLISH LANGUAGE LEARNERS: family literacy programs for, 126–145, 176, 179–180, 304. *See also* Project FLAME

ENVIRONMENTAL PRINT, 52–53, 54*f*

ETHICS OF CHANGE, 143–144

EVALUATION: of adult/child interactive reading skills, 282–301; assessment tools for, 255–261, 258*f*, 259*f*, 288–301, 300*f*–301*f*; of Boots Books for Babies project, 206–221; of community collaboration, 260; curriculum and, 295–296; design of, 254; external evaluator for, 260–261; family literacy portfolios in, 260–280; of family literacy programs, 250–265; formative, 251; framework for, 253, 253*t*; future directions for, 264; general guidelines for, 252–255, 253*t*; goals of, 251–252, 254–255; information sources for, 255, 265; National Institute for Literacy and, 262–263; qualitative vs. quantitative approaches to, 253, 253*t*; school-based portfolios in, 278; scope of, 259–260; standardized tests in, 255–256, 257*f*; summative, 251; uses of, 261–262. *See also* assessment tools

EVEN START, 2, 10–11, 168–182, 250, 251, 257; core components of, 172–173, 250; evaluation of, 257, 259*f*; family involvement in, 170–171; family literacy initiatives in, 175–180; goals of, 168–169, 172; overview of, 171–173; partnership model of, 170–171; results of, 12–15; target population for, 172, 173; theoretical orientation of, 169–171

EVERYONE POOPS (GOMI), 193

EXPERIMENTAL READING AND WRITING PHASE, 37–41, 39*t*, 64–66

EXTRAFAMILY MANAGEMENT, 91–92

F

FAMILIA CONCEPT, 132, 135–137, 144–145

FAMILIES AND SCHOOLS TOGETHER (FAST), 227–247; history of, 228–229, 235–236; home-school partnership in, 233–234; operational strands in, 231–232; participants in, 230, 233–234; principles and goals of, 229–233; sociocultural context for, 232–235; texts in, 234–235; as wealth-model program, 229–231, 233–235

FAMILIES LEARNING TOGETHER TRUST (FLT), 227–247; curriculum for, 237; history of, 228–229, 235–236; participants in, 230; principles and goals of, 229–233; theoretical framework for, 236–245. *See also* Parents and Schools Learning Clubs/Families Learning Together Trust (PASLC/FLT)

FAMILY INITIATIVE FOR ENGLISH LITERACY, 179–180

FAMILY LITERACY: ABCs of, 54–55; adolescents and, 68–83 (*see also* adolescents); for children with disabilities, 147–165 (*see also* children with disabilities); community support for, 82; deficit model of, 170, 175–176, 229–230, 233, 309; definitions of, 1–2, 16; diverse practices in, 286–288; home-school partnerships for, 23–24, 24*f*, 70–73, 80–81; overview of, 303–309; as panacea, 2; research on, 2, 12–21; research studies of, 118–120; restrictive view of, 119–120, 308–309; school support for, 80–83; sociocultural context for, 129, 134–137; wealth model of, 229, 233–235, 247, 308–309

FAMILY LITERACY: YOUNG CHILDREN LEARNING TO READ AND WRITE (TAYLOR), 1

FAMILY LITERACY PORTFOLIOS, 266–280. *See also* Home-School Portfolio Project

FAMILY LITERACY PROGRAMS, 8; for adolescents, 68–82; assessment of, 250–265; for babies, 184–224; based on existing literacy practices, 78; Basic Skills Agency's Demonstration Programmes, 15–16; benefits of, 10–13; Birmingham Bookstart project, 203, 204; book bags in, 59–60; books in (*see* book[s]); Boots Books for Babies project, 202–224; in Canada, 304; child care for, 136–137, 143; classroom lending libraries in, 58–59; components of, 10–11; comprehensive, 307–308; cultural context for, 127–129, 134–137, 232–235, 239–245; debate over, 11–12; deficit-model, 170, 175–176, 229–230, 233, 309; diversity of, 304; duration of, 307; Effective Partners in Secondary Literacy Learning, 76–77; for English language learners, 126–145, 176, 179–180 (*see also* Project FLAME); ESL instruction in, 131; ethics of change and, 143–144; Even Start, 2, 10–11, 12–14, 168–182, 250, 251; *familia* concept in, 132, 135–137; Families and Schools Together, 227–247; Families Learning Together Trust, 227–247; Family Initiative for English Literacy, 179–180; family literacy portfolios in, 268–280; Family Reading Program, 75–78; fathers in, 99–118, 136, 143; federally sponsored, 169–171; future of, 308–309; goals of, 10, 119–120, 254, 296; Head Start, 2, 10–11, 168–182; as home-school partnerships, 23, 24*f*; Home-School Portfolio Project, 268–280; instructional approaches in, 13–21; intensity of, 306–307; intergenerational, 17–19, 136; Intergenerational Literacy Project, 17–19; joint reading in (*see* joint reading); Keeping Up With the Children, 20; literacy focus in, 307; for low-income African American fathers, 106–122; models of, 10–11, 12–21; mother-daughter book clubs in, 78–79; networking in, 135; parenting instruction and, 308; Parents and Schools Learning Clubs, 227–247; Project EASE, 19–20; Project FIEL, 179–180; Project FLAME, 16–17, 128–145; rationale for, 119–120; recruitment and retention in, 259–260; research studies of, 12–21; results of, 21–24; shared reading in, 78–79, 100–101; short- vs. long-term, 22–23; social isolation and, 135; in South Africa, 227–247; storybooks in, 36, 56–57, 60; suggested improvements in, 22–24; supplemental nature of, 307–308; Teachers Involve Parents in Schoolwork (TIPS), 71–72; videotapes in, 60; wealth-model, 229, 233–235, 247, 308–309

FAMILY LITERACY RESOURCE NOTEBOOK (FLRN): assessment tools in, 256–257, 258*f*, 259*f*

FAMILY LITERACY SERVICES: federal definition of, 169–170

FAMILY MANAGEMENT: intrafamily vs. extrafamily, 91–92

FAMILY READING PROGRAM: for adolescents, 75–78

FAMILY TREES, 242

FATHERS, 86–122; absent, 96–98, 107–108; African American low-income, 102–122; availability of, 91, 92; as caregivers, 93–98; children's academic achievement and, 95–96; divorced, 92, 93, 96–98; encouragement of reading by, 73–75, 96; engagement of, 91, 92–93; in family literacy programs, 99–118, 136, 143; in family management, 91–92; in family system, 87; Hispanic, 110–122; increased interest in, 88–90; levels of involvement of, 90–94; in literacy development, 98–106; literacy needs and activities of, 109–122; meaning of literacy to, 110–122; presence of, 90–93; race of, 96–98; research on, 88–90, 96–106; responsibility of, 90, 91–92; responsible fathering and, 90; school involvement of, 96; socioeconomic status of, 95, 96–98; types of involvement of, 94–95; unmarried, 93–94. *See also* parent(s)

FATHERS AND LITERACY STUDY, 106–118

FATHERWORK, 92–93

FEDERAL LITERACY PROGRAMS. *See* Even Start; Head Start

FOLK TALES, 242–243

FORMATIVE EVALUATION, 251

FRAGILE FAMILIES STUDY, 105

G

GENERAL EDUCATIONAL DEVELOPMENT (GED) PRACTICE TEST, 256, 257*f*

GROUP-EDITED STORIES, 243–244, 243*f*

H

HEAD START, 2, 10–11, 168–182; family involvement in, 170–171, 174–175; family literacy initiatives in, 175–180; goals of, 169; multidirectional participatory learning in, 171; outcomes of, 173–174; overview of, 171–172, 173–175; theoretical orientation of, 169–171

HEAD START–LIBRARY OF CONGRESS PARTNERSHIP PROJECT, 175

HIGH SCHOOL STUDENTS. *See* adolescents

HISPANICS: child care and, 136–137; family literacy programs for, 126–145, 179–180, 268–277 (*see also* Project FLAME); literacy levels of, 126–127. *See also* English language learners

HOME-SCHOOL PARTNERSHIPS, 23–24, 24*f*; for adolescents, 70–73, 80–81; for English language learners, 127–145; family literacy portfolios in, 260–280 (*see also* Home-School Portfolio Project); in Head Start programs, 176–177; in South Africa vs. United Kingdom, 227–247

HOME-SCHOOL PORTFOLIO PROJECT, 268–280; design and implementation of, 269–274; guidelines for, 278–280; outcomes of, 274–278; parent-child interactions and, 275; parent-teacher collaboration in, 274–280; parent training in, 269–272, 270*f*, 275; participants in, 268–269; portfolio contents in, 269–274, 270*f* 272*f*, 278–280; sample parent form for, 279, 279*f*; teacher training in, 272–274, 273*f*

HOME VISIT LOG, 256–257, 258*f*

I

INCLUSIVE INSTRUCTION: for children with disabilities, 148–149, 156–158

INDEPENDENT AND PRODUCTIVE READING AND WRITING, 46*t*, 47

INFANTS: Boots Books for Babies project for, 202–224; exposure of to spoken language, 51–52; reading to, 184–224, 288–289; Read to Me program for, 184–200

INTERACTIVE READING SKILLS: evaluation of, 282–301. *See also* dialogic reading; joint reading; shared reading

INTERGENERATIONAL READING PROGRAMS, 8, 17–19, 136

INTERNATIONAL READING ASSOCIATION (IRA), 5, 28, 31, 80, 171, 283–284, 304

INTRAFAMILY MANAGEMENT, 91–92

INVENTED SPELLING, 38–41

J

JOINT READING: ACIRI assessment tool for, 283, 290–301; with babies, 184–200; benefits of, 185, 283–286; dialogic, 55–56, 185, 285–286; diverse literacy practices and, 287–288;

evaluation of reading skills in, 282–301; importance of, 283–286; instruction in, 185–186, 287; interactive behaviors in, 284–286; parent-child relationship and, 186, 286–288; sociocultural aspects of, 286–288; tips for, 56–57; zone of proximal development and, 285. *See also* shared reading; dialogic reading

JULIUS, the BABY OF THE WORLD (HENKES), 198–199

K

KEEPING UP WITH THE CHILDREN, 20
KENAN TRUST MODEL, 172–173, 304

L

LADDER TO LITERACY, 150–151, 162, 163–164
LATINOS. *See* Hispanics
LEARNING COMMUNITY, 178–179
LIBRARIES: Boots Books for Babies project and, 206–208, 211–214, 217, 218–219, 222–223; classroom lending, 58–59; Parents and Schools Learning Clubs and, 238; toy, 245
LISTENING: to children, 55
LISTENING VOCABULARY: development of, 51
LITERACY: definitions of, 1, 150; emergent, 28–46; family sense of, 149–150; meaning of to low–income urban fathers, 110–122; metaphorical ladder to, 150–151, 162, 163–164; restrictive views of, 150, 161–164, 308–309; social generation of, 153–155. *See also* reading; writing
LITERACY DEVELOPMENT: ABCs of, 54–55; age-appropriate activities for, 64–67; awareness and exploration phase of, 30–37, 33*t*, 64–66; benchmarks for, 29–30; in children with disabilities, 147–165 (*see also* children with disabilities); continuum of, 28; dialogic reading in, 55–56, 185; early, 28–47 (*see also* emergent literacy); early reading and writing phase of, 41–47, 43*t*, 67; environmental print in, 52–53, 54*f*; experimental reading and writing phase of, 37–41, 39*t*; father's involvement in, 98–118; independent and productive reading and writing phase of, 46*t*, 47; joint reading in, 185–186, 282–301 (*see also* joint reading); ladder model of, 150–151, 162, 163–164; one-size-fits-all approach to, 150–151, 162, 163–164, 304; overview of, 29; phases of, 28–47; representational thinking in, 52–53; spoken language development and, 32–36; spoken language exposure in, 51–52; the Talking Home and, 63; transitional reading and writing phase of, 45–47, 46*t*
LITERACY INSTRUCTION: assembly line model of, 150–151; bilingual, 304; for children with disabilities, 147–152; in family literacy programs (*see* family literacy programs); one-size-fits-all approach in, 150–151, 162, 163–164, 304
LITERACY INVOLVES FAMILIES TOGETHER (LIFT) ACT, 170
LITERACY LEVELS: of Hispanics, 126–127; of low-income African American fathers, 109–114. *See also* parental education
LITERACY PORTFOLIOS, 260–280; suggestions for, 278–280. *See also* Home-School Portfolio Project
LOCAL UNDERSTANDING: definition of, 152; development of, 164–165; examples of, 152–162

M

MAINSTREAMING, 148–149, 156–158
MENTAL RETARDATION. *See* children with disabilities
MIDDLE SCHOOL STUDENTS: Family Reading Program for, 75–78. *See also* adolescents
THE MOTHER-DAUGHTER BOOK CLUB (DODSON & BARKER), 78–79

MOTHER-DAUGHTER BOOK CLUBS, 78–79
MOTHERS: encouragement of reading by, 73, 96. *See also* parent(s)
MR. FINGER (GOMI), 193
MRS. MUSTARD'S BABY FACES (WATTENBERG), 191
MY LEFT FOOT (movie), 153

N

NATIONAL ASSESSMENT OF EDUCATIONAL PROGRESS (NAEP), 8
NATIONAL ASSOCIATION FOR THE EDUCATION OF YOUNG CHILDREN (NAEYC), 5, 28, 31,
    283–284
NATIONAL CENTER FOR FAMILY LITERACY, 10, 11, 101
NATIONAL CENTER FOR SERVICE LEARNING IN EARLY ADOLESCENCE (NCSLEA), 75
NATIONAL CENTER ON FATHERS AND FAMILIES (NCOFF), 90, 106–118
NATIONAL INSTITUTE FOR LITERACY, 10, 11, 101; electronic discussion list of, 263–264
NATIONAL STUDY OF EARLY HEAD START, 104
NETWORKING: in family literacy programs, 135
NO CHILD LEFT BEHIND ACT, 304
NON-ENGLISH BOOKS: for reading aloud, 193–194

O

101 THINGS TO DO WITH A BABY (ORMEROD), 197
ONE-SIZE-FITS-ALL APPROACH, 150–151, 162, 163–164, 304
ORAL STORY SACKS, 242–245

P

PARENT(S): of children with disabilities (*see* children with disabilities); literacy instruction for,
    10–13; local understanding by, 152–153; support for adolescent reading by, 73–75. *See
    also* family; fathers; mothers
PARENTAL EDUCATION: children's academic achievement and, 8–9; home literacy practices
    and, 9–10; socioeconomic status and, 9, 11 (*see also* socioeconomic status)
PARENT AS READER SCALE (PARS), 288
PARENTING INSTRUCTION, 308
PARENTS AND SCHOOLS LEARNING CLUBS/FAMILIES LEARNING TOGETHER TRUST
    (PASLC/FLT), 227–247; activities in, 237–239; curriculum in, 237; history of, 228–229,
    235–236; language for learning in, 239–240; library usage and, 238; local genres and
    text forms in, 240–245; outcomes of, 245–247; parent workshops in, 237–239; partici-
    pants in, 229–231; principles and goals of, 229–233; sociocultural context for, 232–235,
    239–245; teacher training in, 245; theoretical framework for, 236–245; toy library in, 245;
    as wealth-model program, 229–231; writing activities in, 240–246
PARENTS' FAIR SHARE DEMONSTRATION, 103
PARENT-TEACHER COMMUNICATION, 278–280; family literacy portfolios in, 260–280. *See also*
    Home-School Portfolio Project
PATTERN SEEKING, 50–51
PEABODY PICTURE VOCABULARY TEST (PPVT), 256, 257*f*
PHONEMIC AWARENESS, 30
PHOTOGRAPHS: in Read to Me program, 189–190
PICTURE BOOKS. *See* book(s)
POEMS: praise, 240–241, 241*f*

PORTFOLIOS: family literacy, 260–280 (*see also* Home-School Portfolio Project); school-based, 278

POVERTY. *See* socioeconomic status

PRAISE POEMS, 240–241, 241*f*

PRESCHOOLERS: Read to Me program for, 184–200

PROJECT EASE, 19–20

PROJECT FIEL, 179–180

PROJECT FLAME, 16–17, 128–145; child care in, 136–137, 143; community liaisons in, 138–139; design and focus of, 129–132; development of, 129; duration of participation in, 141; ESL instruction in, 131; vs. ESL program, 137–138; *familia* concept and, 132, 135–137, 144; fathers' involvement in, 136; follow-up services and, 141–143; graduates of, 141–143; home-school partnership in, 140–141; implementation of, 129–132; length of service in, 141; parents as learners in, 129; parents as school volunteers in, 129, 142–143; parents as teachers in, 129, 132–134, 142; parents as trainers in, 129, 142; participants in, 137–138; planning and implementation in, 140–141; recruitment and retention for, 138–139; *respeto* concept and, 133–134; sociocultural context for, 129, 134–137; students' academic gains in, 130–131; supplemental services in, 139, 141–143; teacher participation in, 140–141

R

READING: dialogic, 55–56, 185, 285–286; early, 41–47, 43*t*, 67 (*see also* emergent literacy); embedded conversation in, 35–36; experimental, 39*t*, 41–47, 64–66; independent and productive, 46*t*, 47; interactive (*see* joint reading); shared (*see* shared reading); transitional, 45–47, 46*t*; word vs. text, 42–44. *See also* literacy

READING ALOUD. *See* joint reading

READING AND TALK (R&T) CLUBS, 82

READING EXCELLENCE ACT, 170

READING LISTS: for adolescents, 79*f*

READ TO ME program, 184–200; activities in, 188*f*, 189–199; ancillary activities in, 200; English language books in, 194–196; goals of, 187; history of, 187; non–English books in, 193–194; Polaroid pictures in, 189–190; theme books in, 196–200; wordless books in, 188*t*, 190–193

RECEPTIVE VOCABULARY: development of, 51

RECRUITMENT AND RETENTION: evaluation of, 259–260

REEP WRITING ASSESSMENT, 256, 257*f*

RELIABILITY: of assessment tools, 292–293

REPRESENTATIONAL THINKING, 52–53

REREADING: of storybooks, 36

RESPONSIBLE FATHERING, 90

RHYMING BOOKS, 195–196

RHYMING GAMES, 32

R&T CLUBS, 82

S

SCHOOLS: family outreach efforts of, 23–24, 24*f*, 70–73, 80–81, 127–128, 176–177, 227–247. *See also* home-school partnerships

SCRIBBLE WRITING, 30–31

SELF-PUBLISHING, 246